PATERNOSTER THEOLOGICAL MONOGRAPHS

The Justifying Judgement of God

A Reassessment of the Place of Judgement in the Saving Work of Christ

PATERNOSTER THEOLOGICAL MONOGRAPHS

A full listing of all titles in this series and Paternoster Biblical Monographs
will be found at the close of this book

PATERNOSTER THEOLOGICAL MONOGRAPHS

The Justifying Judgement of God

A Reassessment of the Place of Judgement in the Saving Work of Christ

Justyn Charles Terry

Foreword by Murray Rae

WIPF & STOCK · Eugene, Oregon

Wipf and Stock Publishers
199 W 8th Ave, Suite 3
Eugene, OR 97401

The Justifying Judgement of God
A Reassessment of the Place of Judgement in the Saving Work of Christ
By Terry, Justyn
Copyright©2007 Paternoster
ISBN 13: 978-1-55635-662-9
ISBN 10: 1-55635-662-5
Publication date 1/8/2008

This Edition Published by Wipf and Stock Publishers by arrangement with Paternoster

Paternoster
9 Holdom Avenue
Bletchley
Milton Keyes, MK1 1QR
PATERNOSTER Great Britain

Series Preface

In the West the churches may be declining, but theology—serious, academic (mostly doctoral level) and mainstream orthodox in evaluative commitment—shows no sign of withering on the vine. This series of *Paternoster Theological Monographs* extends the expertise of the Press especially to first-time authors whose work stands broadly within the parameters created by fidelity to Scripture and has satisfied the critical scrutiny of respected assessors in the academy. Such theology may come in several distinct intellectual disciplines—historical, dogmatic, pastoral, apologetic, missional, aesthetic and no doubt others also. The series will be particularly hospitable to promising constructive theology within an evangelical frame, for it is of this that the church's need seems to be greatest. Quality writing will be published across the confessions—Anabaptist, Episcopalian, Reformed, Arminian and Orthodox—across the ages—patristic, medieval, reformation, modern and counter-modern—and across the continents. The aim of the series is theology written in the twofold conviction that the church needs theology and theology needs the church—which in reality means theology done for the glory of God.

Series Editors

David F. Wright, Emeritus Professor of Patristic and Reformed Christianity, University of Edinburgh, Scotland, UK

Trevor A. Hart, Head of School and Principal of St Mary's College School of Divinity, University of St Andrews, Scotland, UK

Anthony N.S. Lane, Professor of Historical Theology and Director of Research, London School of Theology, UK

Anthony C. Thiselton, Emeritus Professor of Christian Theology, University of Nottingham, Research Professor in Christian Theology, University College Chester, and Canon Theologian of Leicester Cathedral and Southwell Minster, UK

Kevin J. Vanhoozer, Research Professor of Systematic Theology, Trinity Evangelical Divinity School, Deerfield, Illinois, USA

To Cathy, Sophia and Lydia

Contents

Foreword

There can hardly be anything more central to the Christian proclamation than the news that in Christ God has acted to overcome the
sinfulness of humanity and to reconcile the created order to himself.
The cross of Jesus Christ, furthermore, is confessed to be in some
manner a decisive turning point of the drama through which human
sinfulness is overcome and right relationship with God is established. So the church confesses. But how is the logic of this event to
be thought through and articulated? Since Gustav Aulen's seminal
work on the metaphors of atonement was published in 1931, theologians have generally recognised that the New Testament offers a
number of ways of explicating the logic of the saving event of the
cross. The question confronted by Justyn Terry in this volume, however, is whether there is an overriding logic that draws the various
strands of New Testament witness together. He argues that there is.
The logic of divine judgement, Terry contends, makes good sense of
the drama of the cross and also of the New Testament witness, and
enables us to proclaim a gospel that is genuinely good news for the
world.

The proposal has various obstacles to overcome, not the least of
which is a widespread distaste in contemporary culture for judicial
language. The investigations of this volume show that preachers
commonly shy away from the proclamation of divine judgement,
despite encountering it plainly enough in the texts on which they are
called to preach. An important contribution of this volume, therefore, is to guide us toward a reformulation of what exactly is meant
by judgement. It is not synonymous with condemnation, as is so
often assumed, but is best understood as the means by which God's
justice is established in an unjust world. The establishment of justice
is an act of grace. It is precisely not the withdrawal of God's love, as
many suppose, but the fullest expression of divine love.

In a world that resists the notion of judgement but cries out for
justice, Terry's theological exploration of these themes deserves careful attention. His proposals will help the church toward a more faithful and a more joyful preaching of the gospel with which it has been
entrusted and which it has been charged to proclaim.

Among the range of theologians considered in this book, Terry
draws most appreciatively upon the work of Karl Barth and Colin
Gunton, the second of whom was the supervisor of this work during
its early formation as a doctoral thesis. Colin's death soon after the
project's completion is a cause of continuing sadness but the theo-

logical work that Colin's teaching inspired among his students and of which this work stands as a further example, is a cause for gratitude and joy.

Murray Rae
University of Otago, New Zealand

Preface

The judgement of God is not a popular topic. It is widely thought to be synonymous with condemnation, which some consider to be out of character with the God of love. Judgement is also generally held to be something we should not make on someone else. Surely, they say, this is what Jesus taught when he said, 'Do not judge, so that you may not be judged' (Mat. 7:1). This book touches on both of these issues, although they are not its primary target. It is aimed instead at the problem of proclaiming the work of Christ: how are we to speak of atonement in terms of sacrifice, victory, redemption and judgement without undue confusion or over simplification? Karl Barth takes the judgement of God, understood as the whole process as bringing justice, as the main metaphor by which to expound God's reconciling work. My aim in this book is to show how that account might be used to draw the other New Testament imagery into a more co-ordinated statement of the gospel message, and to relate this to the responses it elicits.

This monograph was developed as a PhD thesis at King's College, London, and I am particularly indebted those who helped me in that project. I would like to thank Professor Francis Watson, who helped shape the early stages of this study before moving to the University of Aberdeen to take up the Chair of New Testament Exegesis. Professor Colin Gunton, who had been involved from the inception of this work, then took over the supervision of this thesis. His support, guidance and encouragement throughout have been invaluable, and his death so soon after its completion was a great loss.

I am also thankful to Dr. Murray Rae, who assisted with the supervision of the work, made valuable comments on a draft of this thesis and provided constant encouragement. I am also grateful to him for writing the foreword. Early drafts of the chapters were greatly improved by the insights of Dr. William Ingle-Gillis, and I would like to express my thanks to him. I was also helped by members of the Research Institute in Systematic Theology at King's College, London. I especially benefited from their comments on two papers based on Chapters 6 and 7 of this material, and on a paper I gave at a Day Conference on the Doctrine of Atonement which drew mainly on Chapters 5 and 6.

The work was carried out in the context of parish ministry in London, initially as a Curate at St John's Hyde Park, then as vicar of St Helen's North Kensington. I am very grateful to the Bishop of London, the Rt Rev'd Dr Richard Chartres, and the Bishop of Ken-

sington, the Rt Rev'd Michael Colclough, for encouraging me in
this undertaking and for grants they supplied to support it. I am
also aware how much the congregations of St John's and St Helen's
helped me not only in providing the context in which it was written
but also for being the first to hear some of the ideas it presents.

I also owe debts of gratitude to David Jackman, who, as minister
of Above Bar Church, Southampton, taught me so much theology
in his preaching, and to Dr. Philip Luscombe, my tutor in Systematic Theology at Cranmer Hall, Durham, who helped alert me to the
problem I address here.

Some of the material in Chapters 5 and 6 originally appeared in
'The Justifying Judgement of God', published in Anvil Vol. 22 No.
1 (2005), and I am grateful for permission to reproduce it here. I am
also thankful for the use of quotations from Karl Barth by kind permission of T & T Clark, an imprint of Continuum.

I would like to express my appreciation to Dr. Robin Parry of
Paternoster Press for bringing this work to publication, and to Jer-
emy Mudditt, Dr. Anthony Cross and John and Sue Longridge for
their generous help in a preparing the text for the press.

Finally, I would like to thank my wife Cathy and daughters Sophia
and Lydia, both born during the writing of this thesis, whose love
has been an inspiration throughout. I dedicate this work to them.

Justyn Terry
London, July 2005

CHAPTER 1

Introduction: Problems in Proclaiming the Atonement

Introduction

> There is something lacking in our preaching by general consent. It
> lacks the note, the energy of spiritual profundity and poignancy as
> distinct from spiritual sympathy, and of moral majesty as distinct
> from ethical interest. And I am convinced that this is ultimately
> due to the loss of conviction as to a real, objective, and finished
> redemption, and to the disappearance from current faith of a real
> relation to the holiness and the wrath of God. The note of judge-
> ment has gone out of common piety... It does not break men to
> Christ, but only train them, or at most bend them. And it does not
> embody that break with the world which, after all, has been a lead-
> ing note in all the great victories of the Cross.[1]

So said the Scottish Congregationalist theologian and preacher Peter
Taylor Forsyth at the turn of the twentieth century. He was lament-
ing the general feebleness of the proclamation of the message of the
cross, and directed his attack against preachers who saw the cross
as primarily, or even exclusively, an inspiration to moral reform,
whereby the love of God revealed in Christ crucified evoked a love
for God in the human heart. For him, such preaching lacked the stat-
ure required to subdue sinners and bring them to their knees in worship before Jesus Christ the Lord. So concerned was it with education
that it avoided confrontation; so keen to inspire, it would not unsettle. It was an inoffensive ministry but wholly ineffective in bringing
about the radical changes God intended for men and women in his
new creation.

The cause of problems with gospel preaching may have changed
over the last century but the effect is much the same. Moral response
may no longer be a dominant motif in sermons today, and yet we
cannot say the 'something lacking in our preaching' has been supplied. The proclamation of the good news of Jesus Christ remains
largely anaemic and uncompelling, giving the words of Forsyth a

---

1   P.T. Forsyth, *Positive Preaching and the Modern Mind* (London: Independent
    Press, 1907), p. 254.

contemporary resonance. Too often, the Christian gospel is presented in ways that demean the moral, intellectual and spiritual grandeur of the atoning work of Christ, and as a result, lack conviction and authority.[2]

It is the purpose of this essay to investigate the problems which currently beset proclamation of the saving work of Christ and to put forward a proposal to address them. As we shall see in the first section of this work, the current problem in presentations of the work of Christ lies in the use being made of a multiplicity of biblical images like redemption, sacrifice, law and victory. They are being treated as if they are essentially independent. Either one of these images is therefore given particular priority and allowed to stand alone, or else a number of them are held together but without any co-ordination. In the first case, important aspects of the atonement are omitted, and in the second, the combination of apparently unrelated images of atonement serves to confuse rather than to clarify the message. It is the contention of this author, as will be explained in the second section, that by giving greater prominence to judgement and treating it as the paradigmatic metaphor of atonement we not only restore what is often an overlooked aspect of atonement, as Forsyth points out, but also provide a means to make the doctrine of atonement more systematic and incisive. Our concerns are therefore not with issues of homiletical structure and presentation, but with the content of the message of atonement to be proclaimed. As such we are following Professor Karl Barth in saying dogmatic theology, 'tests the orthodoxy of contemporary kerygma.'[3]

That is not to say that this is the only problem with contemporary preaching of the gospel. Several major changes in British society have contributed other difficulties: the loss of confidence in authority-fig-

---

2   Forsyth also bemoans the loss of authority in preaching. He says, 'It is the absence of the note of authority that is the central weakness of so many of the churches; and it is the source of their failure to impress Society with their message for the practical ends of the Kingdom of God'. Forsyth, *Positive Preaching*, pp. 27f.

3   Karl Barth, *Church Dogmatics* (translation by G.W. Bromiley, editors G.W. Bromiley and T.F. Torrance, Edinburgh: T. & T. Clark, 1975), vol. I, part 1, p. 82. Future references to the *Church Dogmatics* will be in the form: 'I/1, p. 82' and given in the main text. Barth expands on his view of the relationship between Christian doctrine and preaching in his Münster *Ethics*, where he defines dogmatics as, 'the science of the content of Christian preaching, i.e., of the relation of preaching to God's revealed Word. The concern of dogmatics is that God's Word is heard in Christian preaching.' Karl Barth, *Ethics* (translation by G.W. Bromiley, New York: Seabury Press, 1981), p. 15.

ures in general and preachers in particular, the decline in Christian education, the growth in demand for entertainment, and the use of Sundays for shopping, recreation and preserving relationships in ever more fragmented families. There are no doubt many other factors, not least what Steve Holmes describes as 'the one great "triumph" of Christian pastoral theology this century: we have learned how to convince sinners with tender consciences that they have no need of Christ's atoning work.'[4] Important as these issues are, however, they lie beyond the scope of this study. It is to the particular problem of the treatment of New Testament atonement imagery that our discussion is directed.

We begin in this chapter with a brief survey of recent preaching and teaching on the atonement in order to present evidence of continuing weakness and to articulate the questions it raises before turning in later chapters to the main task of analysing the root problems and proposing a remedy. In order to narrow the scope of this work, we shall only be concerned with the current situation as we find it in Britain.

We shall take 'atonement' to mean the bringing together of two parties who have become estranged, literally at-one-ment.[5] It will also be used to refer to the state of harmony brought about through such an action.[6] As such, atonement will be treated as a synonym for reconciliation, which, as R.S. Paul shows,[7] is how it has been treated throughout its history in the English language. And we shall refer to 'atonement images' in this chapter so as not to prejudice the question of whether they should be treated as theories, models or metaphors of atonement.

---

4   Steve Holmes, 'Edwards on the Will' *International Journal of Systematic Theology* vol. 1, no. 3, (1999) p. 271.
5   Colin Grant points out that this is the only major theological word of English origin. C. Grant, 'The Abandonment of Atonement', *Kings Theological Review* (1986), IX, p. 3.
6   F.W. Dillistone notes that this second usage predates the first in English usage. F.W. Dillistone, 'Atonement', in Alan Richardson and John Bowden, ed., *A New Dictionary of Christian Theology* (London: SCM Press, 1983), p. 50.
7   R.S. Paul, *The Atonement and the Sacraments* (London: Hodder and Stoughton, 1961), pp. 20ff. So, whilst the term 'atonement' has come to be commonly associated more especially with the cross of Christ, we shall take it to embrace every aspect of the work of Christ by which God and his creatures are reunited. This also means that we shall treat reconciliation not simply as one of the New Testament images of the atonement, but as the defining image.

A. Uncertain Images[8]

One useful source of insight into contemporary preaching of the atonement is *The Times Book of Best Sermons* which has been published annually since 1995. Each book contains thirty sermons recommended by members of the congregation and short-listed by a panel of judges. All but the first book also include the sermon which won the Preacher of the Year award the previous year at a special service for the six finalists short-listed from the thirty. The selection of sermons does, of course, reflect the editorial views of the judges and no claim is here being made that they offer a basis for rigorous statistical analysis. They do, however, provide a wide variety of recent sermons from many different church traditions which illustrate the problems we seek to identify. In them we find two general approaches to the doctrine of reconciliation. The first is to take one image of the atonement and develop that alone, and the second is to try to combine several of them. We shall look at each of these in turn to assess their effectiveness.

Single image approaches

In the first category, one of the most popular images is of sacrifice. Many times this arises as no more than a passing reference. For instance, Ian Knox of St John the Baptist, Westwood, Coventry, said that before confession we hear the words, 'the blood of Jesus Christ makes us clean from all sin.'[9] Nigel Freestone told Holbeach Baptist Church, Catford, that, 'the sacrifice of the cross has been accepted, God has proved it by raising Jesus from the dead.'[10] The Old Testament scholar Dr. Gordon Wenham told the congregation of Holy Trinity, Platt, Manchester, that the basis of the call to living for others lies in our relationships is Jesus Christ who 'gave himself that we might live.'[11] And Canon Michael Botting, speaking on the subject of time, interprets John 12:23, 'The hour has come for the Son of Man to be glorified,' as meaning, 'laying down his life for the sins

---

8   This subtitle and the one that follows, 'Trivializing Illustrations', themselves echo two of the three main criticisms P.T. Forsyth makes of preaching in 1907: triviality, uncertainty and complacency. Forsyth, *Positive Preaching*, p. 115.

9   Ian Knox, 'Marriage at Cana', in Ruth Gledhill, ed., *The Times Book of Best Sermons*, (London: Cassell, 1995), p. 105.

10 Nigel Freestone, 'Hope for Hereafter' in Ruth Gledhill, ed., *The Fourth Times Book of Best Sermons*, (London: Cassell, 1999), p. 75.

11 Gordon Wenham, 'Relationships' in Gledhill, *The Fourth Times Book of Best Sermons*, p. 47.

of the world.'[12] Occasionally sacrificial language is developed a little more fully, as when Ian Knox, short-listed for a second time in 1996, used the parable of the Good Samaritan as an allegory of Christlike self-sacrifice.[13] Knox, however, like the other preachers who mention Christ's sacrifice, assumes that the congregation already knows what it means to say that Christ died as a sacrifice for sins. But how is it that the blood of Christ cleanses us from sin? And what does it mean to say that the sacrifice of Christ has been accepted? Unless these things are already understood, these sermons are of little help.

We also find many other images of atonement being used, although less frequently. Paul Walker at St Winfrid's Church, Moorside, Sunderland, described the gospel as 'a victory.'[14] Dr. Arnold Kellett, preaching on the second coming of Christ, reminded his congregation that, 'The Jesus who is our Judge is also our Saviour.'[15] Gill Dascombe at Wood Lanes Methodist Church, Adlington, referred to another sermon in which she had described the cross as, 'a symbol of coming together, and of reaching out in Christ.'[16] Dr. Edmund Marshall preaching on the pearl of great price at Howden Methodist Church, Humberside, describes Christ as 'our oyster, opening up for us the world of eternal life by the precious pearls made of his infinite agonies on the cross.'[17] Colin Williamson preached on Salvation at Aberdalgie Parish Church. Referring to the bronze serpent Moses raised up in the wilderness, he explained that, 'Lifted up on his cross, Jesus drew out all the poison which spelled our eternal death and bore it away.[18] Here again, the assumption each time is that we already know what Christ has achieved. But what exactly is this victory that Christ has won? In what sense was his death a

---

12 Michael Botting, 'Instant Gratification or Patient Expectation' in Gledhill, *The Fourth Times Book of Best Sermons*, p.109. This biblical quotation and those that arise subsequently, are taken from the New Revised Standard Version (Oxford: Oxford University Press, 1989), unless there is an indication to the contrary.

13 Ian Knox, 'The Good Samaritan' in Ruth Gledhill, ed., *The Times Best Sermons of 1996*, (London: Cassell, 1996), pp. 99ff.

14 Paul Walker, 'The Beheading of John the Baptist' in Ruth Gledhill, ed., *The Times Best Sermons of 1998* (London: Cassell, 1997), p. 140.

15 Arnold Kellett, 'A Thief in the Night' in Gledhill, *The Fourth Times Book of Best Sermons*, p. 10.

16 Gill Dascombe, 'The Widow's Mite' in Gledhill, *The Times Book of Best Sermons*, p. 144.

17 Edmund Marshall, 'The Pearl of Great Price' in Gledhill, *The Times Book of Best Sermons*, p. 155.

18 Colin Williamson, 'Salvation' in Gledhill, *The Times Best Sermons of 1996*, p. 83.

judgement? How did it bring about reconciliation? And what made his suffering and death redemptive?

So we find that these single image approaches to expounding the work of Christ give little more than very partial glimpses of what he has achieved.

Multiple images approaches

A second line of approach to this subject matter is that of a combining several images of atonement. So, for instance, Alexander Gunn at Aberfeldy Parish Church, Perthshire, employs sacrificial and military language, saying Jesus achieved, 'forgiveness and access to God', and that, 'The victory over death and evil has been won.'[19] Mark Ashcroft also combined sacrificial and military language when he said at St Margaret's, Burnage, Manchester, 'Jesus has won the victory over sin, over death, over Satan, and the powers and principalities of this world...by the blood that Jesus shed on the cross at Calvary'[20] which purifies us from sin. Dilys Owen-Quick at St Mary's Church, Swansea, makes extensive references to atonement in her discussion of Gen. 1:31, 'God saw everything that he had made, and indeed, it was very good.' She describes how Jesus, 'took death upon Himself when He died on the Cross. He conquered Death, He conquered evil, and rose again. His sacrifice was acceptable to the God of all righteousness as a propitiation for our sins.' And she finishes her sermon with the words, 'All this is ours through the amazing love of God for His creation, and the grace of His Son Jesus Christ, who gave His life as a ransom for the sin of us all,'[21] adding redemption to victory and sacrifice as images of atonement.

But how does it help to say that victory was secured by sacrifice? It is, no doubt, faithful to the New Testament witness,[22] but what does it mean? Either it adds very little, since it is well known that battles are generally only won at the cost of many lives which may be seen as sacrificed for the cause. Or else it adds too much, by diverting one line of thought into another with which there is no obvious connec-

19   Alexander Gunn, 'Remembrance Sunday' in Gledhill, *The Times Best Sermons of 1996*, p. 149.
20   Mark Ashcroft, 'The Lion, the Lamb and the Scroll' in Gledhill, *The Times Best Sermons of 1996*, pp. 17f.
21   Dilys Owen-Quick, 'And God saw Everything that He had Made' in Gledhill, *The Times Best Sermons of 1998*, pp. 112f.
22   Rev. 12:11, 'But they have conquered him by the blood of the Lamb and by the word of their testimony.' We shall examine the use of the Bible in formulating a doctrine of the atonement in chapter 3.

tion, like victory and the forgiveness of sin. And adding redemption to sacrifice and victory only further obscures the subject. If more than one image is to be taken, something needs to be said about how they relate to one another.[23]

Two of the short-listed preachers directly address the question of how multiple images might be combined. Bernard Thomas, preaching on Passion Sunday in St. Michael's Church in a hilltop community in South Wales, referred to the numerous discussions of theories of the atonement and concludes, 'Ideas of the atonement, ransom and sacrifice have had their place and continue to do so, but essentially atonement is felt and experienced by each believer.'[24] So Thomas attempts to resolve the problem by appeal to the feelings of each believer rather than discussion of any theory of atonement. But that leaves him vulnerable to the criticism that Feuerbach makes against experience based Christology: that it may be merely a dream of the human mind rather than something based on an objective reality. We need to know what Christ has done, not what we feel as if he has

---

23 Many introductory courses on the Christian faith also simply lay out several images of atonement without trying to explain how they might be interrelated. For instance, the *Christianity Explained* course by Michael Bennett takes judgement, reconciliation and redemption and describes them without comment on their interconnection. *The DC (Discovering Christianity) Course* by R.M. Cunningham again treats the cross by appeal to a range of biblical images of atonement: propitiation, redemption, justification, reconciliation and victory. His guiding principle is set out at the start, 'This sacrificial, vicarious death on our behalf transcends our ability to understand it; it is at bottom, a mystery which we cannot fully grasp. Nonetheless, the New Testament offers a number of different images to help us gain at least a glimpse of what is involved.' Richard Cunningham, *The DC Course* (Leicester: UCCF, 1994), p. 69. Some notable evangelists also take much the same approach in the preaching. David Watson combined the imagery of sacrifice with that of redemption and reconciliation in interpreting the death of Christ, as we see in his book, *My God is Real* (Eastbourne: Falcon, 1980), pp. 45ff. Elsewhere he expounds the cross in terms of justification, reconciliation and redemption. David Watson, *I Believe in Evangelism*, (London: Hodder and Stoughton, 1976), pp. 72ff. Michael Green presents redemption, judgement and sacrifice as an array of atonement images. Michael Green *Why bother with Jesus?* (London: Hodder and Stoughton, 1979), pp. 37, 41f. And J. John uses many images including sacrifice, redemption and judgement. J. John, *Calling Out* (Milton Keynes: Word, 2000), pp. 54, 58f. But how these images are related to each other, none of them attempts to say.

24 Bernard Thomas, 'Passion Sunday' in Gledhill, *The Times Best Sermons of 1996*, p. 38. As he goes on to explain, the experience to which he refers is that of suffering and abandonment, which is, he says, 'redeemed and is a fellowship of his suffering.'

done.

The other attempt to bring the images of atonement together is made by Jim Rea of the East Belfast Mission. He devoted a third of his sermon for Advent to the crucifixion, and says, 'The cross has so many facets that it is impossible even to begin to comprehend. It is essentially the most amazing way that God shows his love to humankind.'[25] So Rea sees the multiplicity of atonement images as evidence that this is such a profound and complex mystery that we should not expect to understand it even in an elementary way. Each image should thus be treated as but one insight that must not be pressed too far.

Rea is by no means alone in this approach. D.W. Cleverley Ford takes a very similar line in his *Preaching on the Crucifixion*. He identifies four general groups of atonement images: legal categories, the demonstration of God's love inspiring love in human hearts,[26] the triumph of good over evil, and, drawing on feminist theologians, childbirth, with the agony of crucifixion yielding new life.[27] He then comments,

> The temptation is to opt for one and reject the others. This is wrong. The Godhead is a profound mystery and so is his work in the crucifixion. We see something, of course we see something, otherwise it would be meaningless. Any explanation, however, we may have can be no more than *one window* through which, possibly, we catch a glimpse, maybe only for a time, of what God was doing for us at Golgotha. Yet we must trust the little we see for by means of it we shall be brought into the presence of God, and that is satisfaction enough.[28]

A similar line of approach is also to be found in some contemporary introductory courses to the Christian faith. In the *Alpha Course*, which is currently being run by over seven thousand British Churches,[29] Nicky Gumbel describes the results of the death of Christ in terms of justification, redemption, sacrifice and reconciliation. All these, says

---

25   Jim Rea, 'Pictures that Last: A Sermon for Advent' in Gledhill, *The Fourth Times Book of Best Sermons*, p. 70.
26   This is an important reminder that although none of the short-listed preachers uses this approach, it is still appropriated by some prominent preachers.
27   D.W. Cleverley Ford, *Preaching on the Crucifixion*, (London: Mowbray, 1993), pp. 97f. This is not an exhaustive list. Cleverley Ford also gives account of the crucifixion in terms of sacrifice and redemption (pp. 7, 43, 83, 113 on sacrifice, and p. 116 on redemption).
28   Cleverley Ford, *Preaching on the Crucifixion*, p. 98.
29   According to *Alpha News*, November 2000, there were then 7,117 *Alpha* courses running in the UK (p. 15).

Gumbel, reveal God's love for us. Commenting on how these many different images may be held together, Gumbel says, 'Like a beautiful diamond, the cross has many facets.'[30] Another popular introductory course, *Emmaus: The Way of Faith*, takes a similar approach. It uses the same four aspects of the atonement: the law court, market, family and sacrifice, and describes them as, 'four pictures'[31] which speak of the meaning of Jesus' death.

So the claim is being advanced that there is an irreducible pluralism here, with no one image commanding special place in a doctrine of atonement, and no particular arrangement of images to be expected to co-ordinate them. None of the images should be developed as if it provides a reliable guide to the doctrine, and no means of combining the images is available to provide a concerted exposition of the gospel message. The *Emmaus* material casts this in a positive light. 'People can normally relate to at least one and they give the beginning of an understanding which can be developed further in the growth section of *Emmaus*.'[32] However, a contemporary Western audience may have largely lost the sense of God as lawgiver and judge, and does not see slaves for sale in the market place or the sacrifice of sheep and goats. Only the need for reconciliation in broken families and the imagery of military conflict are likely to strike a cord. But are we at liberty to discard those other images that fail to make connections with us? There is a real danger here of being left with little more than hints and intimations of the love of God. If that is all we have, we cannot expect preaching on the atonement to be anything other than timid and tentative.

The crucial question here is about the status of these atonement images. To say that they are like the facets of a diamond, pictures, or the windows of a building is to attribute to them an equality of importance and to assign each a unique but partial perspective. It is a move away from regarding them as alternative theories which each give full accounts of the same event, but towards what exactly?[33] Should

---

30   Nicky Gumbel, *Questions of Life* (Eastbourne, Kingsway: 1993), p. 49.

31   Stephen Cottrell, Steve Croft, John Finney, Felicity Lawson and Robert Warren, *Emmaus: The Way of Faith*, Stage 2, Nurture (London: National Society/ Church House Publishing, and Swindon: The Bible Society, 1996), Members' Handouts, p. 13.

32   Cottrell *et al*, *Emmaus: The Way of Faith*, Stage 2, Nurture, Leaders' Guide, p. 22.

33   Cleverley Ford continues to refer to the theories of atonement, but, by describing them as windows, he shows that he has in mind partial and incomplete explanations hardly worthy of the designation 'theory' in any strong sense. Cleverley Ford, *Preaching on the Crucifixion*, p. 56.

they be seen more as working hypotheses, or perhaps as models or metaphors of atonement? And, whichever term may best describe them, how do they relate to one another? If they may indeed be combined, do they together span the whole message of reconciliation, as the diamond analogy suggests, or not, as the window and picture analogies suggest? In order to establish how these images should be regarded separately and collectively, we must seek to articulate what each one contributes to our understanding of the work of Christ and where their limits lie.

B. Trivializing Illustrations

Our second concern is with the way these sermons on the atonement are illustrated. In order to try to make the discussion of reconciliation more concrete and visual, stories are told which are said to illuminate the gospel message. Inevitably, all such illustrations have their limitations, but, we must ask, how well do they function in these cases? For instance, Ian Sweeney, ended his sermon on John 3:16, which won the 1998 Preacher of the Year Award, with the story of a railroad controller, John Griffith. His eight-year-old son fell into the gears that operated the bridge just as the Memphis Express was approaching. If he lowered the bridge his son would die. If he didn't the passengers on the express would die. He chose to sacrifice his son so that the passengers would live. Sweeney then explains that God loves us enough to sacrifice his Son so that we might live.[34]

What are we to make of this story? It does have certain strengths. The language of sacrifice is rendered in a form which is both accessible and relational, and it indicates how the many might benefit from the death of the one. But it also carries with it several problems. The first is that it makes the death of the son seem inevitable. However great the pain of allowing the son to die, if it certainly meant saving the lives of the many passengers of the express train, the decision to sacrifice him was almost unavoidable. Any other action would have been dreadfully selfish. Secondly, it makes the work of the father appear essentially independent of the action of the son. However great the anguish at bringing about his son's death so that the passengers on the train might live, it is his son and not himself that suffers that death, losing the sense of God in Christ reconciling the world to himself.[35] Thirdly, it represents the death of the son as being either his own fault or his father's. If he had not been permitted

---

34   Ian Sweeney, 'It's the Thought That Counts' in Ruth Gledhill, ed., *The Fifth Book of Best Sermons* (London: Cassell, 1999), pp. 201ff.

35   2 Cor. 5:19.

to leave the observation tower then the son was to some extent to blame for his own suffering, and if he had been granted permission the father must bear some share of the blame. For all its strengths, this story lacks the vital ingredient of grace.

Jim Rea, in his sermon on Advent, provides a second example of such illustrations. After saying that the cross is fundamentally multifaceted, he takes up judicial language to develop his theme further and offers the following illustration.

> A story that originates in the United States is that of two young men growing up in a community together as firm friends. However, life went differently for them. One sadly became involved in crime, while the other became successful in the legal profession and ended up as a judge. One day they faced each other across a courtroom. The offender had committed a serious act of fraud. His friend the judge recognised a need to do right by the law, so he greatly shocked his childhood pal when he fined him the highest amount for the crime committed. Moments later the judge went to the centre of the court and paid the fine for his friend.[36]

Rea then explains that the atonement is likewise an act of both justice and mercy in which 'Jesus takes upon himself death as a way of sharing in our judgement. Therefore God forgives us.'

This illustration does have considerable merit. It is to be commended for overcoming the sense of emotional distance between the judge and the defendant in some presentations of judicial accounts of atonement, by making them friends. It is also effective in representing the atonement as an act of grace with the guilty man shocked that he could go free because of what the judge does vicariously for him. It does, however, have important weaknesses. Firstly, it allows the law to be something externally imposed rather than being a gracious gift of the judge himself. This judge does not formulate the law; he only interprets and applies it. Secondly, by making the crime fraud rather than a capital offence like treason, presumably in order to allow the penalty to be borne by another, the sense of sin leading to death is lost. Having the judge impose the maximum possible fine also seems unduly harsh. Thirdly, the payment of the fine by the judge appears almost effortless. The judge could no doubt afford it. He earned a substantial salary and was even able to pay the fine then and there. And lastly, this is a highly individualistic account of atonement. What about the next man or woman in the dock? Does the atonement need to be re-enacted for each? Rea himself was not unaware of some of the limitations of this story. He mentions that

---

36 Jim Rea, 'Pictures that Last: A Sermon for Advent' in Gledhill, *The Fourth Times Book of Best Sermons*, p. 70.

it lacks a sense of the judge being a representative, which could go some way towards addressing the problem of individualism. He also says that this judicial picture is but one aspect of the atonement, although he does not explain how other pictures help to overcome these weaknesses.[37] Commendable as it is that Rea draws attention to some of these inadequacies, they do inevitably greatly diminish the value of using the story to help elucidate the gospel message.

A third illustration of the atonement is provided by Gumbel in his discussion of the question, 'Why did Jesus die?' He says what God has done is best understood in terms of, 'the self-substitution of God', following John Stott.[38] This is illustrated by the story of prisoners of war working on the Burma railway during World War II when a shovel went missing and a Japanese guard threatened to shoot all the prisoners unless it was returned. One man stepped forward and was clubbed to death as he stood silently to attention. On returning to the camp it was found that no shovel was missing. Gumbel explains that one man had died as a substitute to save others. He then interprets Christ's own suffering and death in the light of it, saying it was because, 'he carried our sins.'[39]

This illustration also has its merits. It speaks eloquently of one death that averted the death of many, and of the courage and dignity of the man who was prepared to die for his friends. But, again, it has some serious problems. Firstly, the death threat made by the guard is entirely unreasonable, especially in view of the recovery of the lost shovel. The whole incident rests on a miscounting and a tyrannical imposition of force, both of which are terribly unjust

---

37 Gumble uses the same illustration more adequately by saying that the judged imposed 'the correct penalty' for the crime and by stating the limitations of the illustration more fully. He points out that the relationship between judge and accused is not just friendship but that of father and lost child, and the cost was not just a fine, but the very life of the Son of God. Gumbel, *Questions of Life*, p. 50.

38 John Stott, *The Cross of Christ* (Leicester: IVP, 1986), pp. 133ff. Gumbel separates the question of, 'What has God done?' from, 'What are the results?', with the former focusing on the self-substitution of God and the latter on justification, redemption, sacrifice and reconciliation as facets of the diamond. But this raises the question of whether such a sharp separation may be made between the action of God and the effects of that action. How do justification, redemption, sacrifice and reconciliation result from this self-substitution? In order to address that question, something must be said about how these transformations were brought about by the self-substitution, thus narrowing the separation that Gumbel proposes.

39 Gumbel, *Questions of Life*, p. 49. The story is taken from Ernest Gordon's account of the *Miracle on the River Kwai* (London: Collins, 1967).

and cast the atonement in a very poor light.[40] And secondly, this is not strictly speaking an example of substitution. The man who was killed was already condemned to die and had nothing more to lose by his action. His life was not being offered in exchange for the lives of the others, but so that others should not share the same fate. This illustration, which has been used by so many preachers, not only raises important problems for the doctrine of atonement, it also fails to convey its intended point.

No doubt it is always true that illustrations can only communicate certain aspects of their message.[41] But here much is being expected of them for articulating the good news of Jesus Christ. And we have to say that each of these familiar illustrations is in danger of trivializing the atonement. They diminish the love of God and the morality of his saving action in Christ. His work is either portrayed as inevitable, thus removing the freedom of God, or unjust, thereby undermining the goodness of God. As Forsyth puts it, 'God becomes either a spectacular and inert God, or a God who acts amiably; with the strictness of affection at best, and not the judgement of sanctity; without the consuming fire and the great white throne.'[42] The saving work of Christ is also rendered one saving action among many, in the light of which the work of Christ may be understood. Such an approach can only belittle the atonement. Again, Forsyth puts it eloquently, 'Our salvation becomes a somewhat common thing, and glorious heavens or fiery hells die into the light of drab and drowsy day.'[43]

These problems raise again the question of the status of the biblical images of atonement to which they appeal. Stories are being used in an attempt to capture the essence of the work of Christ in

---

40 It might be possible to correct this weakness if the injustice could be associated with the work of the Sanhedrin and Pilate, but that would require a significant reframing of the story.

41 Barth expresses his own reservations about the use of illustrations in the context of the *vestigia trinitatis*. He says we should not allow any of them to be pressed beyond their intended role of being an, 'interesting, edifying, instructive and helpful hint towards understanding the Christian doctrine' (I/1, p. 338).

42 Forsyth, *Positive Preaching*, p. 244. A similar point is made in *The Preaching of Jesus and the Gospel of Christ*, where Forsyth says, 'The element of divine demand has much faded out of our Christianity before the element of humane blessing; which again does not echo the preaching of Jesus.' P.T. Forsyth, *The Preaching of Jesus and the Gospel of Christ* (Blackwood, South Australia: New Creation Publications, 1915/1987), p. 28.

43 Forsyth, *Positive Preaching*, pp. 244f. This suggests that perhaps Michael Green is right when he goes so far as to say of illustrations of the atonement, 'There aren't any.' Michael Green, *Why bother with Jesus?*, p. 42.

such a way as to suggest that sacrifice, judgement or substitutionary death may be regarded as theories of the atonement which provide an account of how it may be understood. Perhaps they are being expected to encompass too much of the doctrine of atonement and would be more effective given a narrower focus, an idea we shall return to in Chapter 8. And how are the considerable claims being made for these illustrations to be held alongside the caution that some of these same authors express about how much of the atonement we can hope to understand?

Of greater concern than any of these criticisms, however, is that the work of Christ is so rarely developed in any significant way in these sermons, and not once is it used to make a congregation face the radical challenge of the cross and bring about a 'crisis of the will.'[44] Of the hundred and forty Christian sermons in the *Times* collections of best sermons,[45] only three are actually on the atonement. A further twenty-two mention the subject, but many of these are only brief allusions, as we have seen. Most references to the cross of Christ speak of the love of God in the face of human suffering, showing the influence of Professor Jürgen Moltmann and in particular his book *The Crucified God*.[46] We may, in fact, go so far as to say that the cross as theodicy has largely displaced the cross as atonement in these sermons. That the central message of God's reconciling work should arise so infrequently in this sample of sermons should be a matter for the gravest concern, presenting further evidence of what

---

44 Forsyth, *Positive Preaching*, p. 89. Barth makes similar demands when he says, 'The Word confronts modern man, to disturb and attack him in order to lead him to peace with God. This Word must never be distorted or obstructed by laziness or disobedience. The preacher, therefore, must have the courage to preach as he ought, courage that does not flinch from a direct attack and is unmoved by the consequences which may result from his obedience.' K. Barth, *Prayer and Preaching* (translation by B.E. Hooke, London: SCM Press, 1964), p. 108.

45 I.e. excluding the thirteen entries by Rabbis in the fourth and fifth books.

46 Moltmann says, 'There is no loneliness and no rejection which [God] has not taken to himself and assumed in the cross of Jesus,' and, 'all being and all that annihilates has already been taken up in God and God begins to become "all in all".' Jürgen Moltmann, *The Crucified God* (translation by R.A. Wilson and John Bowden, London: SCM Press, 1974), p. 277. We see this echoed by Dr Alan Billings at St George's Church, Kendal, who spoke on the Dunblane massacre saying, 'If we are tempted to ask of Dunblane, 'Where is God in all this?' we answer 'He is here. In the sixteen children and their teacher, Christ is crucified.' Alan Billings, 'The Dunblane Massacre' in Gledhill, *The Times Best Sermons of 1996*, p. 132. And Dr. Imogen de la Bere

Colin Grant has described as a tacit 'abandonment of atonement'.[47]

C. How we shall Approach the Problems

It is the aim of this study to address these problems by arguing that judgement, victory, redemption and sacrifice are not independent images of atonement, but that they stand in mutual relationship as metaphors of atonement with judgement as the paradigmatic metaphor. As such, we are building on what Professor Colin Gunton[48] has argued, that these are metaphors rather than theories or models of atonement, and then showing that judgement is such a profound and wide-ranging metaphor of atonement that victory, redemption and sacrifice should be treated as subordinate metaphors to it.

Our method will be to analyse the texts that have most strongly influenced the doctrine of atonement in Britain over the last century. We shall see from these that victory, redemption, sacrifice and judgement should be seen as metaphors rather than theories of atonement, and that none of these should be discarded, as some authors are inclined to do, but nor can they simply be collected together without any arrangement between them, as others propose. We shall then investigate the proposal made by P.T. Forsyth that the perfect obedience of Christ provides the co-ordinating principle for the doctrine of atonement, and point out how this fails to bring about the unification it promises. Then we shall consider the doctrine of recon-

---

told a congregation at St. Saviour's, St Alban's, that, 'This God, this God who was in Jesus, knows what it is to stand naked in the gas chamber.' Imogen de la Bere, 'Bending God's Ear' in Gledhill, *The Fourth Times Book of Best Sermons*, p. 65. It also arises in Clare Herbert's sermon on God and suffering at St. Anne's Church, Soho, when she says, 'We may see in the one who knows pain that mixture of suffering and strength, that same flame of love in the surrounding darkness, that we perceive in Christ on the cross.' Clare Herbert, 'God and Suffering' in Gledhill, *The Fifth Times Book of Best Sermons*, p. 69.

47 His article, entitled 'The Abandonment of Atonement', was published in the *Kings Theological Review* IX, 1986. Grant here draws on D.M. MacKinnon who wrote in an essay in honour of H.H. Farmer, 'Where the theologian is concerned, we have to reckon with a readiness today to drop (without conscious acknowledgement) the concept of atonement, and to suggest that we content ourselves with that of redemption' in the sense of deliverance from evil. D.M. MacKinnon, 'Subjective and Objective Conceptions of Atonement' in *Prospects for Theology: Essays in Honour of H.H. Farmer* ed. F.G. Healey (Letchworth: Nisbet, 1966), p. 170.

48 C.E. Gunton, *The Actuality of Atonement* (Edinburgh: T. & T. Clark, 1988).

ciliation in terms of the judgement of Jesus Christ as it is expounded by Karl Barth. Judgement will then be seen in its mutual relation to victory, redemption and sacrifice and from this we will argue that it may be seen as the paradigmatic metaphor of atonement. The implications for the response to the saving work of Christ will then be considered.

The plan of work falls into two sections. The first will concentrate on twentieth century British atonement theology, looking at the influence of some of the most important texts on the atonement of last century to see how they approach the subject and how they treat the biblical material to which they appeal. Then we will consider the contribution of P.T. Forysth. The second section will focus on the judgement of Jesus Christ as it is developed by Barth in his exposition of the doctrine of reconciliation and on how this is related to victory, redemption and sacrifice. From this we will conclude that the judgement of Jesus Christ may be considered as the paradigmatic metaphor of atonement with victory, redemption and sacrifice subordinate to it. Finally, we shall look at the implications this has for the response to the message of God's saving work, seeing repentance, baptism, eucharist and growth in holiness in their relationship to judgement, before drawing our conclusions.

The intended result of this work is to provide a more effective way to present the doctrine of reconciliation and to call people to respond to the saving work of Christ. The conclusion will therefore consider what the implications are for evangelistic preaching and introductory courses in the Christian faith.

Conclusion

We have found that contemporary sermons and introductory courses to the Christian faith generally offer either one modest insight into the atonement or a puzzling array of images through which the work of Christ might be understood, with the result that there is either a lack of breadth or of clarity about what this good news actually is. Each in their different way provides no more than a muffled trumpet call which is unlikely to rouse people to make ready to meet with their God. Our task in this thesis is to try to clarify how these different images of atonement may be more effectively related to each other by treating judgement as the paradigmatic metaphor of atonement.

Section 1: Twentieth Century British Atonement Theology

CHAPTER 2

Theories, Images and Metaphors of Atonement

Introduction

Why is it that there is so little confident proclamation of the atoning work of Christ in contemporary preaching and teaching? We have seen some evidence of this malaise in our introduction and expressed concern about it, but from where precisely does the problem stem? What are the assumptions that lie beneath the sermons and introductory teaching materials which give rise to the weaknesses that we have observed?

It is our task in this first section to analyse the atonement theology that has shaped the present generation of preachers and teachers by asking, What have been the dominant approaches to this doctrine in Britain over the last century? As we shall see, there have been a great many different selections and formulations of the material, offering theories, models, images and metaphors which draw on the biblical language of redemption, sacrifice, love, law and victory. Underlying almost all of them is the assumption that these are essentially independent interpretations of atonement with minimal interconnection. In this chapter we shall see how such thinking tends to promote either outright rejection of some elements of the biblical revelation with a resulting narrowness of vision, or else a pluralistic acceptance of many aspects of atonement but without a coherent account of how they relate to one another and produce a concerted solution to the central problem of sin.

One important exception to this general trend is to be found in the writings of P.T. Forsyth. He was deeply concerned about the confusion generated by an inability to inter-relate the three major strands of New Testament teaching on the work of Christ: redemption, justification and sanctification.

> [W]hat we do not find in the classic theologians of the past is the co-ordination of the three aspects under one comprehensive idea,

one organic principle, corresponding to the complete unity of Christ's person, who did the work. We do not find such a unitary view of the work as we should expect when we reflect that it was the work of a personality so complete as Christ, and so absolute as the God who acted in Christ. Yet we must strive after such a view, by the very nature of our faith. A mere composite or eclectic theology means a distracted faith. A creed just nailed together means Churches that cannot draw together. We cannot, at least the Church cannot, rest healthily upon medley and mortised aspects of the one thing which connects our one soul with the one God in one moral world. We cannot rest in unresolved views of reconciliation.[1]

Forsyth ventured a resolution of his own, suggesting that there is a single, central theme at the heart of the atonement, perfect obedience, around which the various elements of this doctrine can be arranged. In our third chapter of this section we shall analyse the effectiveness of Forsyth's solution to the problem he so eloquently states. Then, in the light of his failure to integrate redemption, justification and sanctification under his account of Christ's perfect obedience, we shall turn to Karl Barth in our second section to consider to what extent his own discourse on the judgement of Jesus Christ provides the basis of a more satisfactory approach to this central doctrine of Christian theology.

We begin this section with an analysis of six of the most influential texts on the atonement published in the twentieth century. All but one of them are British and the other is Swedish, by the Lutheran, Gustaf Aulén. His *Den kristna försoningstanken* ('The Christian Idea of the Atonement') was published in English under the title *Christus Victor* just fourteen months after Aulén first delivered the material in the form of Olaus Petri Lectures in the University of Uppsala in March and April 1930. It has had a profound influence on English atonement theology ever since and as such demands a place in this discussion. The other five works are: *The Idea of Atonement in Christian Theology* (1919) by Hastings Rashdall, *The Christian Understanding of Atonement* (1968) by F.W. Dillistone, *Sacrifice and the Death of Christ* (1975) by Frances Young, *Past Event and Present Salvation* (1989) by Paul Fiddes, and *The Actuality of Atonement* (1988) by Colin Gunton, which we shall take in their chronological order.[2]

---

1   P.T. Forsyth, *The Work of Christ* (London: Independent Press, 1910/1938 with memoir), pp. 200f.

2   Strictly speaking, this means Gunton should come before Fiddes. However, Gunton provides a more sophisticated formulation than Fiddes and as such is best treated last.

A. Hastings Rashdall: The Atonement in the Light of Historical Progress

For the 1915 Bampton lectures, Hastings Rashdall, then Dean of Carlisle, took as his subject, 'The Idea of Atonement in Christian Theology'. The lectures were published under the same title four years later with some further elucidations. His aim was to re-examine and, where necessary, reconstruct Christian theology, 'in the light of modern philosophy, modern science, and modern criticism,'[3] by which he meant Hegelian idealism, evolutionary biology, and historical and literary criticism of the Bible. He implements this modernist agenda by a detailed survey of the New Testament, and of patristic (both Greek and Latin), scholastic and Reformation theology. His approach follows the development of the doctrine of atonement under the influence of successive generations of theologians, and results in an impressive sweep across this vast landscape of thought. One of the benefits of his approach is that ideas about ransom, victory, love, justice and sacrifice are seen to rise and fall in their significance over the centuries. Each of them is traced from their New Testament origins through the whole history of Christian theology, not so much as guides to the subject in themselves, but rather as recurring themes in the work of subsequent authors.

That is not to say, however, that Rashdall attributes equal validity to all of these themes. In fact he could see no continuing place for theories of atonement based on ransom, victory, justice or sacrifice. He abruptly dismisses the theory of a ransom paid to the devil, and with it any theory of triumph over the devil, as 'monstrous' and 'hideous.'[4] Even where Gregory of Nyssa gives an account, 'more plausibly worked out by him than by anyone else' he still calls it 'childish and absurd enough to a modern mind.'[5]

When it comes to judicial theories, Rashdall takes great care to delineate a Pauline theology of sin leading to death, and the work of Christ as taking that punishment as our substitute.[6] Then he rejects it by saying, 'It is because for modern minds it does not meet the diffi-

---

3   Hastings Rashdall, *The Idea of Atonement in Christian Theology* (London: Macmillan, 1919), p. vii.
4   Rashdall, *Atonement*, pp. 259 and 350.
5   Rashdall, *Atonement*, p. 306.
6   He says, 'it is clearly St. Paul's conception that Christ has paid that penalty in order that man may not have to pay it. It is impossible to get rid of this idea of substitution, or vicarious punishment, from any faithful representation of St. Paul's doctrine.' Rashdall, *Atonement*, p. 92. Pp. 83 to 143 are devoted to Pauline material, predominantly drawing on Romans but with references to 1 and 2 Corinthians, Galatians and Ephesians.

culty, that St. Paul's theory of the atonement cannot be our theory of
it; and in spite of all St. Paul's authority, it was never really accepted
by a great deal of later Christian thought.'[7] Atonement theories
emphasizing substitutionary punishment, such as those of Eusebius
and Augustine are firmly denied any place in modern atonement
theology.[8] And Anselm of Canterbury, although applauded for his
rejection of the ransom theory, is criticized for suggesting that Christ
satisfied the debt to God's honour, since he relied on notions of justice based on 'the barbaric ideas of an ancient Lombard king or the
technicalities of a Lombard lawyer.'[9]

The important part played by sacrificial imagery in the theology of
atonement is carefully outlined by Rashdall. He sees it particularly
in Paul's writing,[10] in the letter to the Hebrews,[11] and in Athanasius.[12]
Sacrifice does not come under the fierce attacks that ransom and
judicial theories do. It is described as 'primitive' and 'crude,'[13] but
otherwise receives little attention because, he says, 'there is no definite theory as to why there should be a need of propitiation or how

7   Rashdall, *Atonement*, p. 108. Rashdall is referring here not only to the apos-
     tolic Fathers and apologists but also to all the non-Pauline books of the New
     Testament (he accepts all New Testament claims to Pauline authorship ex-
     cept that of the pastoral epistles, p. 84). He claims that they 'shrank from the
     substitutionary theory which St. Paul attempted' (p. 206). This is a highly
     questionable point as Leon Morris and John Stott make clear. L. Morris, *The
     Apostolic Preaching of the Cross* (Grand Rapids, Michigan: Eerdmans, 1965),
     pp. 33ff, and J.R.W. Stott, *The Cross of Christ*, pp. 149ff.
8   The atonement theory of Eusebius is described as 'repulsive' (p. 301) and
     Augustine is deemed to fall short even of Paul's account of substitutionary
     punishment (pp. 335ff). Augustine is further criticized for incorporating the
     theory of ransom to the devil (pp. 330ff).
9   Rashdall, *Atonement*, p. 355. Rashdall does provide a more detailed critique
     of Anselm's theory. He complains that Anselm has a tendency, 'to confuse
     the conception of criminal and civil justice, to identify moral transgression
     with personal affront; the debt, which according to ordinary legal ideas can
     be forgiven by the creditor, with the penalty due to wrong-doing which
     must be supposed to rest upon some moral ground and cannot therefore
     be arbitrarily remitted' (p. 355). He also criticizes the attribution of guilt to
     all humanity for the sin of one, and the payment of a penalty by the sinless
     Christ for each one of them. But his primary concern is that his theory was
     wedded to a bygone era and treated the Bible in ways unacceptable to mod-
     ern criticism.
10   Rashdall, *Atonement*, p. 94.
11   Rashdall, *Atonement*, p. 151.
12   Rashdall, *Atonement*, p. 296.
13   Rashdall, *Atonement*, pp. 66 and 151.

this need was satisfied by the death of Christ.'[14] Sacrifice is always, for him, part of another theory and not a theory in its own right.

In Rashdall's estimation, the only theory deserving a place in contemporary expositions of the atonement was that of the subjective moral response to the example of Jesus Christ. He traces its emergence from the teaching of Jesus: '[O]ur Lord never taught that his death was necessary for the forgiveness of sins, or that any condition was required for forgiveness but the supreme one of repentance and that amendment which is implied in all sincere repentance,'[15] a view that relies on a very selective reading of the Gospel accounts, as we shall see in our next chapter. When he returns to this theme in his concluding chapter, Rashdall presses the point further, saying that a doctrine of atonement based on anything other than moral response is contrary to the teaching of Christ, involving, 'the astounding paradox that what the Founder of Christianity taught to His disciples was not Christianity at all.'[16] He says moral response is present in Paul, in the Johannine writings and all over the Fathers,[17] and concludes, 'what the earliest Christian Church really believed in was salvation by the influence of Christ and his teaching.'[18]

Peter Abelard is identified as the main protagonist of the exemplarist position and is quoted at length.[19] His teaching is welcomed with the exclamation, 'At last we have found a theory of the atonement which thoroughly appeals to reason and to conscience,'[20] and Rashdall bemoans a wrong turn in history when the view of Anselm prevailed over that of Abelard. Abelard is particularly commended for isolating this theory from other atonement theories, especially those based on ransom and satisfaction, and for emphasizing its importance. Rashdall does acknowledge flaws in Abelard's account; chiefly that he allows Christ's death to become somewhat isolated from his life, teaching and work as a whole. Even this, though, is regarded as less pronounced in Abelard than in other Latin authors, and Rashdall believes this weakness can be overcome, as he endeav-

---

14　Rashdall, *Atonement*, p.132.
15　Rashdall, *Atonement*, p. 45.
16　Rashdall, *Atonement*, p. 435.
17　He says of these, 'Whatever else they teach about the death of Christ, they all with one consent teach this – that it was a revelation of the love of God, intended to call forth answering love of man.' Rashdall, *Atonement*, p. 360.
18　Rashdall, *Atonement*, p. 208.
19　Rashdall, *Atonement*, pp. 358-363.
20　Rashdall, *Atonement*, p. 360.

ours to show in his final lecture.[21] So it is clear that, for Rashdall, there is only one theory of atonement worthy of any continuing place in Christian theology and that is moral response.

It is highly significant that Rashdall was writing at a time of great confidence in the human capacity for self-advancement, nurtured by Darwinism and Hegelianism, which provided fertile soil for his ideas. Since then, however, moral response theories have themselves come under mounting criticism. V.F. Storr summarizes the persistent objections effectively in fourfold form before attempting to rebut them: they make light of sin, underplay the objective effect of the cross, stress a relatively minor element of New Testament teaching, and provide no adequate explanation of why Jesus died.[22] They rely on an optimism about human progress that was buried in the cemeteries of two world wars. Meditation on the love of Christ may indeed evoke a response of love, but it does not carry the power to change the human heart without the aid of the Holy Spirit, and if that is the means of change it is not strictly 'moral influence'. Nor can such meditation put right the sins of the past. Communion with God, which is broken by our sin,[23] cannot be restored simply by reducing the rate of sinning, any more than pollution can be removed simply by reducing the rate of polluting. The barrier of sin has somehow to be removed, as Abelard himself recognized by his appeal to sacrificial categories in explaining Jesus' death.[24] The confidence that

---

21 By insisting that it is the life, teaching and work of Christ as a whole that provides his moral example. So he says, 'Christ's whole life was a sacrifice which takes away sin in the only way in which sin can be taken away, that is by making the sinner actually better.' Rashdall, *Atonement*, p. 454. Here Rashdall follows the New England theologian whose work he admired, Horace Bushnell, in describing the forgiveness of Christ in terms parallel to that used of his healing power. 'Christ entered vicariously into men's diseases, just as He is elsewhere shown to bear, and to be vicariously entered into, the burden of their sins.' H. Bushnell, *The Vicarious Sacrifice* (London: Alexander Strahan, 1866), p. 8.

22 V.F. Storr, *The Problem of the Cross* (London: SCM Press, 1924), pp 138ff.

23 '[Y]our iniquities have been barriers between you and your God, and your sins have hidden his face from you so that he does not hear' (Isa. 59:2).

24 This important aspect of Abelard's theology was apparently unknown to Rashdall. We see it in the *Exposition of the Book of Romans* where Abelard says, commenting on Rom 3:25, 'In his blood,' means 'by his death' which he describes as a 'propitiation' for those who believe. *The Library of Christian Classics* vol. X (London: SCM Press, vol. X), p. 279. Abelard also speaks of Christ bearing the penalty of our sins. Commenting on Rom 4:25 he says, 'In two ways He is said to have died for our faults: (1) because the faults for which he died were ours and we committed the sins of which he bore the penalty and (2) that by dying He might remove our sins, i.e. might take

Rashdall places in the ability of the human agent to make themselves right with God overestimates the power of the will and is in the end Pelagian. A moral response to the death of Christ is indeed required as Rashdall suggests, but it cannot provide the key to understanding the atonement.

B. Gustaf Aulén: The Rediscovery of the Classic Idea

Aulén delivered his Olaus Petri Lectures into a theological climate in which discussions of the atonement were dominated by a debate between 'subjectivists' (appealing to the moral example theory attributed to Abelard) and 'objectivists' (appealing to legal formulations like that of Anselm which had played a major role in the Western Church and were therefore dubbed 'Latin' by Aulén). In Britain, this debate could be seen around the moral exemplarists like Rashdall, R.S. Franks and V.F. Storr on the one hand, and the penal substitutionalists like R.W. Dale, James Denney and J.K. Mozley on the other.[25] In Aulén's assessment, the former were in the ascendancy thanks largely to Albrecht Ritschl's powerful advocacy of the sub-

---

away the penalty of our sins introducing us into paradise at the price of His own death and might display such grace as to draw our minds away from the will to sin and incline them to the fullest love of Himself.' Quoted by F.W. Dillistone, *The Christian Understanding of Atonement* (London: SCM Press, 1984), p. 327. Alister McGrath, in an article on *The Moral Theory of the Atonement*, shows that Rashdall is in fact following the Enlightenment theologians Steinbart and Semler rather than Abelard as he claims. McGrath also demonstrates that Rashdall was strangely unaware of Kant's penetrating criticism of the moral theory of atonement: that it lacked the ideas of divine grace and divine pardon. In the end, McGrath says, Rashdall relies on notions of merit which he criticized in medieval theology. A.E. McGrath 'The Moral Theory of Atonement,' *Scottish Journal of Theology* 38 (1985), pp. 206ff.

25 R.S. Franks, *The Work of Christ* (Edinburgh: Thomas Nelson, 1918/1962); V.F. Storr, *The Problem of the Cross*; R.W. Dale, *The Atonement* (London: Congregational Union of England and Wales,1888); J. Denney, *The Atonement and the Modern Mind* (London: Hodder and Stoughton, 1903); and J.K. Mozley, *The Doctrine of Atonement* (London: Duckworth, 1915). P.T. Forsyth comes closer to the latter group since he regards Christ's death as both substitutionary and penal, but he rejects the idea that punishment was somehow transferred to Christ. He prefers the language of representation to that of substitution, and of judgement to that of penalty or punishment. Forsyth, *The Work of Christ*, pp. 134f, 146f, 162 and 181f.

jectivist cause.[26]

Aulén did not so much wish to enter that debate as to reshape it into a three-way discussion with the addition of what he called the 'dramatic' or 'classic' idea, to emphasize its dynamic and its pedigree. He summarized this idea as follows:

> Its central theme is the idea of the Atonement as a Divine conflict and victory; Christ – Christus Victor – fights against and triumphs over the evil powers of the world, the "tyrants" under which mankind is in bondage and suffering, and in Him God reconciles the world to Himself.[27]

Aulén claimed this third element of atonement had too often been subsumed under objectivism or else neglected altogether[28] with seri-

---

26 In his *A Critical History of the Christian Doctrine of Justification and Reconciliation* (translation by J.S. Black, Edinburgh: Edmonston and Douglas, 1872). This was a translation of the first volume of *Die christliche Lehre von der Rechtfertigung und Versöhnung* (1870) in which Ritschl charted the '*Zersetzung*' or disintegration of the 'objectivist' doctrine and the rise of the Abelardian view under Schleiermacher. It is interesting to note that, by contrast, Adolf von Harnack gave a more critical assessment of Abelard's position in his *History of Dogma*. He says, 'Abelard has furnished no strict proof of the necessity of the death on the Cross; his propositions, moreover, are inadequate, because he has not clearly perceived that *that love* is the highest, is indeed alone effectual, which, by taking the *penalty upon itself, reveals at the same time the greatness of the absolution* and the *greatness of the cancelled guilt.*' Adolf von Harnack, *History of Dogma* vol. VI, (translation by W. McGilchrist, London, Edinburgh and Oxford: William and Norgate, 1893/1899), p. 79.

27 G. Aulén, *Christus Victor* (translation by A.G. Herbert, London: SPCK, 1931), p. 20. Here we can see why Aulén identifies the biblical text in which the classic idea of the atonement finds its most 'pregnant expression' (p. 89) as 2 Cor 5:18f, 'All this is from God, who reconciled us to himself through Christ, and has given us the ministry of reconciliation; that is, in Christ God was reconciling the world to himself, not counting their trespasses against them, and entrusting the message of reconciliation to us.' Although there is nothing here about victory, the devil, the forces of darkness, or even of a battle to be won, it focuses attention on the goal of Christ's saving work: atonement. Aulén does appeal to texts about the conquering Lion of Judah (Rev 5:5), Christ's death destroying death and the devil (Heb 2:14), and to the binding of the strong man (Mark 3:22ff and parallels) (pp. 90, 92). But he wants to ensure that the work of salvation is not detached from the work of atonement, either by making salvation prior to atonement (as Schleiermacher did in making *Erlösung* the precursor to *Versöhnung*), or by making atonement prior to salvation (as in the Latin doctrine). For Aulén, the two cannot be separated.

28 Aulén is inclined to exaggerate at this point. F.D. Maurice had a sermon published in his influential book, *The Christian Doctrine of Sacrifice* (Lon-

ous implications for our view of God and of Christian history. He was therefore not attempting to introduce anything new into the theological debate, but rather to restore a lost voice.

Aulén's stated aim was, 'to analyse the actual types of Atonement doctrine so that their characteristics may emerge with the greatest possible clearness, and to fix the actual development of these types in the course of Christian thought.'[29] He set about this task by providing a survey of the New Testament and giving a historical overview of the development of the doctrine of the atonement, with particular attention to the Fathers. It is a considerably less detailed analysis than Rashdall's and focuses mainly on Irenaeus and Luther. Irenaeus is given prominence for his use of the biblical imagery of ransom and for regarding the ransom as being paid to the powers of evil, to death, or to the devil, so that the world can be reconciled to God. Thus God is both reconciler and reconciled, revealing a double-sidedness that Aulén is keen to emphasise since it preserves the doctrine from rationalism. Luther is applauded for having all three essential elements of the classic view: the continuity of the divine action (i.e. it is really God Almighty himself who acts to bring about reconciliation in his Son), a close connection to the incarnation (i.e. it is not just Christ's death but his whole life that demonstrates victory over evil), and for being unashamedly dramatic and dualistic (not in the Manichean sense, but as a radical opposition of good and evil). Aulén then complains that Lutheranism has failed to receive and broadcast this important rediscovery to a wider audience.

Aulén is particularly concerned to distinguish the classic view from the Latin, and he does so not just by making clear how the two accounts differ, but by challenging the validity of the Latin theory itself. He questions some of the biblical support its adherents claim,[30] and criticizes Anselm for allowing a particular legal framework to so determine God's action, and for isolating the effect of the death of Christ from the rest of his life. He also complains that Anselm over-

---

don: Macmillan,1854/1893) which was entitled, 'Christ's death, a victory over the devil' (sermon XV) based on Heb 2:14,15. P.T. Forsyth wrote of the 'triumphant aspect' of the cross in *The Work of Christ*, (pp. 199, 222), and H. Maynard Smith had a chapter on, 'Our Lord's Victory' in his *Atonement* (London: Macmillan, 1925), where he dealt with Christ's victory over sin, evil and the devil.

29 Aulén, *Christus Victor*, p. 28.
30 In particular, he questions whether Rom 3:24,25 ('they are now justified by his grace as a gift, through the redemption that is in Christ Jesus, whom God put forward as a sacrifice of atonement by his blood') really does support the Latin satisfaction theory as some have argued (p. 88).

stresses the humanity of Christ, although this might be more a reflection of Aulén's own overemphasis on his divinity.[31] He describes the
Latin view as 'a side-track in the history of Christian dogma'[32] from
which Luther had to restore atonement theology to its main lines.

Aulén considers the imagery of sacrifice more briefly. He notes
it in Irenaeus, the Eastern and Western Fathers, the Epistle to the
Hebrews, in Anselm and in Luther.[33] Each time it is seen as a component of the classic idea, with its double-sidedness of priest and
victim, but it is not treated as an 'idea' in itself.

The 'subjective' approach is examined chiefly through the work
of Peter Abelard. Aulén reviews his criticisms of both the classic
view and Anselm's satisfaction theory before challenging his inconsistency in adding to the subjectivist idea of human merit (gained
by love awakened) the Latin concept of Christ's merit (completing
human merit by his intercession). The relatively minor emphasis that
Abelard placed on the death of Christ, which marginalized his view
in his own day, seems to make his argument virtually irrelevant to
Aulén, for whom that death is so important.

Aulén is highly critical of the account of the subjective approach
offered by Rashdall. His main concerns are that it obscures the distinction between the human and divine in the incarnation and that
it allows God's forgiveness to be conditional upon ethical improve-
ments in human lives.[34] He is also critical of the modernist agenda
that Rashdall follows, seeing its effects as stifling for theology. Eventually, Aulén concludes that the subjective view, like the Latin, has no
continuing place in Christian theology: 'In the course of the long con-
troversy, the two rival doctrines have thoroughly exposed one anoth-

---

31 Anselm's balance of Christ's humanity and divinity can be seen in *Cur Deus
    Homo?*, where Anselm tells Boso, 'If, then, it be necessary (as we have as-
    certained) that the celestial citizenship is to be completed from among men,
    and that this cannot be unless there be made that before-mentioned satisfac-
    tion, which God alone can, and man alone should, make, it is needful that
    it should be made by one who is both God and man.' Anselm, *Cur Deus
    Homo?* (translation by Rose Corbet, London: Griffith, Farran, Okedan and
    Welsh, 1098/1909), II.6. John McIntyre carefully analyses Anselmic Chris-
    tology in his reinterpretation of the *Cur Deus Homo?* and applauds the bal-
    ance he achieves. J. McIntyre, *St Anselm and his Critics: A Re-interpretation
    of the Cur Deus Homo* (Edinburgh and London: Oliver and Boyd, 1954), pp.
    126ff. In contrast, Aulén's own claim that the classic theory requires Jesus be
    fully man and fully God (pp. 168f), lacks support in his overall thesis. His
    stress on divine continuity of action runs the risk of docetism.
32 Aulén, *Christus Victor*, p. 31.
33 Aulén, *Christus Victor*, p. 47, 73f, 93ff, 104, and 133.
34 Aulén, *Christus Victor*, pp. 155f.

er's weak points; and now it is becoming clearer with every year that passes that they both belong to the past.'[35] A study that set out to restore a missing aspect of atonement doctrine has come to clear the field to such an extent that this view is the only one left standing.

Aulén acknowledges that the classic idea is unpalatable to some. He recognizes that in its patristic formulations 'its mythological dress, its naïve simplicity, its grotesque realism' does 'awaken disgust.'[36] But he calls for a patient search beneath the surface for the religious values they express and for the idea, *motif*, or theme of the atonement to which they bear witness. Here again we see Aulén's deliberate avoidance of a 'rational theory' of atonement.[37] He firmly rejects the idea that there is any self-contained system within which the mechanics of atonement may be understood.

This concern to diffuse any idea that he is offering a theory of atonement is perhaps why Aulén does not develop his main theme more fully. There is surprisingly little said about who exactly the enemy was that Christ went out to face and how it was that this enemy was overcome. Nor does Aulén discuss the question of the relationship between Christ's death, resurrection or ascension in this victory. There is also hardly any consideration of the appropriate response to the triumph of Christ, suggesting that the atonement was an entirely external act of God to which no particular response is required and after which no ongoing earthly struggle with sin should be expected. As a result, Aulén is in danger of allowing the suffering of Christ to be obscured by his final triumph over the devil, and the call to take up our cross and follow him to be drowned by the invitation to celebrate his victory.

There are also problems within the idea that Aulén expounds. What he calls the classic idea is itself in fact a bundle of ideas. The Roman Catholic theologian, J. Rivière, in his *Le Dogma de la Rédemption* discerns in the Fathers three forms of 'The Question of the Rights of the Devil.' They are a 'judicial' ransom theory, a 'political' misuse of demonic power, and a 'poetical' or metaphorical deception of the devil.[38] Aulén denies that such separate categories

---

35 Aulén, *Christus Victor*, pp. 161f.

36 Aulén, *Christus Victor*, p. 63.

37 E.g. Aulén, *Christus Victor*, p. 47. Since it is the removal of supernatural elements of Christian faith by appeal to reason that Aulén repeatedly criticises, it is not so much avoiding *rational* theories, as avoiding *rationalist* theories.

38 He identifies the first chiefly with Origen and Gregory of Nyssa, the second with Augustine and Pope Leo the Great, and the third with Ambrose, Eusebius of Emesa and Pope Gregory the Great. J. Rivière, *Le Dogma de la Rédemption* (Paris: Victoire Lecoffre, 1905), pp. 373ff.

can be maintained,[39] which is perhaps true if we are considering three fully fledged theories. He cannot, however, deny that they are all distinct *ideas* of the atonement to be found in the Fathers. In the same way we must say that even if Aulén rejects the Latin and 'subjective' accounts as theories of atonement he can hardly question their biblical and patristic basis as *ideas* of the atonement. So Aulén's classic idea unravels into a whole set of ideas which, when added to all the other possible ideas of atonement, proliferate into a plethora of ideas, which are unmanageable for a dogmatic theology.

C. F.W. Dillistone: Analogues and Parables of Atonement

Aulén's work, with the support for his discussion of victory over evil as a New Testament theme[40] and for his interpretation of Luther,[41] made a rapid and lasting impression on British theology. It reopened the question of how the atonement is best understood, and spawned many new attempts to articulate its rationale. In 1937, Professor Sydney Cave of London University adopted Aulén's threefold scheme, renaming them Anselmian, moral and patristic to avoid giving the third prominence over the other two, as implied by the term 'classic'.[42] The following year, Professor Oliver Quick of Oxford University separated the Latin theory into two, juridical and sacrificial,

---

39   Aulén, *Christus Victor*, p. 520. When Rashdall comments on the work of Riv-ière, he accepts this distinction between the three forms of the theory of de-monic rights, although he suggests that the second is 'merely an outgrowth of the first' (1919, 354f).

40   *Jesus der Herr* (1935) by Karl Heim was of particular importance in empha-sising God's redeeming victory over satanic powers, as was his *Jesus the World's Perfector* (translation by D.H. van Daalen, Edinburgh and London: Oliver and Boyd, 1959). This emphasis has since continued to gain support from the study of ideas of victory and conflict in the New Testament in *Christ the Conqueror* (London: SPCK, 1955), written in English by the Nor-wegian, Ragnar Leivestad, and from G.B. Caird in his *Principalities and Pow-ers* (Oxford: Clarendon Press, 1956).

41   In Obendiek's *Der Teufel bei Martin Luther* (1931), as J.S. Whale points out in *Victor and Victim* (Cambridge: Cambridge University Press, 1960), p. 27.

42   In *The Doctrine of the Work of Christ* (London: University of London Press and Hodder and Stoughton, 1937). C.F. Rogers, Professor of Pastoral Theol-ogy at King's College, London, included ransom from slavery to the devil in his booklet on *The Atonement* (London: SPCK) in 1932, but since he does not mention Aulén it is not clear whether it was a result of his influence or not.

43   O. Quick, *Doctrines of the Creed* (London: Nisbet, 1938), pp. 221ff.

making four types of atonement theory.[43] In the same year, Professor J.G. Riddell of Glasgow University incorporated Aulén's victory idea into a scheme involving five aspects of atonement: love (moral response), law (forgiveness of sins), life (sacrifice), union (mystical participation in Christ) and conflict (victory).[44] T.H. Hughes of Edinburgh University grouped the modern writings on the atonement around eight rather muddled categories, with a ninth section for miscellaneous theories.[45] The trend towards a proliferation of theories continued largely unchallenged until 1960, when *Victor and Victim* by J.S. Whale was published. Whale returned to a threefold approach, with Christ as victor, victim and criminal, taking victory, sacrifice and judgement as three metaphors, not theories, of atonement. The response to Christ's work appears not as a moral influence on individuals but in a redeemed community entered by baptism and nourished by eucharist. This innovative and important work was, however, soon to be overshadowed by F.W. Dillistone's encyclopaedic work *The Christian Understanding of Atonement*, which returned to the quest for an all-embracing show-case in which to display the doctrine of atonement, and was to play a powerful part in subsequent British atonement theology.

The first edition of Dillistone's book was published in 1968 while he was a Fellow of Oriel College, Oxford. It was structured around

---

44 J.G. Riddell, *Why did Jesus die?* (London: Hodder and Stoughton, 1938). Essentially the same framework is used with great analytical clarity by the Reading Professor of Philosophy, H.A. Hodges, in *The Pattern of Atonement* (London: SCM Press, 1955). H.E.W. Turner also follows a fivefold course in *The Meaning of the Cross* (London: Mowbray, 1959), replacing Riddell's sacrificial category by a psychological one (overcoming sin in the form of personal frustration). K.C. Thompson takes Riddell's five aspects in his book *Once for All: A Study of the Christian Doctrine of Atonement and Salvation* (London: Faith Press, 1962), but adds a sixth, the 'remedy', meaning the grace of incarnation from which the others flow. Professor D.M. Baillie of the University of St Andrews, whose work, *God was in Christ* (London: Faber and Faber, 1947) does not seek to enumerate the New Testament 'figures' of the atonement, but sees them as complementary ways of expressing how Christ overcame sin (p. 200).

45 In his *The Atonement: Modern Theories of the Doctrine* (London: George Allen and Unwin, 1949). Hughes groups theories around satisfaction, penalty, restatements of these two, ethical satisfaction (satisfaction theory with a stronger ethical tone), biblical, moral influence, mystical and psychological theories. Sacrificial terminology was given no section of its own, appearing rather as part of the chapter entitled 'Back to the Bible' and in scattered references throughout the book.

four pairs of analogues and parables, what Dillistone also called 'extended metaphors'[46]:

Analogues	Parables
The Eternal Sacrifice	The Unique Redemption
The Supreme Tragedy	The Decisive Judgement
The All-Embracing Compassion	The All-Inclusive Forgiveness
The Image of Perfect Integration	The Word of Final Reconciliation

Dillistone saw several interpretative frameworks in the New Testament for the work of Christ, including redemption, justification and propitiation, and wanted none of these to be omitted. He said, 'My own conviction is that the New Testament contains a richly comprehensive interpretation of the death and resurrection of Christ and that we cannot afford to neglect any facets of this interpretation in any age.'[47] And he set out to place all these aspects of the doctrine of the atonement within his eight categories.

The project resulted in two striking successes. Firstly, Dillistone was able to give an account of atonement that equally stressed its corporate and individual aspects, in contrast to Rashdall with his emphasis on the individual response and to Aulén with Christ obtaining a corporate victory. His use of analogues ('patterns of corporate experience') and parables ('examples of individual achievement')[48] is scrupulously maintained in each aspect of the process around which every chapter is structured: analysis of universal human experience, of Old and New Testament texts, of the Fathers, of later theologians, and of contemporary thought. The one place where this balance is noticeably lacking, the introduction, is reworked in the second edition of the book published in 1984, where Dillistone adds a discussion of pollution to that of alienation in order to provide the corporate aspect of the problem met by the atonement.

Secondly, the scheme Dillistone proposed could embrace a huge breadth of material. Old and New Testament teaching on sacrifice, victory over evil, law and judgement are considered, as are family life, covenant friendship, reconciliation and initiation into the people of God, providing an unusually wide-ranging coverage of the biblical basis of Christ's atoning work and human responses to it. It also

46   Dillistone, *The Christian Understanding of Atonement* p. vi.
47   Dillistone, *The Christian Understanding of Atonement* p. 26.

encompasses the writings of a great many theologians of the atonement and relates their work to the wider field of religious behaviour of groups and individuals, and to history, philosophy, literature, poetry, art, music, psychology and law. As such, Dillistone provides a remarkably thorough introduction to the doctrine of atonement and locates its place amongst many different disciplines of thought.

The eight-fold structure and the breadth of scope do, however, introduce conflicting demands. In order to maintain the shape of the book, without omitting any notable writer on the atonement, Dillistone is obliged to make difficult decisions about which single aspect of a given author's thought is to determine their primary location in the book. Surprisingly, Abelard is considered under, 'The Image of Perfect Integration' as part of a discussion of Christian mysticism, not under 'The All-Inclusive Forgiveness' in the section on the importance of human response to the cross of Christ. Emil Brunner is discussed under 'The All-Inclusive Forgiveness' rather than 'The Decisive Judgement,' with the penal substitutionary theorists. And P.T. Forsyth is introduced under the psychological response category in 'The All-Inclusive Forgiveness' chapter, making Forsyth's discussion of the objective redemption by the perfect obedience of Christ secondary to that of the human response of confession. Each one of these could be regarded as a matter of emphasis, but together they call into question whether the distinctions made between the eight categories can be maintained without doing violence to the views of the theologians that Dillistone seeks to represent.

In his final chapter, 'The Idea and the Event', Dillistone attempts to consolidate the work, and identifies sacrifice and redemption as 'two basic shapes or patterns'[49] around which much of his material may be understood, giving his first analogue and parable a precedence over the others. Unfortunately, how the other sections relate to these two, and how these two relate to each other, Dillistone does not explain. We are therefore left without a coherent Christian *understanding* of atonement, but rather with innumerable Christian *understandings*. Dillistone's commitment to set his discussions of the atonement within the wider context of universal human religious experience also means that the particularity of the *Christian* understanding of atonement is sometimes lost. So this commendable quest for a comprehensive account of the atonement eventually serves to illustrate the inherent difficulties in trying to give an orderly account of atonement without making informed selections from all the possible material.

48   Dillistone, *The Christian Understanding of Atonement* p. 27.
49   Dillistone, *The Christian Understanding of Atonement* p. 410.

D. Frances Young: Sacrificial Images of Atonement

In 1975, Frances Young, then lecturer in Biblical Studies at Birmingham University, presented and developed some of the conclusions of her PhD thesis on sacrificial ideas in early Greek Christian writers in a book entitled *Sacrifice and the Death of Christ*.[50] It has had the effect of securing sacrificial imagery a more prominent place in British atonement theology.

Young's aim was 'to clear away misunderstanding' and 'to rediscover the original meaning of the sacrificial language of the Church' in the hope of showing Jesus Christ meets 'ultimate needs, concerns and values.'[51] She provides an analysis of sacrificial imagery as it is found in the Bible, in Greek and Roman philosophies and in the early Church, and addresses concerns about the enduring relevance of sacrificial imagery for Christian doctrine and practice. It is this second part, where Young relates sacrifice to other accounts of the atonement, that is of particular interest to us.

In chapter five, 'Atonement and Sacrifice', Young briefly surveys the theories of Abelard and Anselm and raises objections to them both. Abelard is criticized for obscuring the centrality of the cross, for making salvation too subjective, and for insufficient stress on the new relationship resulting from Christ's reconciling work. And Anselm is criticized indirectly, and therefore rather ineffectively, for sowing the seeds of penal substitutionary theories which, she says, endorse the immoral punishment of an innocent victim instead of the guilty sinner and set a wrathful heavenly Father against his loving Son.[52] Young then welcomes Aulén's reintroduction to atonement theology of Christ's victory over Satan and his angels, although she criticizes him for minimizing the place of sacrifice because he regards it as incompatible with his ideas about ransom. Young argues that sacrifice can be to avert evil powers, in which case it comes very close to Aulén's victory motif. Sacrifice and ransom are thus parts of the same cosmic drama and do not need to be treated as rival alternatives.

---

50 F.M. Young, *Sacrifice and the Death of Christ*, (London: SPCK, 1975). The PhD thesis was later published with minimal modifications in the Patristic Monograph Series, No.5 under the title *The Use of Sacrificial Ideas in Greek Christian Writers from the New Testament to John Chrysostom* (Cambridge Massachusetts: The Philadelphia Patristic Foundation, 1979).

51 F.M. Young, *Sacrifice and the Death of Christ*, pp. 12 and 16.

52 Since Anselm himself made Christ's *satisfactio* (satisfaction) of God's honour the means by which *poena* (punishment) was avoided, not implemented (*Cur Deus Homo?* I.xiv,x,v), the criticisms Young makes of his work fall short of her target.

Young hoped to do for sacrifice what Aulén had done for victory,[53] and she employed a similar method, showing the importance of sacrifice in expounding the death of Christ in the Bible and in the early Church. Where Aulén gave particular prominence to Irenaeus, Young gives it to Athanasius, although she is disinclined to make her own theology as systematic as his.[54] Young delights in the bipolar nature of Christ's sacrifice as priest and victim,[55] just as Aulén rejoiced in the bipolar nature of his victory. She also follows Aulén in avoiding claims that she is setting out a rationalist 'theory' of the atonement, preferring to talk of sacrificial 'imagery' of atonement, although she was apparently unaware that Aulén rejected the designation, 'theory' for his classic idea.[56] Sacrifice, she says, could be understood to effect the expiation of sin, the propitiation of God or the aversion of evil, and no one model could faithfully express all three.[57]

Young sees her contribution as threefold: (1) opening up wider perspectives on the atonement by reconsidering the imagery of a sacrifice offered by God and to God, (2) healing a divorce between atonement and response by an emphasis on a sacrificial response to the sacrifice of Christ,[58] and (3) restoring the corporate dimension of atonement by making the worshipping community the context in

---

53 We should note, however, that the theme of sacrifice has never been as neglected as victory in atonement theology, largely because of its greater significance in eucharistic prayers. See Dom Gregory Dix, *The Shape of the Liturgy* (London: A. & C. Black, 1945), p. 77, R.S. Paul, *The Atonement and the Sacraments*, pp. 257ff, and John McIntyre, *The Shape of Soteriology* (Edinburgh: T&T Clark, 1992), pp. 8f, for further discussion of this point.

54 Young rejoices in 'the rich and varied range of meaning implicit in the [sacrificial] imagery' because 'it leaves open the possibility of unsystematic thinking and unresolved paradoxes.' Young, *Sacrifice and the Death of Christ*, p. 91.

55 'There are two sides to [Christ's] sacrificial act, the removal of evil and sin by God, and the offering of perfect homage by man.' Young, *Sacrifice and the Death of Christ*, p. 95.

56 Young refers to Aulén's '"classic" theory' of the atonement. Young, *Sacrifice and the Death of Christ*, p. 89.

57 Young makes it clear that these different aspects cannot be seen as aspects of one theory. For instance, she says about aversion and propitiation: 'There is a fundamental inconsistency between thinking of Christ's sacrifice as an act performed by God to avert the devil and thinking of it as an offering made to God to appease wrath.' Young, *Sacrifice and the Death of Christ*, p. 91.

58 She takes this too far when she says, approvingly, 'the sacrificial language of the early Church represented not merely response to, but participation in the sacrifice of Christ,' if this indicates that the atonement is achieved in part by our own actions. Young, *Sacrifice and the Death of Christ*, p. 97.

which Christ's sacrifice is received and celebrated.[59] In each respect she has achieved some measure of success. It is, however, her avoidance of a detailed consideration of what exactly Christ has achieved and how he has achieved it that weakens her thesis. The discussion moves too quickly to how the eucharist 'sums all this up,'[60] before she has explained what it is that it summarizes. We are left with not one but three unresolved and unrelated images of sacrifice: expiation, propitiation and aversion, none of which has been described in any detail.[61] Like Aulén, she has rejected other theories of the atonement and replaced them with a set of ideas which are only preserved from the kind of criticism she has leveled against others by reducing their claims from being 'theories' to being, in her case, 'images.'

E. Paul Fiddes: Overlapping Images of Salvation

The next important developments in British atonement theology came a decade after Young's work, when three influential works were published: *The Cross of Christ* (1986) by John Stott, *The Actuality of Atonement* (1988) by Colin Gunton, and *Past Event and Present Salvation* (1989) by Paul Fiddes. All three gave justice, sacrifice and victory prominent roles in interpreting the atonement, and considered appropriate responses to the death of Christ. Stott argued the case for a recasting of a penal substitutionary theory in the light of its critics, based on the self-satisfaction of God by his self-substitution. His work makes extensive use of biblical exegesis and is less concerned to delineate and interrelate aspects of justice, sacrifice and victory and as such contributes little to our discussion. For reflections on the use of theories, images and metaphors of atonement, it is Gunton and Fiddes who demand our attention here. We shall take Fiddes first.

Paul Fiddes, then tutor in Christian doctrine at Regent's Park College, Oxford, set out to explore how the completed work of Christ relates to contemporary experience of salvation. By so doing, he undertook to address one of the two central questions posed by Kant's moral philosophy: How does a present course of right living relate to the past satisfaction for sins?[62] Fiddes was concerned

---

59   Young, *Sacrifice and the Death of Christ*, p. 95ff.
60   Young, *Sacrifice and the Death of Christ*, p. 98.
61   The nearest Young comes to explaining what it is that Christ has achieved in these three respects is given on pp. 121-124, but even here the brief discussions are dominated by their accessibility to modern culture and to their psychological effect.
62   This question, along with that of whether we can be saved by an agent other than ourselves without losing our moral freedom and autonomy, is raised sharply by Kant in his *Religion Within the Limits of Reason Alone*, especially

that this aspect of the atonement was too often being 'glossed over.'[63] With this in mind, he examined the issues addressed by the atonement, the 'images' (rather than theories) by which atonement has been understood, and the experiences that should flow from that atonement. It is his use of these images that we shall consider here.

Fiddes selects four images: sacrifice, justice, victory and the act of love, which he regards as incomplete in themselves and overlapping. He says,

> That the effect of the cross can never be fully or properly explained is witnessed to by the wide range of images and metaphors created through the ages to express it; atonement has been portrayed in pictures drawn (among many others) from the temple, the battle-field, the law-court, the slave-market, courtly love, family life and medicine [psychology].[64]

Here we see some of the influences of Dillistone, Fiddes' teacher. There is no expectation of arriving at an account of the atonement. Instead, the subject is to be considered through a kaleidoscope of images, each of which has established a place in the history of Christian doctrine.

Fiddes makes several important advances on Dillistone in the framework within which he proposes to argue his case. Firstly, by confining the images to four, Fiddes achieves a higher degree of clarity, selecting major doctrines of the atonement rather than trying to include them all. Secondly, by setting himself the task of relating the past event to present salvation, Fiddes allows himself to treat only those elements of Christian tradition that make important connections between the first century and the twentieth. Thirdly, Fiddes investigates the individual and corporate aspects of all four images he considers rather than trying to allocate different aspects to different images. And fourthly, by providing a brief history of the doctrine of sin from the New Testament to the modern era he is able to integrate the problem addressed by the atonement and the means of its resolution more effectively than does Dillistone in his introductory

---

in the discussion of *Verschuldung* (moral debt). I. Kant, *Religion Within the Limits of Reason Alone* (translation by T.M. Greene and H.H. Hudson, New York: Harper and Row, 1794/1960), pp. 66ff. Fiddes comes to very different conclusions from those of Kant, who sees satisfaction in the suffering of punishments by the new man (who has adopted a good disposition) for the sins of the old man (who is morally regarded as another).

63 P.S. Fiddes, *Past Event and Present Salvation: The Christian Idea of Atonement* (London: Darton, Longman and Todd, 1989), p. ix.

64 Fiddes, *Past Event and Present Salvation*, p. 4.

discourse on alienation and pollution.[65]

Fiddes, like Young, wants to overcome the distinction between the 'objective' and 'subjective' theories of atonement. He says, 'The question then is not whether a view of atonement is objective *or* subjective, although much fruitless argument has been spent on this by Christian thinkers in the past; the question to be asked is how well it *integrates* the two elements.'[66] He undertakes to do so by emphasizing the continuing process of salvation and the present experience of restored relationships.

There is, however, an important problem with the way Fiddes implements this programme. He does so by conflating images of sacrifice, justice and victory with 'the act of love', the image which draws heavily on Abelard. We find Fiddes concluding his chapter on justice with a strongly subjective reinterpretation:

> This legal model of atonement tells us not that [Christ] endures a penalty instead of us, but that he can create a penitence within us. Such penitence is expiating, in that it wipes out sin by replacing an attitude of sinful rebellion with an attitude of home-coming.[67]

In his discussion of sacrifice, Fiddes makes the remark, 'the sacrificial death of Christ expiates sin; it expiates sin by changing sinners,'[68] which replaces the sacrificial removal of sin with a moral response to Christ's self-sacrifice.[69] The victory of Christ is also recast and seen as facilitating our victory: 'it is an event that creates and enables a

---

65 Fiddes himself uses alienation as evidence of a fallen world, but to this he adds failure to fulfil potential and rebellion against God (p. 6). The integration he achieves also makes clear how theories of the atonement cannot be separated from their corresponding doctrines of sin.

66 Fiddes, *Past Event and Present Salvation*, p. 26. Fiddes is critical of the way that Aulén challenges the objectivists and subjectivists. He says that, despite his denials, Aulén is advocating another theory, and a theory that sets God's wrath against his love, and neglects the fact that Satan became an over-zealous guardian of the law by making it absolute rather than provisional (pp. 132f).

67 Fiddes, *Past Event and Present Salvation*, p. 110.

68 Fiddes, *Past Event and Present Salvation*, p. 79. He claims support from Isa 52:13-53:12 and from Origen's phrases: 'propitiated sin' and 'propitiated men to God.' But these make different points, since each of them involves the removing of past sin, not just changing the sinner for the future.

69 He also, in the end, distances himself from seeing Christ's work as being sacrificial because of 'the circumstances of his death.' Fiddes, *Past Event and Present Salvation*, p. 82. There may indeed be forsakeness and shame, Fiddes says, but it is hardly a cultic sacrifice of the kind he had earlier discussed. Here he overlooks the metaphorical connection between the death of the passover lambs and that of Christ, a connection made in different ways by

victory in our lives here and now'[70] by the revelation of the victories Christ achieved and the formation of a community committed to emulating his example. Jesus' victory was not so much over Satan as over sin,[71] and benefits his disciples not so much by a past defeat as by a present influence. In the end, Fiddes' concern to stress the subjective aspects of each theory has the effect of transforming them into being aspects of the fourth: the act of love. His concern to raise the profile of present salvation is achieved at the price of reducing the significance of the past event, and of the eschatological fulfilment yet to be realized.

Fiddes claims he espouses a multiplicity which is to be welcomed because of the expectation that it will mean that the atonement will 'touch life at many points.'[72] However, as we have seen, his desire to stress the subjective element of the so-called 'objective' images results in a much narrower outcome than he had promised.[73] The atonement for Fiddes is about the transformation of life now by the inspiration of the work of Christ two thousand years ago. Salvation is gained by responding to the cross, not by the cross itself. The rivalry between the different approaches to the atonement is removed not so much by seeing them as overlapping images as Fiddes claims, as by reworking them into several aspects of moral response, and is subject to the problems which we have already seen with relying on that approach alone.

F. Colin Gunton: Metaphors of Atonement

In his *The Actuality of Atonement*, Colin Gunton, Professor of Christian Doctrine at King's College, London, set out to 'show that metaphor is both a pervasive feature of our language and that it is a

---

all the Gospel writers, as Gunton points out. Gunton, *The Actuality of Atonement*, p. 122.

70 Fiddes, *Past Event and Present Salvation*, p. 135.
71 He is quite explicit about this, 'Better to speak of defeat of sin, than defeat of Satan.' Fiddes, *Past Event and Present Salvation*, p. 133.
72 Fiddes, *Past Event and Present Salvation*, p. 5.
73 This is further evidence to support Colin Grant's argument that all attempts to reconcile objective and subjective explanations of atonement are doomed to failure because they operate in different paradigms. C. Grant, 'The Abandonment of Atonement' *Kings Theological Review* IX, 1986, p. 6. This is, however, not so much because the objective had to give way to the subjective as a result of the Enlightenment as Grant suggests, but because subjective theories do not strictly constitute an atonement theory at all; in them, the barrier of past sin remains in place.

way of telling things as they are,'[74] and then to apply his findings to the doctrine of the atonement.[75] From the start, these twin concerns give the book a markedly different shape from that of the previous five. We have for the first time a substantial criticism of prevailing contemporary thought patterns rather than an attempt to provide an account of atonement from within their assumptions (like Rashdall, Dillistone and Fiddes) or broad-brush rejections of rationalism (like Aulén and Young). Gunton instead targets the rationalisms of morality, experience and concept stemming from Kant, Schleiermacher and Hegel respectively, which have done so much damage to pre-modern expositions of the atonement. This is not in order to justify reusing past formulations of the doctrine of atonement, but as a preparation for reinterpreting traditional atonement imagery in terms of metaphor, and thereby to transcend the narrow confines of rationalism.

To establish his case, Gunton draws on recent scholarship, largely from the philosophy of science, which almost unanimously rejects the view propounded by Hobbes and Locke that metaphor is an abuse of language, and instead advances the claim that it is a major clue to what language is and does. He considers its characteristics in comparison to those of the rationalist conception of language mirroring reality and concludes that 'simply in virtue of the greater modesty of the claims for comprehension, metaphor is a primary vehicle of human rationality and superior to the pure concept (if such exists, as must be doubtful).'[76] Here, indeed, lies the importance of metaphor: it enables us to speak of things without which we could only remain silent. As Gunton later says, '[A] metaphor or family of metaphors takes its shape from the divine and human story it seeks to narrate, and so enables aspects of the meaning of an unfathomable mystery to be expressed in language.'[77] Having secured his use of the term,

---

74 Gunton, *The Actuality of Atonement*, p. 25.
75 As he acknowledges, Gunton was by no means the first to use metaphor to describe the relationship between biblical imagery and the work of Christ. We see it, for instance, in Rashdall (*Atonement*, pp. 159, 356, 370), Storr (*The Problem of the Cross*, chapter.VIII), and prominently in Whale (*Victor and Victim*, pp. 36f, 46f, 69, 78), whose influence Gunton acknowledges in his preface (p. xi). Gunton's contribution is to harness recent philosophical writing on metaphor in order to spell out more precisely how traditional atonement imagery relates to the work of Christ itself, without diminishing the claim to the objective reality of the ontological change in relationship which it has secured.
76 Gunton, *The Actuality of Atonement*, p. 39.
77 Gunton, *The Actuality of Atonement*, p. 113.

Gunton then examines the New Testament imagery of victory, justice and sacrifice as metaphor, reconsidering each of them in the light of this research.

Gunton's discussion of 'The Battlefield and the Demons' is largely occupied with analysing Aulén's *Christus Victor*. He argues that by taking the victory over Satan metaphorically rather than literally some of the historic problems with this theory, such as the attribution of rights to the devil, can be avoided. It is, in Gunton's view, precisely because Aulén presses the imagery too far that the cosmic battle becomes a 'myth,' placing it, 'in a sphere outside the course of concrete divine-human relations.'[78] This is by no means to withdraw the claim that by his death Christ gained a mighty victory. It is instead to say that we have here a metaphorical way of expressing the victory that Christ has achieved. As Gunton puts it, 'These biblical metaphors, then, are ways of describing realistically what can be described only in the indirect manner of this kind of language. But an indirect description is still a description of what is really there.'[80] And since this is a victory in which the evil and lies of an enemy are overpowered not by force but by goodness and truth, it is an example of how a metaphor can transform our understanding of a word (such as 'victory'), our understanding of the world in which this victory has occurred, and our understanding of the God whose victory it is.

The beneficial results of such a conscious use of metaphor continue to be seen in the chapters on justice and sacrifice. Gunton gives Anselm a sympathetic reappraisal, not least because he avoids being bound by a literal reading of cosmic law; Jesus after all freely offers himself to the Father, and God is not primarily a judge exacting compensation. Anselm also makes a rather limited use of the so-called 'classic theory' of overcoming the devil, which shows an awareness that his judicial account does not entirely stand alone. Gunton then takes two accounts of atonement in terms of justice, one by P.T. Forsyth in *The Justification of God* and the other by Karl Barth in volume IV of his *Church Dogmatics*, and shows how these can be seen as two different uses of judicial metaphor each with their own strengths and weaknesses.

When Gunton comes to the metaphor of sacrifice he engages primarily with the nineteenth century Calvinist, Edward Irving, applaud-

---

78 Gunton criticizes Aulén for failing to provide the basis for a theory (p. 61), although, as we have seen, Aulén did not intend to produce a theory.

79 Gunton, *The Actuality of Atonement*, p. 63f. A 'myth,' says Gunton, is what results when a metaphor is allowed to dictate reality.

80 Gunton, *The Actuality of Atonement*, p. 65.

ing his consistency and originality, his development of Calvin's theology of Christ's human priesthood, and the cosmic context in which
Irving uses the sacrificial metaphor. Gunton concludes, 'What, then,
is potentially an abused and overused metaphor can also become
the most living and expressive of all, the heart of the doctrine of the
atonement as an expression of the unfathomable power and grace of
God.'[81]

Having made a persuasive case for the use of the term 'metaphor'
to describe the use of the images of victory, justice and sacrifice to
interpret the work of Christ, Gunton then moves to set these three
metaphors in a wider context. He asks, What do they say about God,
his creatures and their mutual relationships? All three metaphors
considered are at root about relationships, but Gunton now wants to
explore 'whether a consistent pattern can be discerned in the various
relationships which have come to light.'[82] Gunton then considers
these metaphors in terms of the twin themes of creation and eschatological redemption, which provide common origins and ends but
no particular connection in between. He does not, however, address
the question of how the metaphors of victory, justice and sacrifice
are to be regarded in connection to each other. His earlier assertion
that sacrifice stands at 'the very centre of the doctrine of the atonement,'[83] with its suggestion of primacy amongst these metaphors, is
not pressed further here with a view to clarifying their inter-relation-
ship.[84] As he said from the outset, Gunton's aim is to reappraise traditional presentations of the atonement in terms of metaphor, rather
than to examine how they might relate to one another.

---

81   Gunton, *The Actuality of Atonement*, p. 141.
82   Gunton, *The Actuality of Atonement*, p. 144.
83   Gunton, *The Actuality of Atonement*, p. 141.
84   Gunton develops this metaphor more fully elsewhere, such as in a chap-
     ter entitled, 'The Sacrifice and the Sacrifices: From Metaphor to Transcen-
     dental?' which he contributed to *Trinity, Incarnation and Atonement* edited
     by R.J. Feenstra and C. Plantinga Jr (Indiana: University of Notre Dame
     Press, 1989). But here again sacrifice is 'one of several central metaphors'
     (p. 213) which is used to illustrate and defend his claims about the value
     of metaphor for Christian doctrine, rather than to draw together the other
     metaphors. He takes the same position in his chapter 'Christ the Sacrifice:
     Aspects of the language and Imagery of the Bible' contributed to *The Glory
     of Christ in the New Testament* edited by L.D. Hurst and N.T. Wright, (Oxford:
     Clarendon Press, 1987), material from which he uses in chapters 2 and 5 of
     The Actuality of Atonement.

G. Problems with the Theories, Images and Metaphors in their Present Form

More recent British publications on the atonement, which have claimed to offer fresh insights, have tended to do little more than place greater emphasis on sacrifice.[85] Those that have made different contributions have not significantly affected the shape of atonement theology as we have described it.[86] We are therefore now in a posi-

---

85 Prominent among these is S.W. Sykes, the former Bishop of Ely, who edited a collection of essays under the title, *Sacrifice and Redemption* (Cambridge: Cambride University Press, 1991) and wrote, *The Story of Atonement* (London: Darton, Longman and Todd, 1997) in which sacrifice is one of many narratives in the story of atonement. He also wrote the forward to *The Sacrifice of God* (Norwich: Canterbury Press, 1992) by Dr. John Moses, then Provost of Chelmsford, which is subtitled 'A Holistic Theory of Atonement'. Here, Moses embraces the term 'theories of the atonement' (chapter15) and makes sacrifice primary among them, whilst giving continuing prominence to victory and to moral response, but without suggesting how they relate to one another. In *The Power of Sacrifice* (London: Darton, Longman and Todd, 1995) the Church of Scotland minister, Ian Bradley, sets out to remove propitiatory distortions of the idea of sacrifice and to make its centre a mysterious and tragic power whose source lies in divine life-giving. Richard Swinburne also gives sacrifice prominence in his *Responsibility and Atonement* (Oxford: Clarendon Press, 1989). Michael Winter, one of very few notable British Roman Catholics publishing on the atonement in the twentieth century, draws attention to the plethora of Catholic scholarship on sacrifice in his *The Atonement* (London: Geoffrey Chapman, 1995), p. 12. Winter himself rejects traditional solutions to the problem of atonement and proposes what he sees as a new solution, that Christ's work is to be understood in terms of intercession for forgiveness, apparently unaware of the discussion of perfect confession in *The Nature of the Atonement* (London: Macmillan, 1878) by J. McLeod Campbell or of the awakening of the spirit of penitence in *Atonement and Personality* (London: John Murray, 1902) by R.C. Moberly.

86 Peter Selby, Bishop of Worcester, has offered a new approach to the metaphor of redemption in his *Grace and Mortgage* (London: Darton, Longman and Todd, 1997), but his emphasis is on international debt and its forgiveness rather than the application of such terminology to the atonement. There have also been feminist theologies of atonement, such as Mary Grey's *Redeeming the Dream* (London: SPCK, 1989) in which she describes atonement as essentially about self-affirmation and right relations. Here, she is focusing on the effect of atonement rather than reworking its metaphors. And *The Message of the Cross* by Derek Tidball (Leicester: Inter-Varsity Press, 2001) is essentially a discussion of the biblical theme of atonement which advocates penal substitution, like *The Cross of Christ* by John Stott and *The Work of Christ* by Robert Letham (Leicester: Inter-Varsity Press, 1993). But he offers no fresh insight on the question of the relationship between the various elements of the biblical teaching on the doctrine of reconciliation.

tion to begin to draw conclusions from our survey.

Twentieth century British atonement theology was heavily dominated by the belief that there are several independent theories, images or metaphors of the atonement with no significant interconnection. They are treated in one of two ways: either by seeing them as a collection of understandings from which only one need be selected (e.g. moral response for Rashdall, victory for Aulén, sacrifice for Young), or from which several or all should be held together in some balance (e.g. Dillistone, Fiddes and Gunton), as we have seen reflected in recent preaching. These two alternatives each bring their own advantages and disadvantages. The former promises greater clarity about what it is that Christ has achieved in his life, death, resurrection and ascension, and therefore about how that is to be appropriated. However, as we have seen, such approaches either fail to reflect the breadth of Christ's achievement as attested in the Scriptures (e.g. Rashdall), or they themselves subdivide into a multiplicity of ideas or images (e.g. Aulén and Young). In this case, they give rise to the same problems that beset the second alternative, namely, that whilst the scope of Christ's achievement is more fully proclaimed, exactly what it has achieved remains elusive. Greater breadth is bought at the expense of perspicuity.

Why is this so? The root of the problem lies in the sheer number of atonement metaphors to be found in the Bible and in two millennia of Christian theology. They defy any doctrinal statement that would engage with them all, which is why Dillistone eventually founders. We are forced to make selections from the material, with all the attendant risks of omitting some crucial aspect of atonement and arousing the just criticism of those like Aulén and Young who identify such flaws. The necessity to select is ever present in theology, but rarely is it so difficult or so influential as it is in atonement theology.

Having made a selection, there is then the second problem of deciding what material rightly belongs to each metaphor we have chosen to consider. Can we safely assume that different biblical authors have in mind the same thing when they use the same term, for instance *lutron*, ransom, or even that they mean precisely the same thing each time they use it? And is it legitimate to suppose that any reference in Christian tradition to, say, victory, may be drawn into a single composition? Our considerations of the insights of Rivière would suggest that the answer must be negative. The judicial, political and poetical aspects of victory over the devil each demand separate treatment. Perhaps it would be safer to speak of 'clusters of metaphors' rather than 'metaphors' in order to make it clear that there are several forms of redemption, victory, sacrifice and judgement which can illuminate different aspects of the atonement.

There is also a third methodological difficulty which arises once we have chosen and described the metaphors we have selected: if we take two or more metaphors, how do they relate to each other? With accounts drawing on such different contexts as the battlefield, the altar and the courtroom, and appealing to such different processes as military victory, ritual killing, and legal verdict, it is far from clear that they are images or metaphors relating to the same thing.[87] This is theologically problematic for three reasons. The first is that it does not make it clear that Christ came to die for the sin of the world. In the form we currently have this multiplicity, it appears that human-kind needs deliverance from many different and apparently unre-lated problems: enthrallment to the devil, slavery to sin and fear of death. Yet, in the Bible we find that there is a single primary problem of sin, which manifests itself in many ways and results in enslave-ment and eventually death because it separates us from God. How do these images or metaphors expound the solution to that central problem? In the form in which we currently find them, it is not clear that they do.[88]

It is also, secondly, not sufficiently clear that this is the saving work of the one Jesus Christ. As we saw earlier in this chapter, For-syth complains that, 'We do not find such a unitary view of the work as we should expect when we reflect that it was the work of a per-sonality so complete as Christ, and so absolute as the God who acted

---

87 This was a concern of R.W. Dale. In *The Atonement,* the lack of consistency between theories of ransom, propitiation and vicarious death, and, in his view, the impossibility of usefully combining them, are cited as driving forces for his work on penal substitution (p. 356).

88 John McIntyre, who is well aware of the problems of differing and often conflicting theories of atonement undermining each other, outlines seven possible ways of relating the different atonement theories: pluralism, his-torical relativism, complementarity, dimensionality, perspectivism (a vari-ant of pluralism), centripetal axial reference (a central hub approached along many spokes), and horizons (intersecting at the cross). J. McIntyre, *The Shape of Soteriology* (Edinburgh: T. & T. Clark, 1992), pp. 54ff. In terms of our study, Dillistone is an example of pluralism, Rashdall of historical rela-tivism, Fiddes of complementarity, and Aulén and Young of dimensionality. McIntyre favours dimensionality with its scope for polarity and paradox, but, it must be said, with all its diffuseness on the central questions of the atonement. He rejects the metaphorical approach taken by Gunton because of the unavoidable differences between a metaphor and that which it il-luminates. But this reflects the inescapable problem for the use of language for theology, and is only exacerbated by invoking the status of theory, which McIntyre prefers, with all its attendant claims to completeness and predic-tive power.

in Christ.' If we really cannot draw these different elements of the doctrine of atonement together, what does it say for our christology? Is it sufficiently clear that we are speaking of the one work of the one Christ? Ought we not be able to say how Christ as redeemer, victor, sacrifice and judge works out our salvation in a more coherent way?

And thirdly, as a result, it makes for great difficulties in proclaiming the atonement. We have already seen evidence of this in our introduction. How does it help to say that Christ's victory was secured by his sacrifice; that his sacrifice brought about our redemption; or to speak of a ransom for sin? Such ideas as victory, sacrifice and redemption need to be explained. And if they are then to be brought together, some account of how they relate to one another is demanded. It is to this problem in particular that this thesis is addressed.

Conclusion

Our consideration of twentieth century British atonement theology through six of its major exponents has served to reveal some of the serious problems associated with addressing this doctrine through just one interpretation or through an array of unconnected theories, images or metaphors. The tendency is either to make the doctrine unrealistically transparent or impenetrably opaque. Such a situation is bound to impoverish the proclamation of this central doctrine of the Christian faith. In order to address this problem, we must consider the use of Scripture on which these accounts rely. Our next task, then, will be to assess how the theologians considered in this chapter appropriate the biblical texts to which they appeal in order to better clarify the nature of the problem and to begin to trace a more promising way forward.

---

89 Forsyth, *The Work of Christ*, p. 200.
90 See Chapter 1, section A.

CHAPTER 3

Biblical Hermeneutics and the Metaphors of Atonement

Introduction

Having identified the problems associated with treating atonement metaphors as a set of independent insights into the divine work of reconciliation, our concern now is to consider how the British atonement theologians we have been considering handle the biblical material to which they appeal in formulating their positions. By so doing, we hope to identify strengths and weaknesses in their uses of the Bible with a view to finding a more systematic way of presenting the doctrine of the atonement which does justice to the teaching of Scripture. We shall therefore examine how Rashdall, Aulén, Dillistone, Young, Fiddes and Gunton address the five most prominent atonement metaphors arising in the atonement texts considered in the previous chapter: love, victory, redemption, sacrifice and judgement.

In order to focus the discussion, we shall examine how these theologians address one of these five images. We shall do so by taking three of the four diagnostic questions proposed by Professor Richard Hays of Duke University Divinity School, in his analysis of the use of the New Testament for Christian ethics.[1] These are the descriptive, synthetic and hermeneutic questions, addressing respectively: How accurate is the exegesis of the texts used? How comprehensive is the scope of the texts employed? and How are these texts appealed to? We shall then consider the way in which these authors handle passages where more than one of these metaphors arise together before drawing our conclusions about how best to appropriate these atonement metaphors.

---

1   *The Moral Vision of the New Testament* (Edinburgh: T. & T. Clark, 1996), pp. 212ff. The fourth, pragmatic, question which looks at the fruit of the theological community founded on a given approach, so important to his ethical enquiry, will not be considered here in view of the more indirect effect of atonement theology on Christian behaviour.

A. Rashdall and Fiddes on Love

Hastings Rashdall and Paul Fiddes both make the response of love to the loving initiative of God the centre-point of their discourse on atonement. We shall therefore take them together and see how they both utilize Scripture.

Descriptive

Rashdall gives considerable attention to New Testament texts which have shaped the ideas of Christian atonement theology and he engages with some passages in detail. In particular, he devotes nine pages to a discussion of the genuineness and original meaning of Mark 10:45, 'For the Son of Man came not to be served but to serve and to give his life as a ransom for many,' and a further seven pages of small print in additional notes to examine critical considerations about source materials and the editorial role of the synoptic evangelists.[2] There is almost as much discussion of the institution narratives, and some detailed consideration of Paul's use of *hilastērion* (propitiation) in Rom. 3:25 and of the meaning of Rom. 5:12 regarding the effects of Adam's sin.[3] Clearly, Rashdall takes the exegesis of scriptural passages very seriously. He shows careful attention to the type of text he examines, to its context and to the critical scholarship available on it, consulting very widely before forming his own judgements.

Most of Rashdall's discussion of the biblical material takes the form of a summary of the teaching of Jesus (from the synoptics, not John[4]) and Paul and, to a lesser extent, the other New Testament authors, with Scripture quotations cited for support. This is the form in which Rashdall seeks to unfold his idea of the atonement in terms of a moral response to the love of God.[5] Firstly, he draws on the preaching of Jesus, 'Repent, for the kingdom of heaven has come near,' (Mat. 4:17) and 'I have come to call not the righteous but sinners' (Mark 2:17) as evidence that his message was, 'that the kingdom of heaven was open not merely to the respectable and law-observing scribe or the learned rabbi, but to the poor and outcast, those who knew not the law and those who had broken it, if only they would repent.'[6] From this he draws the implication that 'for-

---

2   Rashdall, *Atonement*, pp. 29ff and 49ff.
3   Rashdall, *Atonement*, pp. 130ff and 133ff.
4   The Fourth Gospel is excluded from this enquiry because he regards it as an unreliable source for the teaching of Jesus. Rashdall, *Atonement*, p. 28.
5   Rashdall, *Atonement*, pp. 23-29.
6   Rashdall, *Atonement*, p. 23.

giveness is dependent upon no condition whatever but repentance, and the amendment of life which is the necessary consequence of sincere repentance.'[7] He then adduces further support for his emphasis on forgiveness being available without prior conditions from several parables, most importantly the prodigal son (Luke 15:11-32) and the Pharisee and the publican (Luke 18:9-14). Finally he attacks those who claim that the forgiveness Jesus offered depended on his own actions, and particularly his death, rather than only on the divine practice of forgiving the penitent, pointing out that Jesus said to the woman who anointed his feet, 'your sins are forgiven' (Luke 7:48) not 'will be forgiven' after his death. This is also the point at which he provides his extensive engagement with Mark 10:45 and the institution narratives in order to dispute their use to suggest Jesus taught that forgiveness was dependent on his death. He does so by questioning the authenticity of the former as 'a report coloured by later doctrinal teachings of the Church,'[8] and by denying any expiatory associations with his death in the latter, by asserting that Luke, who does not say Jesus' blood was poured out, 'for the forgiveness of sins,' provides the most primitive account.[9]

Rashdall is, however, more concerned with detailed exegesis of passages which appear to be hostile to his view than with those that support him. The parables of the prodigal son and of the Pharisee and the tax-collector, and the narrative of the woman who anointed Jesus, to which he attaches such importance, are not examined in any detail. Of particular concern with regard to his thesis is the lack of engagement with the question of the cost of forgiveness to the one who forgives. What did it cost the father of the prodigal son

---

7   Rashdall, *Atonement*, p. 25.

8   Rashdall, *Atonement*, p. 29.

9   Rashdall also disputes claims that the writings of John suggest the death of Jesus is necessary for forgiveness. He says, 'Nothing is said about the saving work of Christ's work which may not be understood of the moral influence of His life and work' (p. 181), and he quotes John 15:13 ('No one has greater love than this, to lay down one's life for one's friends) and 1 John 3:16 ('We know love by this, that he laid down his life for us – and we should lay down our lives for one another') in support. But he is only able to maintain that assertion by claiming that 1 John 1:7; 2:2 and other verses which speak of Jesus' death as being expiatory are the additions of later Church traditions (p. 180). For a detailed refutation of Rashdall's arguments regarding Mark 10:45, see Leon Morris *The Apostolic Preaching of the Cross*, pp. 29ff.

to forgive him for squandering a substantial portion of his estate,[10] and to endure the terrible affront of his son wishing him dead by disposing of that share of the inheritance while he lived?[11] And was it not because the woman had been forgiven such a large debt that she loved so much? Rashdall's exegesis suggests that her debt had been simply erased from the balance sheet, when in fact a debt written off is a debt borne by the creditor. As such, Jesus' announcement of forgiveness prior to his death may be seen as a statement of preparedness to accept the cost rather than a declaration that it has already been absorbed. The parable of the Pharisee and the publican was directed at those who 'trusted in themselves and regarded others with contempt' (Luke 18:9) and should not be pressed too far in determining what it took to be able to offer the repentant tax-collector forgiveness. Had Rashdall been as diligent in scrutinizing the texts to which he turned for support as he was in analyzing those which he regarded as inimical to his view, his doctrine of atonement might have been significantly different.

Paul Fiddes makes considerably less detailed use of biblical texts than does Rashdall when he comes to consider 'The Act of Love.'[12] What use he does make of the Bible here is largely mediated through his discussion of other theologians, and in particular, Peter Abelard. So when he quotes Rom. 5:5, 'God's love is poured into our hearts through the Holy Spirit that has been given to us', Fiddes does so

---

10   The exact proportion of the estate which the younger son might have received is uncertain, but it was probably either a third or two-ninths of the estate. For a fuller discussion see I.H. Marshall, *The Gospel of Luke*, (Exeter: Paternoster Press, 1978), p. 607, J. Nolland, *Luke 9:21-18:34* (Word Biblical Commentary, vol. 35B, Dallas, Texas: Word Books, 1993), pp. 782f, and E. Schweizer, *The Good News According to Luke* (translation by D.E. Green, London: SPCK, 1984), p. 248.

11   Charles Talbert comments on this text, 'The boy treats his father as if he were dead.' and N.T. Wright describes asking for his share of the inheritance as the functional equivalent of saying to his father, 'I wish you were dead.' C.H. Talbert, *Reading Luke* (London: SPCK, 1990), p. 149, and N.T. Wright, *Jesus and the Victory of God* (London: SPCK, 1996), p. 129. Leon Morris replies to Rashdall's exegesis by pointing out that no evidence is given for the amendment of life in the younger son in this parable, nor does the father actively seek out the son, or show his abhorrence of his sin, nor even introduce the figure of Christ. L. Morris, *The Cross in the New Testament* (Grand Rapids, Michigan: Eerdmans, 1965b), p. 79. James Denney makes the same points in *The Christian Doctrine of Reconciliation* (Carlisle, Paternoster, 1918/1959), p. 135.

12   Fiddes, *Past Event and Present Salvation,* pp. 140ff.

because 'it is a key one for Abelard'[13] in explaining how redemption takes place through inciting love in the human heart. John 15:13, 'No one has greater love than this, to lay down one's life for one's friends', is also quoted because it is important to Abelard, this time in establishing a connection between the love of Jesus and his death, but not because Fiddes wants to make use of the verse himself.[14]

When it comes to the direct appropriation of Scripture, Fiddes makes reference to only three biblical texts in this chapter. The first, Exod. 3:13 ('But Moses said to God, "If I come to the Israelites and say to them, 'The God of your ancestors sent me to you' and they ask me, 'What is his name?' what shall I say to them?"') is not actually quoted and is interpreted with the bald assertion, 'Moses wanted to gain power over God by possessing his name.'[15] The second, Rom. 8:26, is used with regard to the work of the Holy Spirit, and is partially quoted: 'with sighs too deep for words.'[16] It does not receive detailed comment, although Fiddes' use indicates an awareness of the context of the verse as part of a discussion of the redemption of creation. The third text, 1 Cor. 12:13, 'For in the one Spirit we were all baptized into one body…', is cited as evidence that Paul required the language of 'Spirit' to speak of our being incorporated into the body of Christ, but he does not use the text to expound the atonement itself.[17] Fiddes thus makes little use of exegetical work to construct his doctrine of atonement in terms of moral response.

Synthetic

Rashdall provides a substantial and serious engagement with every part of the New Testament, with the Gospels, Pauline material and other writings receiving careful attention. They do not, however, enjoy equal weighting. There is a clear hierarchy, with the synoptic Gospels as most authoritative, then Paul, followed by John and the other writings, shading off into the apostolic Fathers and apologists. Rashdall's functional canon would include the synoptics and parts of Paul, but little else. Certainly, the Old Testament would lie outside of it, reflecting the influence of Schleiermacher, whose support for an Abelardian position he applauds.[18] Since so much of the biblical evidence for understanding atonement in terms of a work of expia-

---

13 Fiddes, *Past Event and Present Salvation*, p. 154.
14 Fiddes, *Past Event and Present Salvation*, p. 155.
15 Fiddes, *Past Event and Present Salvation*, p. 160.
16 Fiddes, *Past Event and Present Salvation*, p. 166.
17 Fiddes, *Past Event and Present Salvation*, p. 167.
18 Rashdall, *Atonement*, p. 438.

tory substitution is to be found outside of the synoptic Gospels, it is clear that Rashdall's selection of Scripture plays an integral part in the formulation and defence of his theological position.

Rashdall is also at times highly selective in the Scriptures he quotes. In his study of Pauline theology he says, 'All through his epistles the atonement is presented as an arrangement due to the eternal and unchangeable love of God,' and goes on to say, 'by far the greater part of what he says may well be explained and justified by the subjective effect which the love of God revealed by Christ produces on the soul of the believer.'[19] He cites the reconciliation through forgiveness of 2 Cor. 5:19-21 and the proof of the love of God of Rom. 5:8 in support. But whilst 2 Cor. 5:19 and 20 are quoted, v 21 (Christ being made sin 'who knew no sin, so that in him we might become the righteousness of God') is not, and no comment is offered about how this verse fits within the view he espouses. Nor does Rashdall use Rom. 5:9, 'Much more surely then, now that we have been justified by his blood, will we be saved through him from the wrath of God', which makes the very point he seeks to refute: that the forgiveness which brings justification is available because of the death of Christ. So Rashdall here builds his case on a highly selective reading of the biblical material.

In contrast to Rashdall, Fiddes makes so little use of the Bible for presenting atonement in terms of moral response as to make it almost insignificant. None of the texts presented by Rashdall are even mentioned by him. Indeed, the chapter entitled, 'The Act of Love', which is so central to his overall thesis, includes the least substantial biblical element of any in his book, which is generally rich in engagement with the Bible. As a result, his minimal use of biblical texts in this chapter suggests that he is unable to muster much biblical support for his position, thus weakening his claim that moral response is so central to a Christian understanding of salvation.

Hermeneutic

Throughout his work on the atonement, Rashdall's reading of the Bible is primarily controlled by reason. For instance, as we have seen, it was for being unreasonable that the Pauline doctrine of Christ dying for our sins as our substitute was rejected.[20] The particular form of reason to which Rashdall refers is that of a mind shaped

---

19 Rashdall, *Atonement*, pp. 100 and 101.
20 He says 'for modern minds it does not meet the difficulty.' Rashdall, *Atonement*, p. 108.

by an 'enlightened conscience,'[21] by which he means one that has been illuminated by repentance and the reconciliation with God that ensues. So, he says, 'For those who believe in a righteous God, God must be supposed to act in the way which the moral conscience approves.'[22] Rashdall thus suggests that the human conscience is so perfected by repentance and reunion with God, and is thereafter able to judge the value of the Scriptures, providing a highly selective Kantian filter through which the Bible is read.[23] Only biblical teachings seen to meet the criteria of moral goodness as perceived by the repentant reader can be accepted as truly Christian, locating the source of authoritative teaching in the enlightened reader rather than in the Scriptures themselves.

This stress on reason also means that Christian tradition is given a relatively minor place by Rashdall. Only those doctrines that meet the standards of rationality and goodness that Rashdall applies retain their place in Christian theology. Tradition is on occasion, however, used to support the conclusions of rationality. When Rashdall repudiates the Pauline doctrine of substitution because of its problems for modern minds, he goes on to say, 'and in spite of all St. Paul's authority, it was never really accepted by a great deal of later Christian thought,'[24] a remark whose truth we have already questioned. Otherwise, tradition is rarely considered as an authority. In practice, Rashdall replaces Hooker's three theological sources: Scripture, reason and tradition, with his own triumvirate of the teaching of Jesus, reason and conscience.[25]

For Fiddes, it is experience rather than reason which dominates his hermeneutics. It is 'experience of God', he says, that leads believers to associate 'fellowship' with the Holy Spirit.[26] The emphasis on experience is reinforced in the third section of his book, which

---

21   Rashdall, *Atonement*, p. 49.
22   Rashdall, *Atonement*, p. 21.
23   Kant says, 'If [a Scripture] flatly contradicts morality, then it cannot be from God (for example, if a father were ordered to kill his son, who is, as far as he knows, perfectly innocent).' Kant, *Religion Within the Limits of Reason Alone*, 6:87/82.
24   Rashdall, *Atonement*, p. 108.
25   Rashdall sets out his approach at the end of his first lecture saying that he will test atonement doctrines according to 'how far they are consistent with the teaching of Christ on the one hand, and on the other with the reason and conscience of the present.' Rashdall, *Atonement*, p. 48.
26   Fiddes, *Past Event and Present Salvation*, p. 166. Fiddes appeals to the teaching about the Spirit of adoption who prays within us in Rom. 8:15 and 26 for corroboration.

52

The Justifying Judgement of God

is devoted to the consideration of the experiences of forgiveness, politics and suffering. The first of these is of particular significance for understanding his formulation of moral response. It is here that Fiddes explains what he means by forgiveness, and he does so by an extensive interaction with literature, drama and poetry, and to a lesser extent with the Bible and Christian tradition. Human experience thus plays the primary role for Fiddes not only in setting the questions theology is to answer, but also in formulating the response it is to make.

Taken together, Rashdall and, to a much lesser extent, Fiddes, adduce considerable scriptural evidence to show that the atonement is an act of God's love and should inspire love in all who hear of it. But they present no biblical mandate for claiming that the response of love is the means of atonement itself. Rashdall only separates the death of Christ from the provision of divine justification by overlooking the cost of forgiveness, and Fiddes only incorporates the death of Christ into the story of salvation by appeal to other images, such as sacrifice, redemption and victory, following the example of Abelard.[27] The scriptural case for atonement through repentance cannot be said to have been established by either author.

B. Aulén on Victory

In his *Christus Victor*, Professor Aulén makes relatively little use of the Bible, concentrating instead on the teaching of the Fathers and Luther to establish the 'classic' idea. He does however devote a chapter of his book to the New Testament, and it is to this that we now turn.

Descriptive

In his study of the New Testament, Aulén only rarely engages with exegetical work on particular texts, even those most germane to his argument. Where he does, it tends to be brief and heavily dependent on the work of other scholars. So when he considers Col. 2:15, '[God] disarmed the rulers and authorities and made a public example of them, triumphing over them in [the cross]', he cites work by Martin Dibelius, drawing attention to the importance of Christ's victory over demonic powers and quotes some of the parallel passages referred to by Dibelius.[28] With the notable exception of Col. 2:15,[29]

---

27   See Fiddes, *Past Event and Present Salvation*, pp. 155ff.
28   1 Cor 15:24f; Phil 2:10 and Rom 8:35f . Aulén, *Christus Victor*, p. 86.
29   This is notable not least because, as Colin Gunton points out, Wesley Carr

Aulén refers to the context of each of these verses, not so much to interpret the texts as to signify their importance by showing that they occur in close proximity to what he regards as Paul's central concern, the love of God in Christ. Surprisingly, Heb. 2:14, '...so that through death he might destroy the one who has the power of death, that is, the devil', is quoted without any comment despite his observation that this is 'perhaps more often quoted by the Fathers than any other New Testament text,'[30] and the very direct bearing that it has on his thesis.[31] Nor does he explore the references to the victorious lamb that was slain in Rev. 5:12 and 12:11. Even the verses in which Aulén finds the most 'pregnant expression' of the classic idea, 2 Cor. 5:18f, 'All this is from God, who reconciled us to himself through Christ, and has given us the ministry of reconciliation; that is, in Christ God was reconciling the world to himself, not counting their trespasses against them, and entrusting the message of reconciliation to us,'[32] receive no further discussion at all, despite the fact that they do not explicitly mention redemptive victory.

Where Aulén does examine the meaning of particular texts, he is not always a careful reader. In his discussion of Rom. 3:24f, '...[Christ Jesus], whom God put forward as a sacrifice of atonement by his blood, effective through faith...,' Aulén is primarily concerned to remove it from the body of evidence purported to support the satisfaction theory. He says it lacks the sense of a sacrifice made by Christ to satisfy God, which would need an offering 'made to God from man's side, from below.'[33] Yet this is one aspect of the 'sacrifice of

---

has since called into question the use of Col. 2:15 as evidence for a victory over the rulers and authorities. After an examination of the first century social background, Carr argues that the verse could be paraphrased, 'He laid aside his battle dress (his flesh); He publicly paraded his army of the heavenly host; He there on the cross, led them in triumphal procession.' A.W. Carr, *Angels and Principalities* (Cambridge: Cambridge University Press, 1981), p. 65; Gunton, *The Actuality of Atonement*, p. 55. This corresponds to the usage of rulers and authorities as angelic beings which G.B. Caird finds in the Septuagint. G.B. Caird, *Principalities and Powers* p. 11. Walter Wink has, however, criticised Carr's analysis for pressing the Roman victory procession metaphor too far, and for making too little of the sense of humiliation of the defeated foe. W. Wink, *Naming the Powers* (Philadelphia: Fortress Press, 1984), pp. 55ff.

30 Aulén, *Christus Victor*, p. 90.

31 Leivestad observes that this and Col. 2:14f represent 'the most dramatic interpretation of the death of Jesus in the New Testament.' R. Leivestad, *Christ the Conqueror*, pp. 182f.

32 Aulén, *Christus Victor*, p. 89.

33 Aulén, *Christus Victor*, p. 89.

atonement' (*hilastērion*) described in the text, as Aulén later acknowl-edges in another context.[34] His strong reservations about the Latin view may here cloud his exegetical judgement.

Most of Aulén's engagement with the Bible is in the form of a summary of the thought of its authors, for which he makes exten-sive use of New Testament specialists. In his work with the Pauline material, Aulén begins by summarizing his theology largely through presenting the findings of William Wrede, who saw redemption as the centre-point of Paul's theology. As such, Wrede and the school of History of Religions following him, provide important exegetical support for the 'classic' idea, interpreted as a redemptive victory. When Aulén addresses the teaching of Jesus himself on the idea of conflict and triumph, he makes considerable use of a paper by Pro-fessor Anton Fridrichsen of Uppsala on 'The Conflict of Jesus with the Unclean Spirits' published in *Svensk teologisk Kvartalskrift*.[35] Aulén makes similarly heavy use of work by Rafael Gyllenberg for his dis-cussion of the sacrifice of Christ in the Epistle to the Hebrews. This form of summary allows Aulén to keep the scriptural texts in their narrative flow and to mention interpretative issues where necessary by making additional comments in footnotes.

Synthetic

Aulén's engagement with Scripture is dominated by his consid-erations of the Pauline Epistles, since it is interpretations of Paul's teaching on the atonement which he regards as playing a formative role in fuelling the dispute between 'orthodox' and 'liberal' scholars. He complains that the exegesis of Pauline atonement texts had been unhelpfully coloured by theological concerns. Aulén also quotes Mark 3:22ff, Heb. 2:14, 1 John 3:8 and Rev. 5:5 as evidence for the 'classic' idea.[36] The Old Testament is only used to illuminate New Testament texts.[37]

---

34   In his discussion of the Epistle to the Hebrews, Aulén affirmatively says the author regards, 'the Sacrifice of Christ both as God's own act of sacrifice and as a sacrifice offered to God.' Aulén, *Christus Victor*, p. 93.

35   Häfte, 4, 1929. It appeared in English translation in *Theology* in March 1931. When Aulén acknowledges the difficulty in interpreting John 16:8ff (espe-cially v 11, 'because the prince of this world has been judged'), he turns to Fridrichsen for advice about what can be safely said about this text and oth-ers relating to the theme of dualism. Aulén, *Christus Victor*, pp. 91f.

36   Aulén, *Christus Victor*, p. 85-92.

37   The descriptions of the Divine Warrior of Isa. 54:16ff and the Good Shep-herd of Ezek. 34:11ff are only mentioned as evidence for a breach between Judaism and Christianity. Aulén, *Christus Victor*, p. 95.

Despite the deliberate brevity of the discussion of Scripture, Aulén does, however, devote a relatively large amount of space to biblical texts using ransom as an image of atonement. After his discussion of Pauline teaching, his 'briefest possible sketch'[38] of the remainder of the New Testament commences with a string of quotations of verses about atonement as redemption. Whilst he justifies this move in terms of their interest to the Fathers, he does not actually support it by establishing their connection to the image of victory, thereby seriously weakening the force of this section.

Hermeneutic

Overall, Gustaf Aulén makes only relatively little direct use of the Bible. His primary concern is instead with Christian tradition, especially that of the Fathers, although he assumes their views are supported by the New Testament.[39] That is not to say Aulén was unaware of ways in which the Fathers differed in their emphasis from the New Testament authors. Indeed, he structures his discussion of Paul's attitude to sin and death, and to the law, around these differences.[40] But Aulén comes to the New Testament primarily to add to the evidence he has already accumulated from the Fathers that a doctrine of atonement formulated as a debate between the so-called objectivists and subjectivists was quite inadequate and needed to be reformulated to allow the 'classic' idea the prominence it deserves. In order to establish his case, Aulén highlights the biblical texts where victory is used as an image of atonement and by so doing demonstrates that it is one of the central atonement metaphors of the New Testament.

C. Dillistone on Redemption

For Dillistone, redemption is, as we have seen, one of the 'two basic shapes or patterns' of atonement, along with sacrifice.[41] We shall now consider how he appropriates Scripture to establish his view.

---

38 Aulén, *Christus Victor*, p. 89.
39 In the summary of the argument at the start of the book, Aulén says, 'We should have the right to expect *a priori* that the view of the Fathers be also that of the New Testament.' Also, the title with which he had been working in his analysis of the Fathers, 'the classic idea of the Atonement' had he says, 'assumed this conclusion.' Aulén, *Christus Victor*, pp. xiv and 77.
40 Aulén, *Christus Victor*, pp. 83ff.
41 Dillistone, *The Christian Understanding of Atonement*, p. 410.

Descriptive

Dillistone rarely uses direct quotations from the Bible, and he does not discuss many biblical texts in detail. Where he does engage in more thorough exegetical work, he, like Aulén, relies heavily on the work of other exegetes. So when Dillistone considers Col. 2:14,15 and Heb. 2:14, they are considered primarily in the light of the comments of R. Leivestad and C.F.D. Moule.[42] For his discussion of Rev. 12, he turns to Martin Kiddle.[43] Of these, it is Leivestad who is the most influential, with Dillistone saying that he provides, 'the finest exposition (in my judgement) available of the ideas of conflict and victory in the New Testament.'[44] On each occasion where the work of these scholars is used, Dillistone does not engage with their arguments. Their findings are simply received and presented, mainly in the form of lengthy quotations, which form almost a fifth of his total analysis of the New Testament material. Where Dillistone does enter an exegetical debate himself, he tends to indicate awareness of exegetical problems with a passage, but avoids disputes by concentrating on what is generally accepted.[45] For the most part, however, Dillistone relies on the work of exegetes that he admires.

Rather than engaging in detailed exegetical discussion, Dillistone is more inclined to provide surveys of biblical teaching. He does this with little reference to the work of other authors. In the Old Testament, Dillistone considers the teaching on God as victor over the forces of chaos in creation, in the exodus, and after the exile. In the New Testament, he examines the synoptic Gospels, Paul, Hebrews, the Gospel and Epistles of John, and the Apocalypse. In these discussions, he shows himself to be well aware of the distinctive emphases of the different biblical authors, and he gives due weight to the context in which the theme of victory over bondage is set.

Synthetic

Dillistone's engagement with the biblical material on redemption is surprisingly patchy. The only explicit references he makes to New Testament texts about redemption or ransom occur in his discussion of patristic writings. The ransom saying of Mark 10:45, and

---

42 Dillistone, *The Christian Understanding of Atonement*, pp. 86-89.
43 Dillistone, *The Christian Understanding of Atonement*, p. 90.
44 Dillistone, *The Christian Understanding of Atonement*, p. 106.
45 He finds, 'the central affirmation of the passage' when he considers Col. 2:14,15, and what is 'at least suggested' by the passages on the harrowing of hell. Dillistone, *The Christian Understanding of Atonement*, pp. 86 and 98.

Paul's phrase, 'You were bought with a price'[46] are only mentioned in quotations from Origen as examples of his embellishment of the Irenaean doctrine of redemption, not for his own reflections.[47] Most of the exegetical work Dillistone does carry out in his chapter about redemption is on texts about Christ's victory over evil, assuming the two to be inseparable but without actually establishing that they are, as we have seen Aulén did before him. So whilst Dillistone says that he understands redemption to mean deliverance from 'all subservience to cosmic powers, all indebtedness to legal systems, all enslavement to self-destroying habits,'[48] which includes victory, justice and redemption, it is the element of victory that is the dominant concern of this chapter.

It is perhaps as a result of Dillistone's concentration on redemption as victory that there are some biblical aspects of redemption that he does not explore. For instance, he gives no attention to redemption as a purchase for service, which we see in 1 Cor. 6:20, 'For you were bought with a price; therefore glorify God in your body,' 1 Cor. 7:23, 'You were bought with a price; do not become slaves of human masters,' and Rev. 5:9, '...by your blood you [the Lamb] ransomed for God saints from every tribe and language and people and nation.'[47] Nor does he take up the ethical implications of being redeemed in these texts and others, such as Tit. 2:14, '[Christ] it is who gave himself for us that he might redeem us from all iniquity.' For Dillistone, redemption is about release from bondage, rather than about the kind of freedom into which that redemption delivers us.

So the concern for comprehensiveness that dominates Dillistone's general approach is less apparent in his handling of Scripture. He presents sufficient evidence from Old and New Testaments to show biblical support for his claims, but he does not attempt to co-ordinate all the texts that may have a bearing on his topic. Even the Pauline epistles, which, following Leivestad, are given extra prominence, are only very partially explored. And by allowing victory to so dominate his understanding of redemption, Dillistone loses clarity about the biblical basis of redemption itself.

---

46 1 Cor. 6:20 and 7:23.
47 Dillistone, *The Christian Understanding of Atonement*, p. 96.
48 Dillistone, *The Christian Understanding of Atonement*, p. 88.
49 For a careful discussion of redemption as acquisition see S. Lyonnet and L. Sabourin, *Sin, Redemption and Sacrifice – A Biblical and Patristic Study* Analecta Biblica 48, (translation by L. Sabourin, Rome: Biblical Institute Press, 1970), pp. 104ff.

Hermeneutic

Dillistone regards religious experience as the lens through which to read the Scriptures, an approach which, as we have seen, influenced his student, Fiddes. Dillistone sets his treatment of the biblical teaching on redemption into the context of the universal human experience of redemption, considering redemption myths in Egyptian, Mesopotamian, Greek and Babylonian civilizations as the context for the Hebrew 'myth' of redemption from Egypt and their hopes for redemption in an age to come. After the sections specifically addressing the Old and New Testaments, he turns to the reflections of more recent thinkers on the experience of redemption. Whilst the Bible occupies a prominent place in his discussion, it is seen as part of a continuum of the religious experience of liberation from bondage. The same approach is taken in the other chapters of *The Christian Understanding of Atonement*, which commence with surveys of their subject in general religious experience.

Dillistone explains the reason for this approach at the end of his introductory chapter:

> We saw how various strands of evidence serve to establish the firm historicity of this death and resurrection [of Jesus] but the bare historical fact would of itself stimulate little interest and carry little meaning. It therefore becomes necessary for some vital connection to be established between the historical event and the transcendent effect. Such a connection, I have claimed, can only be made by means of a *theory*, an imaginative *pattern of comparison* which somehow links the record of the death and resurrection of Christ with the wider experiences of mankind.[50]

Dillistone is thus operating with an Enlightenment dichotomy of naked facts and added values. When he brings the historical facts of the death and resurrection of Jesus Christ into the arena of human experience, he does so in search of values that may be attached to them so that they may be generally understood. Thus when he introduces the Bible into his enquiry about the experience of redemption, Dillistone is looking for further evidence of redemptive experiences common to human life, rather than an authoritative guide to what those experiences might mean in the light of the redemption of Christ. As a result, after providing evidence for the historical death and resurrection of Christ, Dillistone gives the Bible more of an illustrative than a formative role in unfolding his doctrine of atonement. He demonstrates that redemption is used as a biblical metaphor of atonement, but makes little use of his findings in shaping the conclusions that he draws.

---

50   Dillistone, *The Christian Understanding of Atonement*, p. 27.

D. Young on Sacrifice

Frances Young wrote her *Sacrifice and the Death of Christ* as a lecturer in Biblical Studies in the University of Birmingham, and the book involves a constant engagement with Scripture. We shall now consider how she uses the Bible in her work on the atonement as a form of sacrifice.

Descriptive

Young does not engage in much exegetical work on particular texts. She prefers instead to summarize passages without commenting on the questions of interpretation they raise, or to simply refer to texts which she claims support her point. Some of her closest engagement with biblical texts comes in the chapter on 'Sacrifice in the Early Church'. Even here, though, she avoids elaborate exegetical argument by indicating an awareness of alternative readings but simply asserting her own viewpoint. So, for instance, Young comments on Jesus cleansing the Temple that, 'This incident was not a repudiation of Temple-worship and the sacrificial system, though later it received this interpretation. Rather it was a protest against turning the place of prayer into a profitable marketplace and banking-exchange.'[51]

Young, like Rashdall, saves her closest scrutiny for the texts which appear unsympathetic to her thesis, and the results are less than satisfactory. The issues raised by the translation of *hilastērion* in Rom. 3:25 and in Heb. 2:17 provide a case in point.[52] Young acknowledges that both verses are in the context of a remedy for the wrath of God, and that *hilastērion* is normally translated 'propitiation' to indicate aversion of the judgement of God. She then argues that the Old Testament background teaches that such an action requires sin be removed, expiated, since it is sin that provokes God's wrath. She therefore prefers to translate it, 'expiation,' describing the idea of propitiating an angry God as a 'pagan' interpretation.[53] However, since by her own admission such expiation would achieve propitiation, this argument does not itself settle the question.[54] Nor does her comment that in Rom. 3:25 propitiation could not be the correct

---

51 Young, *Sacrifice and the Death of Christ*, p. 48.
52 Young, *Sacrifice and the Death of Christ*, p. 72.
53 Young, *Sacrifice and the Death of Christ*, p. 74.
54 Professor J.D.G. Dunn comments on this long running dispute that it displays an unnecessary polarization of alternatives, since the wrath of God is clearly averted by the cleansing sacrifice. J.D.G. Dunn, *Romans 1-8* (Dallas, Texas: Word, 1988), p. 171.

translation because, 'the *subject* of the sentence is God,'[55] since, as Young says of sacrifice, God could be both the subject and object of the atoning action.[56] The decision to use 'expiation' instead of 'propitiation' in the face of philological and contextual evidence is, it seems, governed by her prior commitment to use what she regards as the more sophisticated interpretation of sacrifice rather than the exegetical arguments which she brings to bear.

There is little use of other exegetes in Young's work, and where such use is made it is generally to illustrate historical interpretations. Chief in this regard are Origen and Athanasius but use is also made of Gregory Nazianzen and John Chrysostom, reflecting her interest in early Greek Christian writers. Recent biblical scholarship is rarely explicitly considered. Young prefers instead to survey a wide range of biblical material directly, summarizing what she regards as the most widely accepted views of biblical scholarship, but without mentioning the names of those who have guided her.

Synthetic

By keeping her detailed exegesis to a minimum, Young is able to bring draw together a wide range of Old and New Testament passages in a short space, giving to her arguments a sense of broad biblical support without over reliance on any particular texts. There are, however, some important imbalances in her presentation. Firstly, Young hardly mentions the institution narratives, despite their importance for understanding how Jesus related his death to the passover sacrifice and her own concern to reassess the eucharist in the light of her findings about the death of Christ as a sacrifice. When such a discussion might be expected Young turns instead to the Fathers to see how the spiritual cult developed.[57] Secondly, passages which

---

55 Young, *Sacrifice and the Death of Christ*, p. 72.
56 E.g. Young, *Sacrifice and the Death of Christ*, p. 95. C.K. Barrett in his commentary on the Epistle to the Romans accepts that this verse makes, 'the paradoxical claim that God propitiates God', but he goes on to remark, 'Paradoxical as it is, this assertion comes close to the heart of what Paul has to say, and the paradox is rooted in the nature of God.' C.K. Barrett, *The Epistle to the Romans* (London: A. & C. Black, 1991), p. 74.
57 The section on the 'sacrifices of communion' (pp. 62f) is dominated by considerations of early church practice. Where connection is made between the death of Christ and the passover, it is to 1 Cor. 5:7 and John 19:31 that she refers, before turning to Melito of Sardis, Pseudo-Chrysostom and Gregory of Nazianzen. Young's discussion of how the eucharist sums up the significance of atonement (pp. 98ff) is centred on the question of in what sense the

describe the death of Christ as inaugurating a new covenant, like some forms of the institution narratives[58] and Heb. 8 and 9, receive insufficient attention, being used only as evidence for a typological interpretation of the sacrifice of Christ. 1 Pet. 2:4-10, about the creation of 'a chosen race, a royal priesthood, a holy nation, God's own people,' with its allusions to a new covenant following Exod. 19:5 and 6, is not discussed at all, although R.J. Daly regards it as, 'the richest single source of a New Testament theology of sacrifice.'[59] And thirdly, texts which suggest that the death of Christ averted the wrath of God are either omitted or introduced only in order to suggest an alternative reading. We have already seen this with regard to Rom. 3:25 and Heb. 2:17, but it is also evident in the paucity of references to sacrifice in the Johannine writings, where the call to come out of the darkness and into the light is a call to flee the wrath of God and enter communion with him, which gives the sacrificial imagery propitiatory overtones.[60]

Hermeneutic

Like Dillistone, Young sees the Scriptures in the context of universal religious experience. She identifies three universal types of sacrifice: gift, communion and sin, each of which encompasses a wide range of rituals and a multitude of different interpretations which, she says with a sense of Hegelian progress, gradually evolved in the direction of increasing sophistication from paganism to Christianity.[61] Young notes that there are additional sacrificial rites particularly associated with special Jewish feasts, such as the aversion ritual of the passover (Exod. 12) and the 'super-sin-offering' of the Day of Atonement (Lev. 16 and 23),[62] although these are then grouped under the sin-offering category. Young also points out where she sees cross-fertilisation of

---

eucharist should itself be seen as a sacrifice, with particular reference to the early Fathers.

58 Luke 22:20 and 1 Cor. 11:25, also some manuscripts of Mat. 26:28 and Mark 14:24.

59 R.J. Daly, *The Origins of the Christian Doctrine of Sacrifice* (London: Darton, Longman and Todd, 1978), p. 65.

60 John 1:29 ('Here is the Lamb of God who takes away the sins of the world!') and 1 John 2:2 ('[Christ] is the atoning sacrifice [*hilasmos*] for our sins') are not used by Young. Nor, indeed, are the references to the sacrifice of the Lamb, or to the blood of the Lamb in Revelation (Rev. 5:6, 9, 12; 13:8, and 7:14 and 12:10 respectively).

61 Young, *Sacrifice and the Death of Christ*, pp. 21ff.

62 Young, *Sacrifice and the Death of Christ*, pp. 28ff.

ideas between Greek and Jewish thought,[63] and shows how so many
of these ideas were assimilated into Christianity. She does highlight
what is distinctively Christian, such as the rejection of all material
sacrificial rites and the call to offer spiritual sacrifices instead, but
her emphasis is on the continuities not the discontinuities with religious experience in general.

Young uses the Bible primarily as evidence of historical advance
in the human experience of sacrifice from feeding or placating gods
towards thanksgiving or purification of the offerers. She provides
ample biblical evidence for regarding the death of Christ as a sacrifice but underplays the distinctiveness of his work. As Gunton says,
'there is no altar, but a cross; he is killed by soldiers not (directly
– see John 11:50) by priests; and there is no provision in the sacrificial
regulations as they appear in the canon of the Old Testament for
the sacrifice of a human victim.'[64] It is therefore better to see this as
a metaphorical use of sacrifice, as Gunton says, with considerable
discontinuity with the universal experience of sacrifice, rather than
in the typological relationship advocated by Young.

E. Gunton on Judgement

Professor Gunton takes 'The Justice of God' as one of the three atonement metaphors selected for reconsideration. Whilst sacrifice is, as
we have seen, identified as the metaphor he finds most fruitful, the
three chapters on the metaphors of victory, judgement and sacrifice
are evenly weighted and we shall use Gunton's discussion of the
justice of God to gain insight into his handling of the Bible.

Descriptive

Gunton generally carries out little quotation of Scripture or detailed
exegetical work.[65] He, like Dillistone and Young, prefers to provide
a statement of what he regards to be the general consensus of biblical scholarship. So he remarks, 'In the Old Testament, for example,
there is a certain amount of variety in the way law is conceived to
function in Israel's life, but none about the fact that it belongs firmly
in the context of God's covenant with Israel,'[66] before proceeding to

---

63   Young, *Sacrifice and the Death of Christ*, p. 45.

64   Gunton, *The Actuality of Atonement*, p. 122.

65   There is somewhat more exegetical discussion where Gunton considers the
     victory of God, especially in his consideration of Col. 2:15. Gunton, *The Ac-
     tuality of Atonement*, p. 55.

66   Gunton, *The Actuality of Atonement*, p. 85.

discuss the importance of the covenant context of the Mosaic law. Later, commenting on God's righteousness in Paul's theology, he says, 'although there is some disagreement among recent scholars, many now see with the help of the Old Testament, that an important aspect of the concept's meaning centres on the notion of God's faithfulness to his entire creation.'[67] He also makes reference to scholars who have particularly shaped his thinking, notably M.T. Brauch and E.P. Saunders on Paul's treatment of the righteousness of God.[68]

If one biblical text could be said to receive particular attention and exert special influence on his formulation of the judicial metaphor it is Rom 3:24f, 'they are now justified by grace as a gift, through the redemption that is in Christ Jesus, whom God put forward as a sacrifice of atonement by his blood, effective through faith.' It is quoted twice.[69] Each time it is used to illustrate the meeting of two atonement metaphors, law and sacrifice, and Gunton sees the exegesis of this text as depending on the mutual interpretation of these two metaphors. On the first usage, attention is also drawn to the presence of a third atonement metaphor, redemption, which Gunton takes to be an image from the slave market. Whilst this is probably the best interpretation of *apolutrōsis* (redemption), it is not the only one. The word is also used of the release of criminals condemned to death,[70] of prisoners of war,[71] and of people in the grip of madness,[72] possibilities which Gunton does not explore. This is one occasion when such an overview can mask exegetical complexities, although here it does not affect the flow of the argument.[73]

Gunton is careful to set the texts he uses in their context. In order to understand the meaning of 'justification of sinners' in Romans, he summarizes the argument of the letter as a whole.[74] He also places

---

67 Gunton, *The Actuality of Atonement*, p. 103.
68 Gunton, *The Actuality of Atonement*, p. 104.
69 Gunton, *The Actuality of Atonement*, pp. 85 and 105.
70 E.g. Heb. 11:35.
71 E.g. Plutarch *Pompei* 24 (I, 631b).
72 E.g. Nebuchadnezzar in the LXX of Dan. 4:34. G. Kittel, ed. *Theological Dictionary of the New Testament* vol. I, (Grand Rapids, Michigan: Eerdmans, 1949, 1964), p. 350.
73 Professor Morna Hooker understands *apolutrōsis* in Rom 3:24 in the same way as Gunton in her study of New Testament interpretations of the death of Christ, but she is careful to say that the underlying metaphor, 'appears to be that of buying a slave,' which explicitly leaves open alternative interpretations. M.D. Hooker, *Not Ashamed of the Gospel* (Carlisle: Paternoster Press, 1994), p. 26.
74 Gunton, *The Actuality of Atonement*, p. 102.

Paul's thought within its Old Testament background,[75] so that he sets the legal metaphor in the covenant context that it occupies in Hebrew thought, enabling him to note that, 'Justification is not a legal fiction but a new relationship.'[76] He thus avoids the pitfall of legalism that results from constructing the judicial metaphor around a concept of abstract law. This same concern with context is seen when Gunton insists that texts like Mark 10:45 are not to be plucked out and used over-literalistically as a building block for a ransom theory, but rather kept as a metaphorical reference.[77]

Synthetic

Gunton sees the judicial metaphor chiefly in legal terms. As he says at the beginning of his chapter on the justice of God, 'we shall concentrate attention on the use in the theology of atonement language deriving from the world of the law.'[78] So although he later broadens his purview to questions of justice, justification and judgement, Gunton devotes his initial biblical analysis more narrowly to legal issues. As a result, the Epistle to the Romans dominates the biblical component of Gunton's work in this chapter. When justification is considered later, it is in its relationship to the law in Romans that Gunton turns. It is, perhaps, surprising that the Gospel of John plays no part here, despite the close association there between judgement and the atoning work of Christ,[79] and its importance to P.T. Forsyth and Karl Barth whose development of the judicial metaphor Gunton uses extensively in this chapter. [80]

Hermeneutic

It is the hermeneutical question of how to interpret biblical imagery

---

75   Gunton, *The Actuality of Atonement*, pp. 83-7.
76   Gunton, *The Actuality of Atonement*, p. 104.
77   Gunton, *The Actuality of Atonement*, p. 88.
78   Gunton, *The Actuality of Atonement*, p. 83.
79   The connection is made particularly in John 12:31, 'Now is the judgement [*krisis*] of this world; now the ruler of this world is driven out' as Jesus prepares to be glorified on the cross. It is also made more implicitly in the trial narrative of John 18 and 19 where Christ submits to the unjust judgement of Caiaphas and Pilate, and by so doing reveals God's true judgement, that Jesus is indeed the King of the Jews, thereby condemning those who denied Jesus the honour due to his name and gave it instead to Caesar.
80   E.g. P.T. Forsyth, *The Justification of God*, p. 179 and K. Barth, *Church Dogmatics* IV/1, pp. 265 and 272.

like victory, justice and sacrifice in the construction of Christian theology that dominates *The Actuality of Atonement*. Gunton's careful attention to the exposition of metaphorical readings of these images marks this book out from the others we have considered and gives the study its strength. It is also very significant that Gunton uses the Bible itself, rather than reason, tradition or experience, as the primary guide for how these atonement metaphors should be read. He alone of our authors embraces the Reformers' hermeneutical principle of interpreting the Bible by the Bible.

But Gunton by no means gives scant attention to other sources of authority for theological discourse. Indeed, his book is essentially a reasoned engagement with Christian tradition that is applied to human experience. It is rather that Scripture is given the supreme authority amongst these sources. Anselm is thus defended against criticism for claiming that the infinite weight of the Son of God more than outweighs the vast weight of accumulated sin by reference to Rom. 5:15-21.[81] And Luther is criticized for what Gunton regards as the one-sidedness of his formulation of justification arising from allowing his personal experience and Augustinian heritage to distort the biblical teaching.[82] Gunton then returns to what he describes as 'the biblical fountainhead'[83] of this doctrine. At times, the Bible seems more of an underground spring than a fountain, especially when dealing with Forsyth and Barth, whose two treatments of justice as an atonement metaphor receive no explicit biblical critique. But throughout his discussions, Gunton follows the Reformation maxim, *sola scriptura*, to formulate his theology of atonement.

Of the authors we have considered, Gunton provides the most satisfactory handling of the biblical material. Because of his commitment to *scriptura scripturae interpres*, Gunton seeks to allow the Bible to speak from within its own frame of reference rather than through the grid of Hegelian rationalism, the Fathers or universal human experience. And because he maintains *sola scriptura*, what the Bible says is given supreme authority in determining the shape of his theology rather than certain aspects of reason, tradition or experience. It also means he is concerned to let the biblical message penetrate into the present situation in the Church and the world. Gunton bridges the two horizons of biblical text and reader by the use of metaphor, allowing first century images of atonement to generate twentieth

---

81   Especially v. 20, 'where sin increased, grace abounded all the more.' Gunton, *The Actuality of Atonement*, p. 92.

82   Gunton, *The Actuality of Atonement*, pp. 101f.

83   Gunton, *The Actuality of Atonement*, p. 102.

century images. Gunton therefore provides a responsible means of reading the Bible for the formation of atonement theology, and leaves us with three worked examples: victory, justice and sacrifice.

It is the combined effect of his criticism of other interpretations of these images and the positive case he makes for treating victory, justice and sacrifice as metaphors of atonement that makes Gunton's work so compelling. He harnesses the arguments leveled against the various theories of atonement in order to show that victory, justice and sacrifice should not be treated as 'theories' of atonement. He also shows that they need not instead be labeled vaguely as 'images' or 'ideas' of atonement but that they should be understood as metaphors, since they take words from their familiar setting into another context, atonement, in order to bring illumination to it.[84] We shall therefore follow Gunton in treating victory, justice and sacrifice as metaphors of atonement.

F. Combining the Metaphors

So far we have considered how these authors use the Bible to develop their doctrine of atonement in terms of love, victory, redemption, sacrifice and judgement. Our particular concern for this thesis, however, is to investigate how these atonement metaphors may best be set in their mutual relationship. We therefore ask, How do these authors treat texts where more than one of these metaphors arise?

There are several biblical verses where two atonement metaphors are combined. In John 12:31 justice and victory occur together, 'Now is the judgement of this world; now the ruler of this world will be driven out.' Redemption and justice are combined in Gal. 3:13, 'Christ redeemed us from the curse of the law by becoming a curse for us'. Redemption is said to come by means of sacrifice in both Heb. 9:12, '[Christ] entered once for all into the Holy Place, not with the blood of goats and calves, but with his own blood, thus obtaining eternal redemption', and 1 Pet. 1:18,19, 'You know that you were ransomed from the futile ways inherited from your ancestors, not with perishable things like silver and gold but with the precious blood of Christ, like that of a lamb without defect or blemish'. And in Rev. 12:11, victory is said to come from the sacrifice of Christ, 'But they have conquered him by the blood of the Lamb and by the word of their

---

84 In an important work on the use of metaphor in religious language, to which Gunton refers his readers, Janet Martin Soskice says that a metaphor is established, 'as soon as the reader is able to detect that one thing is being spoken of in terms suggestive of another.' Janet Martin Soskice, *Metaphor and Religious Language* (Oxford: Clarendon Press, 1985), p. 22.

testimony.'

How are these texts handled by the authors we are considering? Generally speaking, they tend only to pick out one of the metaphors present. Aulén, Dillistone and Fiddes all quote John 12:31, but only with regard to the aspect of victory.[85] Rashdall and Fiddes use Gal. 3:13 for its legal metaphor.[86] Aulén cites Heb. 9:12 and 1 Pet. 1:18f just for evidence of ransom.[87] Dillistone and Fiddes use Rev. 12:11 as examples of the victorious aspect of atonement;[88] only Gunton draws out the sacrificial imagery as well as that of victory as twin components of atonement in this text.[89]

There are also biblical passages which incorporate three atonement metaphors. The most important of these is Rom. 3:21-26, where redemption, sacrifice and judgement are interweaved:

> But now, apart from the law, the righteousness of God has been disclosed, and attested by the law and the prophets, the righteousness of God through faith in Jesus Christ for all who believe. For there is no distinction, since all have sinned and fall short of the glory of God; they are now justified by his grace as a gift, through the redemption that is in Christ Jesus, whom God put forward as a sacrifice of atonement by his blood effective through faith. He did this to show his righteousness, because in his forbearance he had passed over the sins previously committed; it was to prove at the present time that he himself is righteous and that he justifies the one who has faith in Jesus.

This passage attracts the attention of all six authors. Aulén does not pick up on any of these metaphors, using it only to dispute its use to support the Latin theory of atonement in view of the absence of any satisfaction payment made by Christ.[90] Young only takes up the sacrificial aspect of the passage, seeing it as evidence for reading *hilastērion* as expiation, not propitiation.[91] Rashdall and Fiddes draw

---

85   Aulén, *Christus Victor*, p. 90, Dillistone, *The Christian Understanding of Atonement*, p. 89, and Fiddes, *Past Event and Present Salvation*, pp. 113 and 119.

86   Rashdall, *Atonement*, p. 93, and Fiddes, *Past Event and Present Salvation*, p. 84.

87   Aulén, *Christus Victor*, p. 89.

88   Dillistone, *The Christian Understanding of Atonement*, p. 91, and Fiddes, *Past Event and Present Salvation*, pp. 113 and 119.

89   Gunton, *The Actuality of Atonement*, p. 56.

90   Aulén, *Christus Victor*, p. 88.

91   Young, *Sacrifice and the Death of Christ*, p. 72.

out the sacrificial and judicial aspects at different times.[92] Only Dillistone and Gunton pick up the references to redemption, sacrifice and judgement.[93] None of them, however, makes use of this passage to throw light onto the question of how these metaphors may be related to each other, using them rather to elaborate the different atonement motifs they find in the Scriptures.

The very combination of these images is itself further confirmation of the conclusion that these are complementary metaphors rather than alternative theories. But these texts do also indicate that we may set these metaphors in relationship to one another. For instance, Heb. 9:12 and Rev. 12:11 describe redemption and victory in terms of sacrifice, suggesting sacrifice has a more fundamental place than either redemption or victory. It is to this question of the mutual relationship of the atonement metaphors that we shall turn in the following chapters.

Conclusion

Each of the major British atonement theologians we have been considering makes appeal to Scriptures to establish their case and criticise alternative approaches. How they do so varies significantly, with consequent differences in their conclusions. By giving such a prominent place to reason (Rashdall), tradition (Aulén) and religious experience (Dillistone, Young and Fiddes), the Bible is left with a relatively minor role in how these authors formulate their atonement doctrine. Only Gunton makes biblical hermeneutics his central concern, thereby giving Scripture a powerful influence in his theology. How these theologians use the Bible is, in the end, a reflection of their theological convictions, supporting David Kelsey's conclusion, 'just how a theologian does finally construe and use scripture is decisively determined, not by the texts as texts, nor by the texts as scripture, but by that logically prior imaginative judgement' about what is the core of the Christian faith.[94]

---

92 Rashdall uses the passage repeatedly in his discussion of Pauline theology to illustrate the problem of sin (v 23), the justification of sinners by virtue of Christ's death (v 24-26), death as a stage in the passage to new life (v 25, 26), and of propitiation (v 25). Rashdall, *Atonement*, pp. 86; 91 and 125; 97; and 99 and 130ff respectively. Fiddes uses it to discuss sacrificial and judicial aspects of atonement. Fiddes, *Past Event and Present Salvation*, pp. 71, 83 and 86.

93 Dillistone, *The Christian Understanding of Atonement*, pp. 180ff, and Gunton, *The Actuality of Atonement*, pp. 85, 105 and 125.

94 D.H. Kelsey, *The Uses of Scripture in Recent Theology* (London: SCM, 1975), p. 206.

What we have seen gives us considerable evidence to support the view expressed by Gunton that a doctrine of the atonement should treat biblical descriptions of the atonement in terms of victory, redemption, sacrifice and judgement, metaphorically. But what we have not seen is how those metaphors relate to one another. We shall therefore turn our attention now to another British writer on atonement, P.T. Forsyth, who endeavoured to integrate the different elements of the doctrine of atonement around the perfect obedience of Christ.

CHAPTER 4

P.T. Forsyth and Perfect Obedience as the Co-ordinating Principle of Atonement

Introduction

As we saw at the beginning of this section, early in the twentieth century, P.T. Forsyth raised concerns about the confusion arising from a lack of co-ordination between the different aspects of atonement. In *The Work of Christ* he said,

> We cannot, at least the Church cannot, rest healthily upon medley and mortised aspects of the one thing which connects our one soul with the one God in one mortal world. We cannot rest in unresolved views of reconciliation. [1]

He was thus aware of the problems that we have sought to delineate with respect to twentieth century atonement theology, and he saw them as a long-standing weakness in this field of theology. Our attention is drawn to P.T. Forsyth, though, not only because he expressed alarm about the problem (an alarm which, as we have seen, has been largely unheeded), but also because he offered a solution to it which involved the combination of atonement metaphors. Forsyth took what he considered to be the three great aspects of the church's understanding of the work of Christ: the triumphant, the satisfactory and the regenerative aspects, or redemption, justification and sanctification, and he set out to relate them to one another as a 'threefold cord.'[2] He did so by offering the co-ordinating principle of 'the perfect obedience of holy love which [Christ] offered

---

1 Forsyth, *The Work of Christ*, p. 201.
2 Forsyth, *The Work of Christ*, p. 199.

amidst the conditions of sin, death and judgement.'[3] Forsyth then explains, 'This one action of the holy Saviour's total person was, on its various sides, the destruction of evil, the satisfaction of God and the sanctification of men.'[4]

Our purpose in this chapter is to consider to what extent Forsyth succeeded in resolving the problem which he so clearly identified. We shall carry out this enquiry by examining Forsyth's view of redemption, justification and sanctification, before seeing how he relates them together in terms of Christ's perfect obedience. Most important for this investigation are three works published while he was Principal of Hackney College, Hampstead, the time that his daughter, Jessie Forsyth Andrews, describes in a memoir as, 'the flower of his life.'[5] They are: *The Cruciality of the Cross* (1909), *The Work of Christ* (1910) and his wartime theodicy *The Justification of God* (1916). Since understanding the cross of Christ remained central to his concerns throughout his later writings, we shall also refer to several others of his works, most notably *Positive Preaching and the Modern Mind* (1907).

A. Redemption

When Forsyth introduces the first strand of the threefold cord and describes it as redemption, he makes it clear that he primarily associates that with the triumphant aspect of atonement, 'the finality of our Lord's victory over the evil power or the devil.'[6] This, he says, is the form that dominated thinking about the atonement in the early Church,[7] but which had little place in the thinking about atonement in his own day.[8] For a fuller exposition of his understanding of

---

3   Forsyth, *The Work of Christ*, p. 201. Whilst Forsyth's work on perfect obedience has received widespread attention, the manner in which it is intended to harmonize the various aspects of atonement has not. J.H. Rodgers and A.M. Hunter are amongst the very few authors to comment on Forsyth's work on the inter-relatedness of these three aspects of the cross, and even they do not discuss how this mutual relationship is to be brought about through the unifying principle of perfect obedience. J.H. Rodgers, *The Theology of P.T. Forsyth* (London: Independent Press, 1965), pp. 56f, and A.M. Hunter, *P.T. Forsyth* (London: SCM Press, 1974), p. 60.

4   Forsyth, *The Work of Christ*, pp. 201f.

5   Forsyth, *The Work of Christ*, p. xx.

6   Forsyth, *The Work of Christ*, p. 199.

7   Despite this remark, Forsyth gives little attention to the Patristic authors, as Gunton points out in his foreword to Trevor Hart, ed., *Justice the True and Only Mercy* (Edinburgh: T. & T. Clark, 1995), p. xiii.

8   This point, to be taken up later by Aulén, Forsyth says arises 'for want of

redemption, however, we must turn to *The Justification of God* where we find Forsyth's most extensive discourse on the subject. It is here that he explains what he means by redemption.

> We mean that the last things shall crown the first things, and that the end will justify the means, and the goal glorify a Holy God. We mean (if we allow ourselves theological language) an eschatology and a theodicy in it – a divine Heaven, a divine Salvation, and a divine Vindication in the result of history. But more. We mean a consummation which can only come by way of rescue and not mere growth. We mean rescue from evil by a God whose manner of it is moral, which is the act of a moral absolute, the act of a holy God doing justice to righteousness at any cost to himself. We mean rectification of the present state of things on His own principles; that is, not mere rectification, mere straightening of a tangle, but justification on a transcendent plane of righteousness, the moral adjustment of man and God in one holy, loving, mighty, final, and eternal act. We certainly mean something more crucial than Meliorism.[9]

Here we find many insights into both the content of Forsyth's thought and the rhetorical style of his writing. We notice, firstly, that Forsyth defines redemption in a deliberately tendentious way. He is concerned not only to say what it is, but, perhaps more importantly, to say what it is not. In particular he issues a declamation against the theological liberalism in which he had been shaped by his teachers Albrecht Ritschl in Göttingen, and F.D. Maurice in London. He had become disillusioned by their Hegelian optimism about human advances and the power of knowledge to improve people. Such thinking, he says, undermines the very need for atonement.

> Sometimes the Godhead is conceived as personal, sometimes as impersonal; but in any case reconciliation would rather be a

---

a belief in the Satan that Christ felt it his supreme conflict to counter-work and destroy.' P.T. Forsyth, *The Justification of God* (London: Latimer House, 1916/1948), p. 175.

9   Forsyth, *The Justification of God*, p. 69. In his apology for using such terms as 'eschatology' and 'theodicy' we notice that Forsyth saw himself as addressing a popular audience and not just scholarly circles. He engages in constant critical dialogue with the influential philosophers of the day, but assumes minimal knowledge of their views. Even *The Work of Christ*, which was written from extempore lectures to what was largely a gathering of young ministers in Norfolk, was reworked for popularization before publication (p. xxx). Forsyth was not thereby denigrating the importance of scholarly debate (see pp. 176f), but expressing his commitment to theological education, teaching the Christian faith in all its sophistication to as wide an audience as possible.

resigned adjustment to this great idea, which, having issued everything, is perpetually recalling, or exalting, everything into fusion
with itself.[10]

Such thinking cultivates a preoccupation with human beings rather
than with God, and produces serious weaknesses in the Church. In
Positive Preaching and the Modern Mind, Forsyth describes the resultant situation as follows:

> Religious sensibility stands where evangelical faith should be.
> Education takes the place of conversion, a happy nature of a new
> nature. Love takes the place of faith, uneasiness of concern, regret
> of repentance, and criticism of judgement.[11]

Forsyth devotes much of his writing to attacking such ideas and
to asserting that only a new creation would do. Thus he stresses that
redemption is about a decisive act of God coming against the powers
of evil in anticipation of the end-time. It is a crisis in history rather
than just a process within it, an event to be acknowledged not merely
an idea to be apprehended. Professor Donald MacKinnon goes to the
heart of the matter when he says Forsyth is concerned not just with
a doctrine of redemption, but with a real atonement.[12]

Secondly, we see here that Forsyth sometimes uses the term
'redemption' in a very broad sense. He speaks of rescue and vindication, of justice and justification, and of rectification and moral adjustment, incorporating elements of what we have identified as redemption, victory, justice and sacrifice. Forsyth brings them all under this
definition of redemption. He is thus here using the term 'redemption' in a much wider sense than when he described it as victory
over evil forces in his description of the threefold cord, using it here
as a synonym for 'atonement.'[13] Sometimes it is clear that this is what

---

10 Forsyth, *The Work of Christ*, p. 69. In *The Justification of God*, there are chapters
on 'Revelation and Teleology' expounding and criticising Hegel (whom he
regards as 'the greatest philosopher the world ever saw,' *The Work of Christ*,
p. 60), and on 'Metaphysic and Redemption' raising objections to the monism of Edward von Hartmann. Against both he argued that process was too
amoral a concept to be given such prominence in their thinking, meaning
that their philosophy would fail to provide the necessary force for good in
society.

11 Forsyth, *Positive Preaching*, p. 244.

12 This comment was made to Stephen Sykes and recorded in his chapter, 'P.
T. Forsyth on the Church' in Hart, *Justice the True and Only Mercy*, p. 7. It
accurately describes the force of Forsyth's remarks, such as his diagnosis of
the feebleness of much of the preaching of his own day to which we referred
at the beginning of Chapter 1.

13 This is, of course, not an unusual use of the word redemption. We have seen

Forsyth has in view, as for instance when he says, 'Redemption, I say, is the great note of the creed...'[14] and speaks of '...redemption, which is the very centre of the Christian faith.'[15] At other times, as we have seen, it is used more specifically of redemptive victory. But there are also times when it is not clear which he has in mind introducing an unfortunate element of ambiguity into his discussion.[16]

Thirdly, Forsyth sees redemption as an eschatological event to be awaited. Redemption concerns the 'last things', 'the end', 'the goal' and 'consummation'. As such, it is something as yet unseen to be anticipated and received by faith. So Forsyth looks not to present realities to build confidence in the goodness of God in the face of times of distress, such as a war; in fact he warns how misleading that is. Drawing faith from the order of the world is one of the chief causes he sees for being 'unhinged' in the face of such a crisis.[17] He points instead beyond the present circumstances to a future which brings hope into that situation.

This definition by no means exhausts what Forsyth has to say about redemption. For instance, whilst he points out here that it is an eschatological event to be expected, he makes it clear elsewhere that it is also an occurrence which has taken place in the past,

> The redemption, therefore, of a race with a conscience and a history means a historic Act of redemption on the part of the Holy, controlling the whole of the race's career, and in command of all the cataclysms and tragedies that seem at times to eclipse its sun.[18]

Forsyth here claims that there was a moment in the past when a decisive action occurred in the light of which the situation of the race (the human race, not just Israel) would be forever altered, irrespective of what someone might think who looked into the trenches of

---

it already in Dillistone who says that redemption means, 'all subservience to cosmic powers, all indebtedness to legal systems, all enslavement to self-destroying habits.' Dillistone, *The Christian Understanding of the Atonement*, p. 88.

14   Forsyth, *The Justification of God*, p. 88.
15   Forsyth, *The Work of Christ*, p. 142.
16   Rodgers makes a similar complaint about the use Forsyth makes of the terms 'revelation', 'gospel', 'religion' and 'moral', which, he says, are used with two or three different meanings. Rodgers, *The Theology of P.T. Forsyth*, p. 263. Interestingly, Forsyth is himself at times aware of using the term 'Gospel' in two different senses and acknowledges the confusion that results, and claims there that one meaning, God's saving action in Christ, is to be taken as more 'ultimate'. Forsyth, *The Preaching of Jesus and the Gospel of Christ*, p. 22.
17   Forsyth, *The Justification of God*, p. 76.
18   Forsyth, *The Justification of God*, p. 74.

the Great War without a knowledge of such an event. The confidence that in the end all will be well is built on something that has already happened, not merely on something still awaited. So he says, 'Victory awaits us because victory is won.'[19] And he goes on to say, 'If [Christ] did not [die], if we cannot be sure he did, we have no teleology for the world.'[20] So Forsyth says confidence for the future is only rooted in an event in the past and is not to be founded elsewhere.

The particular historical redemptive act Forsyth has in mind is that of the cross of Christ. 'The supreme tragedy becomes, in the cross of Christ, the vehicle of the eternal Redemption, and the source of the New Creation.'[21] Here we see the crucicentrism that is so characteristic of Forsyth.[22] That which had brought about Forsyth's own crisis with the theological liberalism of his youth, the cross, was to become the dominant motif of all his later works. As Trevor Hart puts it,

> The way from love to grace lay across a deep chasm of natural human resentment and theological repentance,[23] a chasm bridged only at one point, across which Forsyth himself had stumbled, and which he had henceforth sought to lead his readers and fellow travellers namely the cross of Christ and all that it signified.[24]

J.K. Mozley is thus quite correct to say, 'There is a true sense in which Forsyth was a man of one idea – the cross.'[25]

In his chapter on 'What is Redemption?' in *The Justification of God*, Forsyth expands on what it is that makes the cross so central to all his atonement theology. It is because that is the place where the kingdom of God enters human history decisively, taking up a familiar Ritschlian theme but giving it a more apocalyptic framework. He says, 'The cross of Christ is not the preliminary of the kingdom; it is the kingdom breaking in. It is not the clearing of the site for the heavenly city; it is the city itself descending out of heaven from God.'[26] The cross of Christ is thus the place and the time when God's kingdom is inaugurated on earth. Thus Forsyth asserts the grandeur and

---

19 Forsyth, *The Justification of God*, p. 78.
20 Forsyth, *The Justification of God*, p. 79.
21 Forsyth, *The Justification of God*, p. 76.
22 Forsyth went so far as to place the cross at the very heart of God. 'The death of Christ is the central point of eternity as well as human history. His own eternal life revolves on it.' Forsyth, *The Work of Christ*, p. 154.
23 Here, Hart is referring to the way Forsyth described his own conversion, 'from a Christian to a believer, from a lover of love to an object of grace.' Forsyth, *Positive Preaching*, p. 193.
24 Hart, *Justice the True and Only Mercy*, pp. 17f.
25 J.K. Mozley, *The Heart of the Gospel* (London: SPCK, 1925), p. 109.
26 Forsyth, *The Justification of God*, p. 77.

significance of redemption, taking it far beyond its original context of a close relative coming to the aid of someone in need. It is the king of the universe who is the redeemer; it is the Lord of all who comes to our aid.

Forsyth is also clear that this redemption is not only a matter of a defeat of the devil in the past, but also, more personally, a defeat of sin in the present. 'We are redeemed *from* the ban of sin's magic circle by the only One who has the secret of the unseen powers; we are joined with the sin-destroying death of Christ.'[27] The Redeemer went out to battle not against flesh and blood but against the invisible forces of destruction whose activity is still to be seen in sinful human actions. As such, Forsyth steers the image of redemption away from a narrowly historical reading of the events around Caiaphas and Pilate towards the moral realm and all rebellion against God. He sees the incarnation itself as being not so much about the manifestation of God in human history, as the Son of God taking sinful flesh in order that it might be redeemed.[28] The person of Christ is thus, for Forsyth, to be understood from the work of Christ,[29] again stressing the centrality of the cross.

> And for experience it is the atoning Redemption that is at the practical base of belief in the Incarnation and prescribes its nature. And, if we invert that order, as the school theology did, is it not bound to affect the whole relation of religion to ethic and to society?[30]

Much depends, for Forsyth, on making the cross the starting point for Christian theology. It is only in the light of it that we can see who Jesus is, and only then can we understand how it is that the devil has been defeated and the power of sin broken so that we may live together as redeemed human beings.

Forsyth also asserts that this work of redemption could only be carried out by the Creator. He says,

> [W]e are driven back before the foundation of the world – to a Redeemer who was *there*, who is deeper and older than His human

---

27 Forsyth, *The Work of Christ*, p. 217. In Ritschlian terms, this brings about deliverance from the 'kingdom of sin.' A. Ritschl, *The Christian Doctrine of Justification and Reconciliation* vol. 3, translation by J.S. Black, (Edinburgh: T. & T. Clark, 1876/1900), p. 334.

28 'The real Incarnation lay not in Christ's being made flesh for us, but in His being made sin.' Forsyth, *Positive Preaching*, p. 250.

29 As Forsyth puts it, 'soterology springs from soteriology,' thus reversing the order of Samuel Coleridge. P.T. Forsyth, *The Cruciality of the Cross* (Carlisle: Paternoster Press, 1909/1997), p. 50. Cf. 'The true key to Christ's person is in His work.' *Positive Preaching*, p. 242.

30 Forsyth, *The Justification of God*, p. 91.

nature, whose Redemption of the world is only possible because of His part in its creation, who took the responsibility of creating because He knew He possessed the power to redeem and retrieve whatever creation might come to.'[31]

The God who in Christ redeemed the world is the God who through Christ created the world. The redeemer was not only the ruler of the world, but also the maker of it. No one could comprehend the magnitude of the abysmal crisis that beset humanity, says Forsyth, except the One who had created the world. And no one ever had the power to make good a world that had become so deeply corrupt except the One who made it. It is only as creator that Christ could be redeemer. Forsyth may not have a great deal to say about creation, as is often pointed out,[32] but it is intrinsic to his understanding of redemption, and therefore to his whole theology.

Redemption thus goes even beyond the forgiveness of sins. 'Man's chief end', says Forsyth, 'is to be forgiven and redeemed.'[33] To be redeemed is not only to be forgiven, although it is certainly that; it is to be restored after the ravages of sin. It is, as we saw in Forsyth's definition of what redemption is, a rectification. It is thus greater than a victory alone; not only is the enemy destroyed, but the very wounds he had inflicted are also healed.[34] As Forsyth says,

> And this Act assures the perfecting, both of the race and of its units and of each through the other, in a reciprocity founded in that of Creator and creature, Redeemer and saint – perhaps even of Father and Son. It means the glory, honour, and immortality of the one in the other, by an Act whose nature is moral to the pitch of a holiness that destroys all sin and guilt by the omnipotence of

---

31 Forsyth, *The Justification of God*, p. 32. He goes on to make the paradoxical statement, 'To redeem creation is a more creative act than to create it' (p. 123). In asserting that redemption is a greater work than creation Forsyth follows Augustine and Luther. See E. Jüngel, 'On the Doctrine of Justification', *International Journal of Systematic Theology* vol. 1, no.1 (1999), p. 26.

32 For example, Rodgers, *The Theology of P.T. Forsyth*, p.263, and Hart *Justice the True and Only Mercy*, p. 19.

33 Forsyth, *The Justification of God*, p. 39. Cf. Ritschl, who said that redemption is 'an idea which embraces justification and renewal.' Quoted by G.W. McCulloh, *Christ's Person and Life-Work in the Theology of Albrecht Ritschl with Special Attention to Minus Triplex* (Maryland: University Press of America, 1990), p. 32.

34 This point is reminiscent of one made by Athanasius as he explains why repentance alone is not enough to make good the transgression of humankind. It is because sin corrupts, and no amount of repentance can repair that corruption. God alone can recreate incorruption out of what has become corrupt (*On the Incarnation* ii.7).

righteousness.'[35]

Forsyth's presentation of redemption is not without its weaknesses. His discussion is so dominated by the imagery of victory that it leaves little room for the imagery of ransom, as we also found with Dillistone.[36] Unlike Dillistone, however, he is very clear about the effect of redemption on the redeemed. He also recognizes that to call Jesus the Redeemer is to use the term metaphorically, since understanding redemption in terms of a show of force, a military conquest or some compensation payment to those who held the world in captivity, break down when applied to Jesus Christ. It was through apparent weakness and foolishness that victory came. The cross is, for Forsyth, the supreme tragedy that overcomes all other tragedies.[37] Forsyth delights in such paradox,[38] seeing redemption as a mighty victory that took effect in the form of a death, with every appearance of defeat.

Forsyth thus provides one of the most impressive accounts of redemption available in our survey of British atonement theology in the twentieth century, holding together the triumph and the suffering of redemption. For Forsyth, redemption is a multifaceted action by which the creator and ruler of the universe comes to reclaim and restore what appeared lost in the world that he had made. The kingdom of God comes against the kingdom of Satan with their decisive battle fought on the cross. There it is that redemption takes place and the rule of God is revealed in the midst of the starkest rejection of it. By it the human race is delivered from its bondage to the forces of evil, healed of the ravages of sin and restored into relationship with God.

B. Justification

The second great aspect of the work of Christ in the threefold cord Forsyth entitles 'satisfactionary.' He also calls it 'justification.'[39] Here he has in mind the issues of justice and of purification from unright-

---

35   Forsyth, *The Justification of God*, pp. 74f.

36   Ransom is mentioned by Forsyth, but only peripherally (e.g. *The Work of Christ*, p. 240, and *The Cruciality of the Cross*, p. 68).

37   Forsyth means by that term what is seen in the tragedies of Ibsen, who Forsyth describes as, 'this great prophet'. Forsyth, *Positive Preaching*, p. 83. For an analysis of tragedy in P.T. Forsyth see the work of George Hall in Hart, *Justice the True and Only Mercy*, chapter 6.

38   Paradox, Forsyth says, is 'vital to religious experience'. Forysth, *The Justification of God*, p. 53.

39   Forsyth, *The Work of Christ*, p. 200.

eousness, the forms under which the atonement was most discussed at the time of the Reformation. The problem addressed by it is this: How can the righteousness of God be satisfied in an unrighteous world? Forsyth brings together in this second cord what he treats elsewhere under the two categories of judgement and sacrifice. We shall therefore consider what Forsyth has to say about justification under those two sub-headings.

Judgement

Forsyth has a great deal to say about judgement, indeed it is one of his most frequently recurring themes. He provides his fullest discourse on the meaning of judgement in *The Justification of God*, although there is also an important discussion in *The Work of Christ*. We shall take these as our primary guides.

The title of the first chapter which Forsyth devotes to a discussion of judgement in *The Justification of God*, 'Saving Judgement', makes clear where his emphasis lies. Judgement is not primarily condemnation, but the means of bringing salvation. So Forsyth writes of 'the judgement of God, and therefore His salvation,'[40] and points out that, in the Old Testament, the final judgement was connected with the great salvation and was as such, 'not a terror, as we view it, but the grandest hope.'[41] For Forsyth, judgement is an act of severe and invasive surgery which, despite the appearance of bringing life to an end, is in fact the means by which life is restored in all its fullness. Judgement is the process that turns the course of history from the path leading to death and destruction, towards the way of life and prosperity. As Gunton points out, this means Forsyth proclaims the salvation of the created order, rather than salvation from it as the Western tradition traditionally has it.[42]

Judgement, for Forsyth, is thus an act of grace and not the withdrawal of it. 'Perfect grace', writes Forsyth, 'was and is final judgement.'[43] He develops this more fully shortly afterwards in terms of another of his central themes: morality.

> How can Christ be at once the living embodiment of the moral law (and so both standard and judge) and also the living grace of God

---

40   Forsyth, *The Justification of God*, p. 170. He also speaks of, 'the Lord whose judgements are salvation.' P.T. Forsyth, *The Soul of Prayer* (London: Independent Press, 1916/1949), p. 47.

41   Forsyth, *The Work of Christ*, p. 147.

42   Gunton, 'The Real as the Redemptive,' in Hart, *Justice the True and Only Mercy*, p. 51.

43   Forsyth, *The Justification of God*, p. 171.

and the agent of reconcilement? This is the issue in the Cross, and for many it has been its offence. And the line of answer is that the grace is the judgement; that grace, acting by way of atonement, has in its very nature a moral element, which does not leave the indifferent immune, but becomes their judgement.[44]

Forsyth sees the moral fabric of the universe, which reflects the holiness of God its creator, as torn and distorted by his creatures. Christ comes to restore it not only by declaring the holiness of God in his own life, but also by bringing to bear the grace of God in judging the corruption of the world. The justice of God is therefore not only revealed in Christ but also implemented by him, especially in his cross. As such, judgement is an expression of the restoring, gracious presence of God in his creation. It is the form in which grace expresses the holy love of God.

Judgement is, therefore, essentially a force for the moralizing of the world. Forsyth is concerned to show that the atonement, rightly understood, should be the basis of Christian ethics and not, as in some formulations, a gross travesty of it. It is, indeed, morality which provides the ontological basis for Forsyth, as Trevor Hart points out.[45] What actually took place on the cross was the purification of the world by the judgement of God. The holy love of God, repelled by the evils of the world, is drawn to them in order to judge them and liberate his beloved. Without this element of judgement to restore the moral order, Forsyth says that the Christian religion loses its claim to have a message for the good of society. 'With the loss from the heart of our religion of the note of judgement goes the sense of public righteousness and national responsibility; thereupon come in the end public meanness, madness, infatuation, and collapse.[46] He therefore tried to restore the emphasis on morality after its loss in Schleiermacher to a preoccupation with feelings, not by placing the emphasis on Christ's effect on society as Ritschl had done, but by focusing on the cross as the judgement of God on all ungodliness.[47] It was not enough to speak of the love of God, as Ritschl had; nothing short of the *holy* love of God would do. It is for this reason that judgement could bring hope to a generation engulfed by war.

---

44 Forsyth, *The Justification of God*, pp. 179f.
45 Hart, *Justice the True and Only Mercy*, pp. 18ff. Gunton draws attention to the 'metaphysic of conscience' in Forsyth's work on Christology and shows that, although Forsyth claims he has no need of an ontology, he operates with a Kantian presupposition of the primacy of morality. C.E. Gunton, *Yesterday and Today* (London: SPCK, 1997), pp. 169ff.
46 Forsyth, *The Justification of God*, p. 174.
47 Forsyth, *The Work of Christ*, pp. 228f.

As such, there is a moral context for human life, despite all appearances to the contrary, and the atonement reveals that moral order to a world blinded to it, by bringing God's judgement against it. Forsyth's achievement in placing the holiness of God at the centre of atonement without making it either a purely personal morality or a subjective response to the love of God,[48] stands as perhaps his greatest contribution to the doctrine.

Judgement is, for Forsyth, a form of painful discipline and is as such an act of God as Father. He says, 'The father has to discipline his children. He institutes certain laws, the children disobey; they must be punished, or, using the more dignified term, judged.'[49] And he says, 'It is an element of Fatherhood, and not a device,'[50] by which he means to distance his remark from the Grotian theory of the cross as a penal example. What he wants to stress here is that judgement is an action, and an action of true love.[51] Despite the severity of judgement, it is carried out for the well-being of the beloved, and not because that love has been withdrawn. As Forsyth says, 'True love is quite capable of being angry.'[52] God's judgement is both a display of his standards and a purging of the transgression of those standards in order to reinforce them. Forsyth thus distances himself from the prevalent view of his day that punishment should be justified only in terms of its power to reform, insisting instead, with Kant and Hegel, that there had to be an element of retribution.

But judgement goes beyond an act of fatherly discipline. That, Forsyth says, 'will not carry a nation's conscience; it will not save it from national egoism.'[53] Judgement, like redemption, needs to be seen as a manifestation of the kingdom of God. As Forsyth says, 'The more we believe in the kingdom of God, the more we must believe in judgement.'[54] For him, the coming of the kingdom of God is the coming of the king as judge.

---

48   As Forsyth says, 'To moralize religion is to make it personal as the Reformation did, and yet to rescue it from the subjectivity of Modernism and its collective egoism.' P.T. Forsyth, *The Principle of Authority in Relation to Certainty, Sanctity and Society* (London: Independent Press, 1912/1952), p. 389.
49   Forsyth, *The Work of Christ*, p. 119.
50   Forsyth, *The Justification of God*, p. 171.
51   The criticism of A.E. Garvie, one time Principal of New College, London, that Forsyth emphasizes the holiness of God at the expense of his love is thus wide of the mark. A.E. Garvie, 'A Cross-Centered Theology,' *Congregational Quarterly* 22 (1944), p. 325.
52   Forsyth, *The Work of Christ*, p. 105.
53   Forsyth, *The Justification of God*, p. 174.
54   Forsyth, *The Justification of God*, p. 170. It is surprising, then, that at times Forsyth describes judgement as something prior to the coming of God's

Judgement by God is in the Bible a function of His action as King. And to this day, when the due sense of God's kingship goes, the sense of judgement goes with it; and the type of religion, however winsome, sinks accordingly in one king to moral pusillanimity, and in another to racial ferocity.[55]

The erosion of the belief that God is king is thus a serious matter, diminishing the deity either to the status of a feeble figurehead lacking moral authority, or to that of an earthly dictator preoccupied with national supremacy. In other words, it is precisely this misconception that Forsyth sees at the root of both Protestant liberalism and the nationalistic ambitions which fuelled the First World War. The kingdom of God is not to be understood in the light of either of these viewpoints. It is instead to be regarded as the realm of God's perfect justice, and where those standards impinge on a world which rejects them, the result is judgement.

Forsyth thus makes it clear that he is not thinking only of something negative when he speaks of judgement. There is the positive element of the vindication of God's faithful people, as well as the negative element of judgement on his enemies. Forsyth sees this expounded in the Old Testament, where the kingship of God is given in the interest of Israel. He says, 'It involved, first, the judgement of Israel's foes, and, second, Israel's justification, *i.e.* the public establishment of that righteousness for which Israel was to stand and suffer.'[56] The righteous rule of God rewards the good and punishes the evil, and these are both to be understood as aspects of God's judgement. Forsyth is not wholly consistent on this point. He also uses the term judgement to mean only the destructive part of the establishment of justice. As he says, 'Judgement is the negative side of love's positive righteousness.'[57] Which meaning he is taking, therefore has to be read from the context, something which at times leaves his argument unclear. Overall, however, Forsyth wants to stress the sense in which judgement is to be welcomed into a sinful world. Thus it is that he seeks to reconcile justice with mercy; it is through judgement that God expresses his mercy. As he says, 'His mercy is by

---

kingdom. For instance, 'All the Old Testament told [Jesus] that the Kingdom of God could never come without the prior judgement of God' (*The Work of Christ*, p. 163), suggesting an inconsistency here about the chronology of the arrival of the kingdom in relation to the judgement of God. However, the point remains that the coming of the king is inseparable from the judgement of God.

55 Forsyth, *The Justification of God*, p. 174.
56 Forsyth, *The Justification of God*, p. 177.
57 Forsyth, *The Justification of God*, p. 180.

judgement unto holy victory and endless peace.'[58]

For Forsyth, then, judgement is much more than punishment alone. 'Mere punishment' he says, 'is less true than judgement.'[59] It is 'the 'indirect and collateral necessity' of judgement.[60] Forsyth thus distances himself from advocates of penal substitution theories like Dale, Denney and Mozley. He complained that they emphasized but one aspect of the judgement of God and thereby distorted the biblical picture of what Christ achieved on the cross. His opposition to such theories is seen explicitly when he says, 'it cannot be true that God punished Christ'[61] because God was well pleased with him. And 'it cannot be true that Christ was in our stead in such a way as to exclude and exempt us,'[62] because he was acting in sympathy with us. Forsyth accepts the term 'penal sacrifice' but only once these interpretations have been prohibited. He would prefer to say not that Christ was punished by God but that he 'bore God's penalty on sin'[63] and 'God did not punish Christ, but Christ entered the dark shadow of God's penalty on sin.'[64] Alan Sell, amongst others, has questioned whether this is any more than a semantic device, asking, Is it possible to bear a penalty and not to bear a punishment?[65] But there is a subtle distinction in Forsyth's usage. He sees the term 'penalty' as carrying less of a sense of something inflicted on an involuntary victim than the term 'punishment'. Whether or not he succeeds in this regard, however, should not be allowed to detract from the importance of Forsyth's achievement in stressing judgement over punishment and penalty in understanding the cross of Christ. It is another very significant contribution to the doctrine of atonement, offering a constructive critique of penal substitution theories.

Forsyth wishes to minimize his use of 'substitution' in relation to the atonement because of its 'unfortunate and misleading sugges-

---

58   Forsyth, *The Justification of God*, p. 58.
59   Forsyth, *The Justification of God*, p. 172.
60   Forsyth, *The Work of Christ*, p. 135.
61   Forsyth, *The Work of Christ*, p. 146.
62   Forsyth, *The Work of Christ*, p. 146.
63   Forsyth, *The Work of Christ*, p. 147.
64   Forsyth, *Positive Preaching*, p. 248. Forsyth seeks support from an unlikely source for his position: John Calvin. Forsyth does not attempt to deny that Calvin spoke of the punishment of Christ (which he clearly did), but in saying that Calvin made it clear that in no sense did Jesus feel chastised or condemned for anything in himself, but only for the sin of the race. Forsyth, *The Cruciality of the Cross* p. 103. See J. Calvin, *The Institutes of the Christian Religion* (translation by Henry Beveridge, Grand Rapids: Eerdmans, 1536/1989), 3.4.30.
65   Hart, *Justice the True and Only Mercy*, p. 121.

tions', although he does not rule out its use completely.[66] He also has reservations about the term 'representative'. Although he regards it as more ethical and constitutional than substitution, he fears that it has too many associations with democracy, suggesting authority is vested in Jesus by those he represents. Forsyth prefers to see Christ's work as 'solidary', by which he means a collective act of a company of people performed by one of them. So Forsyth describes Jesus as 'head of the human race by his voluntary self-identification', as 'a federal person', and he says, 'all humanity is in him and in His act...'[67] He speaks of a 'solidary judgement' and a 'collectivist redemption'.[68] There is no atomic individualism here, but a corporate bond of solidarity. Forsyth bases this claim on the observation that we live in the same moral world, as is manifested in conscience, even in 'sinful conscience'.[69, 70] Humankind is irreducibly social and the remedy for the sinful human condition is to be found in a corporate act of the race in the person of Jesus Christ.

As God's chosen people, Israel was not exempt from God's judgement. Forsyth goes on to say,

> Nay, further, there was involved a third thing – the judgement of Israel itself in the interest of that same righteousness. And this carried with it both the threshing out of a small remnant of the nation, and the use of the heathen as the divine flail.[71]

The calling to be the people of God is for the display of the right-

---

66 Forsyth, *The Work of Christ*, p. 210. He does, however, still endorse the term when sufficient caveats are included. For instance, he says, 'Atonement is substitutionary, else it is none... We may replace the word substitution by representation or identification, but the thing remains... It was not simply on our behalf, but in our stead – yet not quantitatively, but centrally.' Forsyth, *The Atonement in Modern Religious Thought* (London: James Clarke, 1902), p. 83.

67 Forsyth, *The Work of Christ*, p. 159, 172.

68 Forsyth, *The Work of Christ*, p. 114.

69 Quoted in M.W. Anderson, ed. *The Gospel and Authority: A P.T. Forsyth Reader* (Minneapolis: Augsburg, 1971), p. 173. cf. Forsyth, *The Work of Christ*, p. 122. Forsyth therefore sees in 'man's self-condemnation...the reflection of his judgement by God.' Forsyth, *The Work of Christ*, p. 250. Conscience is thus the location at which the likeness of the holiness of God is to be found in human form. Such a careful grounding of the concept of solidarity in the shared moral realm means that the fear expressed by Alan Sell and others that the idea is too metaphysical is ill-founded. Hart, *Justice the True and Only Mercy*, p. 121.

70 The emphasis on conscience and on the corporate nature of atonement both reflect the influence of F.D. Maurice.

71 Forsyth, *The Justification of God*, p. 177.

eousness of the Lord, and the judgement of God comes to his own people to purify them for that purpose. So, also, to be in the Church is not to be exempt from God's judgement. It is, however, to face a different sort of judgement:

> When we have entered the kingdom through the great judgement in the Cross, we do not escape all judgement; we escape into a new kind of judgement, from that of law to that of grace. We escape condemnation, for we are new creatures, but chastisement we do not escape. Our work may be burned, to our grief, that we may be saved (1 Cor. 11:32). We are judged or chastened with the Church to escape condemnation with the world.[72]

Again, the effect of judgement is to bring righteousness, something needed by those who have responded to the call to be the people of God as well as those who have not.[73]

With these things in mind, we come to what Forsyth regards as the central revelation of the judgement of God: the cross of Christ. This is the locus of the saving judgement as the kingdom of God breaks into the world. Forsyth says, 'The Cross of Christ is God's last judgement on all sin, for its destruction by a realm of infinite grace and love.'[74] The final judgement is thus an event of the past; it has already taken place in the death of Christ. In making such a statement, Forsyth is well aware of the surprise with which it will be widely received.

> It is to many an incredible, and even unintelligible thing to say that the last judgement took place in principle in that Cross as God's last word and Self-vindication to the world, that we are living in the midst of it, and that all history is working it into detail, whether by way of order or of convulsion.[75]

In the past judgement of Jesus Christ, Forsyth says we see the future. So decisive is what took place on the cross that the eternal destiny of each person and community is determined by that one death.

---

72 Forsyth, *The Justification of God*, p. 181. We notice here that Forsyth makes no real distinction between the kingdom of God and the Church, a point observed out by Rodgers. Rodgers, *The Theology of P.T. Forsyth*, p. 289, footnote 104. For Forsyth, to have faith in God as king is to be in the kingdom of God and therefore to be in the Church of Christ.

73 As such we have to say that the criticism of T. Hywel Hughes that, 'The God of Forsyth seems to be more concerned with Himself, with His holiness, His judgement, His satisfaction, than with the sinner, whereas in the Gospel the supreme object of interest is not law, judgement, not even sin, but the sinner,' (1940, 37), fails to do justice to Forsyth. T.H. Hughes, 'Dr Forsyth's View of the Atonement', *Congregational Quarterly* 18 (1940), pp. 30-37.

74 Forsyth, *The Justification of God*, p. 183.

75 Forsyth, *The Justification of God*, p. 182.

So what was that judgement that took place in the cross? It was, Forsyth says, an action in which Jesus willingly and obediently shouldered the burden of judgement upon the sin of the world in such a way as to bring about the destruction of that sin. 'Christ bore evil, He did not avenge it. He so bore it as to judge and destroy it.'[76] When Jesus hung on the cross under the judgement of God against the sin of the world, it was not in order to bring final condemnation on a world in rebellion against him, but to diffuse and denature that sin by bringing it under the condemnation of God's judgement. It was the moment when the wrath of God against all ungodliness took effect, the effect of consuming sin and guilt as they were borne by Jesus Christ in his death. For, as Forsyth puts it, 'The sinner's reconciliation to a God of holy love could not take place if guilt were not destroyed, if judgement did not take place on due scale, if the wrath of God did not somehow take real effect.'[77] God therefore managed, 'to make sin further the purpose it seemed to foil,'[78] harnessing its destructive energy to bring about its own demise. Such a purifying judgement was necessary for the salvation of the world. 'Not until sin had been brought to do its very worst, and had in that culminating act been foiled, judged, and overcome; not until then could individuals receive the reconciliation.'[79] Only when the fire of judgement had burnt up all the stubble of unholiness could God dwell with his people again.

This judgement which brought about the destruction of sin was implemented by Christ in his perfect obedience, who both declared the righteousness of God and endured the condemnation of God on all unrighteousness.

> Christ accepted the judgement holiness must pass upon sin, and did so in a way that confessed it as holy from amidst the deepest experience of it, the experience not of a spectator but a victim. His obedience was not merely a fine, perfect, and mighty harmony of His own will with God's blessed will; but it was the acceptance on man's behalf of that judgement which sin had entailed, and the confession on man's behalf in a tremendous act that the judgement was good and holy. For the holiness of God makes two demands: first, for an answering holiness in love, and second, for a judgement on those who do not answer but defy. And Christ met both, in one and the same act.[80]

---

76   Forsyth, *The Justification of God*, p. 172.
77   Forsyth, *The Work of Christ*, p. 132.
78   Forsyth, *The Cruciality of the Cross*, p. 100.
79   Forsyth, *The Work of Christ*, p. 133.
80   Forsyth, *The Work of Christ*, p. 206.

This dual aspect of the obedience of Christ makes it clear that judgement in Forsyth's thinking was both the demonstration of what was right and the destruction of what was wrong. This takes us to the very heart of Forsyth's understanding of judgement, which encompasses both the condemnation of sin and the vindication of righteousness. George Hall expresses Forsyth's position elegantly when he says that, 'In Christ, the world passed judgement on God and in the selfsame event God passed judgement on the world – and Christ took both judgements.'[81]

The judgement declared and borne by God the Son is carefully placed alongside the judgement declared and borne by God the Father. Referring to the work of the Father, Forsyth says, 'He set up reconciliation by an act of judgement on His Son, cutting off his own right hand that we might enter the kingdom of heaven.'[82] Forsyth thus again distinguishes his view from any penal substitutionary theory which might suggest that the Son bears the punishment of the Father for the sin of the world in a way that drives a wedge between Father and Son. The Father not only inflicts judgement but endures it; he not only shows his anger and wrath against sin but also takes that upon himself in the Son. As such, Forsyth anticipates work by Jürgen Moltmann in considering the effect on the Father of the death of the Son.[83] Forsyth also draws attention to the involvement of the Holy Spirit in this saving work, saying that 2 Cor. 5:19, 'in Christ God was reconciling the world to himself,' makes reference to God the Father, the Son and the Holy Spirit.[84] It was the triune God who came to our salvation, and not the Son only.

That judgement on the cross is, Forsyth says, to be seen worked out in history, and in particular, in war. He says war is 'God in judgement of godlessness,'[85] and that, 'War as judgement is the servant of righteousness, and righteousness is the twin of grace.'[86] This forms the central plank of his theodicy. War is not to be seen as evidence that God is no longer sovereign over the universe or that God no longer cares for the world, but that his rule is being implemented in his judgement and that his love is being expressed in his chastisement. These things cannot be seen from a study of a war in itself or even by noting who wins the victory. Forsyth himself comments that victory in war, 'might go to military efficiency, to the side that

---

81   Hart, *Justice the True and Only Mercy*, p. 91.
82   Forsyth, *The Work of Christ*, p. 134.
83   Moltmann, *The Crucified God*, especially pp. 200ff.
84   Forsyth, *The Work of Christ*, p. 152.
85   Forsyth, *The Justification of God*, p. 23.
86   Forsyth, *The Justification of God*, p. 172.

has the best machine and the least scruple,'[87] not to the side that best manifests the kingdom of God.[88] The only vantage point from which to see how the rule of God is worked out in the affairs of men and women is the cross of Christ. The revelation of judgement in history is therefore to be seen not in the study of history itself, as Hegel would suggest, but in the cross of Christ where God's judgement of the world is revealed.

There is, however, also judgement still to come. Forsyth is concerned to root that expectation into the present so its implications can be felt: 'We are all standing before the judgement seat of Christ. And one day we shall know it.'[89] The future element of judgement is thus a declaration of something that is already true but currently concealed, the day when our lives will at last be seen in the light of the past judgement of Jesus Christ. It is therefore not an empty threat to instill a sense of moral seriousness in a dissolute world, but an inevitable outworking of an action that has already taken place and is continuing to shape world history. And yet because it is Jesus who will be our judge, it will be the judgement of the one who has undergone judgement for us so that we may be justified. Such future judgement, therefore, need not be a day for despair but for hope.

On what basis shall that judgement take place? It is on the basis of relationship, our relationship with God, expressed in faith. 'It is a judgement of our faith and its personal relation to the true Christian, rather than of our works, which are the fruit of the relation.'[90] Forsyth here steers a course between two opposite poles. The first pole is that of those Protestants who singularly stress the importance of responding to the Scriptures with the declaration that Jesus is Lord. To this Forsyth replies, 'Lip confession of Christ is nothing; but soul

---

87 Forsyth, *The Justification of God*, p. 186.
88 In the context in which he wrote, a world war in which Christian nations were ranged against each other, Forsyth's point may be understood. He is, however, in danger of overlooking the important sense in which Israel's military victories were seen as signs of God's blessing, and their defeats as signs of God's displeasure. Without such a sense of vindication and condemnation, albeit often at terrible cost to both sides, Forsyth is not sufficiently clear in what sense war is the judgement of God.
89 Forsyth, *The Justification of God*, p. 187.
90 Forsyth, *The Justification of God*, p. 81. 'The great sin,' writes Forsyth, 'is not something we do, but it is refusing to make ourselves right with God in Christ's Cross. We are judged in the end with our relation to the Cross of Christ', because that is the test of our relationship with Christ, which is in turn the test of our relationship with God. Forsyth, *The Work of Christ*, p. 168.

confession, life confession, there must be.'[91] At the second pole stand those Catholics who would see justification in terms of being communicant members of the Church by virtue of adhering to its laws. Forsyth instead wants to stress that judgement is on the basis of lives transformed as a result of turning to Christ and being restored in relationship with God. He thereby avoids taking the judicial metaphor in a narrowly legalistic sense by not allowing judgement to become a question of obedience to abstract law.[92] The decisive matter is not an acknowledgement of the authority of the law of Scripture nor of the law of the Church as extension of the incarnation, but rather transformation by the Gospel itself. Forsyth was thus an Evangelical in the strict sense of the word, making the *euaggelion* the fulcrum of his theology. Judgement is about the effect of the gospel, and that is to be discerned from the whole tenor of life, whether it is set towards or against the holy purposes of God, and especially whether or not it displays the fruit of accepting Christ's gracious invitation into the holy presence of God.

Such a sharp disjuncture between the friends and the enemies of God makes it clear that Forsyth regards judgement as a sifting and a separating of people according to their relationship with God, making a clear distinction between those who should look forward to judgement as a final vindication and those who should face judgement with dread. He speaks of 'boon' or 'doom,'[93] of preachers who, 'are adding to the judgement of some as well as to the salvation of others,'[94] and of 'the reality of damnation.'[95] These remarks are, however, modified by those of a more universalist tendency, reflecting the influence of Ritschl and Maurice. He writes of God's, 'justification of all the world,'[96] and says, 'To the whole of Humanity, with faith and hope eclipsed by world catastrophe, the infinite and most merciful Majesty yet says, "Fear not, little flock, it is the Father's good pleasure to *give* you the Kingdom.'[97] He explains how this view may be integrated with a doctrine of election by saying:

> From the non-elect in one stage comes the elect for the next. And so on, in an ascending series of elects, till the whole human lump is refined, till all are brought in – the worst and most intractable last,

---

91 Forsyth, *The Justification of God*, p. 181.
92 Judgement, 'is not between a soul and a law.' Forsyth, *The Justification of God*, p. 180.
93 Forsyth, *The Justification of God*, p. 187.
94 Forsyth, *The Soul of Prayer*, p. 72.
95 Forsyth, *The Justification of God*, p. 87.
96 Forsyth, *The Justification of God*, p. 187.
97 Forsyth, *The Justification of God*, p. 76.

since freedom may not be forced. There is all eternity to do it.[98]

Such a dynamic conception of election means that in the end the elect embraces everyone. How this is to be held alongside his affirmation that there is doom as well as boom he does not – and perhaps could not – say. But what is clear is that he wants to avoid any narrowly individualistic reading of justification. There is corporate sin which invokes corporate judgement and, by God's grace, yields corporate salvation. Treating war as judgement is itself to broaden the concept from any narrow focus on the individual standing before the judgement seat of God to one in which whole nations stand or fall together under his judgement. Forsyth does, however, make it clear that future judgement is not to be treated with complacency, especially by those who count the delay in the coming of that last judgement as evidence of its cancellation. Even here, though, he maintains the hope of universal mercy. As Forsyth says, magnificently:

> The non-intervention of God bears very heavy interest, and He is greatly to be feared when He does nothing. He moves in long orbits, out of sight and sound. But He always arrives. Nothing can arrest the judgement of the Cross, nothing shake the judgement-seat of Christ. The world gets a long time to pay, but all the accounts are kept – to the uttermost farthing. Lest if anything were forgotten there might be something unforgiven, unredeemed, and unholy still.[99]

Forsyth's account of the judgement of God does have its weaknesses. One of the chief amongst these is the uncertain relationship between judgement and death. At times he sees a close connection between sin and death, and suggests that death is judgement on sin. He says, 'Death as punishment for sin was absorbed in Christ's sacrifice,'[100] and God 'converted death itself from the destructive service of sin to His own redeeming service.'[101] But at another time he says that death, 'is not the result of sin' since, he says, 'it was there before sin',[102] showing the influence of evolutionary theory. There is also a reluctance to see the form in which judgement was brought to bear on Jesus as being explicitly in his death. Too often, the ambiguous term 'cross' is allowed to stand in the place where Christ's death

---

98 Forsyth, *The Justification of God*, p. 161.
99 Forsyth, *The Justification of God*, p. 207.
100 Forsyth, *The Work of Christ*, p. 156.
101 Forsyth, *The Justification of God*, p. 148.
102 Forsyth, *The Soul of Prayer*, p. 89.

should be expounded.[103] The sin of the world is said to be 'over-come' on the cross rather than put to death in the death of Christ as God's judgement on sin. As a result, Forsyth might be taken to imply that the judgement of God could have been fulfilled in Christ had he been rescued from the cross before he died. It is probably as a result of this weakness that Forsyth gives the resurrection of Jesus from the dead comparatively little attention, since a reduced stress on his death *per se* inevitably diminishes the significance of the resurrection of Jesus from the dead.[104]

There are, however, many strengths in Forsyth's account of judgement. It is far more than a legal construct, but a metaphorical description of the implementation of the reign of God in all the world. It is the transformative action by which the holy rule of God is established on earth, the rule of a loving Father, a wise King, and a gracious Saviour. We do not find here the clinical detachment of the law-court, but a thoroughly relational and moral judgement. As such Forsyth has contributed a great deal to this often neglected aspect of the atonement.

Sacrifice

Forsyth's most sustained discussion of the sacrificial aspect of the atonement is found in, *The Work of Christ*. Here, his primary concern is to identify where the sacrifice of Christ differs from sacrifice as it occurs in human societies, a radically different approach from that taken by Frances Young, who concentrates on similarities. By so doing Forsyth makes it clear from the outset that he sees references to the sacrifice of Christ as a metaphorical use of the term sacrifice.[105]

For his starting point, Forsyth takes the story of a potential train

---

103 This becomes particularly clear when a comparison is made with the account of judgement in Karl Barth: 'Death, as it actually encounters us men, is the sign of God's judgement on us' (III/2, p. 596). We shall consider Barth's teaching on judgement in Chapter 5.

104 Forsyth does mention the resurrection (e.g. *The Justification of God*, p. 215; *The Preaching of Jesus and the Gospel of Christ*, p. 17 and *The Cruciality of the Cross*, p. 87), but remarkably rarely considering its importance to the doctrine of atonement.

105 Cf. 'The metaphor [of the blood of Christ] denotes the radicality, totality, and finality of the whole action in the realism of the moral world – which even high sacrifice, not resisting unto blood, only slurs or shelves – when it does not toy with it.' Forsyth, *The Cruciality of the Cross*, p. 103. We notice here, as elsewhere, that Forsyth uses the term 'sacrifice' to refer only to sin and guilt offerings; he does not include communion or thanksgiving offerings, as Young does.

collision averted by a Belgian signalman who threw himself between the tracks and held the points together with his hands as the train went overhead.[106] He survived the experience and returned to his duties as the train continued on its journey. Forsyth acknowledges two parallels between this action and that of Christ. Firstly, there was a kind of dying and rising again, and, secondly, the passengers were unaware of his saving action. Beyond that, however, he says the analogy breaks down. Firstly, because if the passengers were told about the action of the signal-man they would be grateful, whereas that response does not automatically follow from hearing of the sacrificial act of Christ. That response, says Forsyth, needs to be created. Secondly, not only does the sacrificial death of Christ fail to arouse gratitude, it instead arouses shame and self-contempt leading either to repentance or to antagonism. From the outset, then, Forsyth is clear that the sacrifice of Christ stands significantly apart from the general human experience of sacrifice.

Forsyth therefore objects to those who see the sacrifice of Christ as heroic. Such an action would arouse universal admiration whereas Christ's does not. So Forsyth says, 'Christ's death was not a case of heroism, it was a case of redemption.'[107] Here again, Forsyth takes up his case against Liberal Protestantism in which Jesus is the ideal man who dies the death of ideal heroism. To that he responds, 'A Cross which is nothing but a revelation of divine sacrifice and service to us is an indulgent and demoralising Cross. It is a piece of indiscriminate charity.'[108] The sacrifice of Christ, he says, goes far beyond being an outstanding example of self-sacrifice. It was an action that actually changed the state of humankind in the universe.

Secondly, Forsyth wants to make it clear that the death of Christ is not the sacrifice of man to God, but rather the sacrifice of God for man. '[The cross] was not heroic man dying for a beloved and honoured God; it was God in some form dying for man.'[109] Thus Forsyth stresses the divine initiative in the atonement, maintaining his strong theocentrism in reaction to the anthropocentrism prevalent

---

106 Forsyth, *The Work of Christ*, pp. 11ff.

107 Forsyth, *The Work of Christ*, p. 16.

108 Forsyth, *The Principle of Authority*, p. 379.

109 Forsyth, *The Work of Christ*, p. 25. Cf. 'The cross does not in the New Testament exhibit God as accepting sacrifice so much as making it.' Forsyth, *The Cruciality of the Cross*, p. 94.

at the time.[110] It was not that humankind had repented of their sin and offered a sacrifice acceptable to God, but that God came among the people he had made whilst they were still in the grip of sin, and offered a sacrifice on their behalf. But that is not to say that this was only a divine sacrifice. Forsyth also speaks of the twofold nature of sacrifice: 'On the one hand it was God offering, and on the other it was man confessing.'[111] Forsyth also portrays Jesus as the human being who represents the human race.[112] So if there is a hint of mono-physitism here, it is no more than a hint. But Forsyth is determined to ensure that the centrality of the grace of God is in no way obscured by the offering made by man.

In saying, 'it was God in some form dying for man,'[113] Forsyth also speaks very directly about the death of God. Forsyth is aware of the risk he is taking, but he is not prepared to retract it. He says, 'He cannot do without it.'[114] To say less would, he believes, be to understate the atonement. It also reinforces his Trinitarian outlook in that he does not want to speak of the death of the Son in isolation from the death of the Father and the Spirit. The atonement is, 'an eternal act of the whole God, one drawing on the whole Trinity…'[115] By including the phrase 'in some form' Forsyth indicates his concern about suggesting that God died, with all the problems that raises for the continuity of God and the sustaining of the universe. But his primary concern is to convey the significance of what God has done in Christ, even if that leaves unresolved problems for other areas of theology.

Thirdly, the sacrifice of Christ is an act of love, not an act of duty. What the signal-man did was in the line of duty; it was his job to keep trains on the right tracks and to prevent collisions. It would have been understood if he had chosen to avoid the risk to his own life in climbing onto the rails, but what he did was, in a sense, expected

---

110 As he says in his synopsis of *The Person and Place of Jesus Christ*, he saw the great religious issue of the hour in terms of 'a God that serves Humanity or a Humanity that serves God.' P.T. Forsyth, *The Person and Place of Jesus Christ*, (London: Independent Press, 1909), p. iv. He also says, 'There is even what we might call a racial egoism, a self-engrossment of mankind with itself, a naïve and tacit assumption that God were no God if he cared for anything more than he did for his creatures.' Forsyth, *The Justification of God*, p. 11.
111 Forsyth, *The Work of Christ*, p. 148.
112 Forsyth describes Jesus as 'head of the human race by his voluntary self-identification'. Forsyth, *The Work of Christ*, p. 159.
113 Forsyth, *The Work of Christ*, p. 25.
114 Forsyth, *The Work of Christ*, p. 25.
115 Forsyth, *The Cruciality of the Cross*, p. 101.

of him. The same could not be said of the sacrifice of Jesus Christ. A people who had brought themselves under the judgement of God by their own defiance of the commands of God could hardly see it as a duty of God to come to their aid. God's action in Christ to offer a sacrifice on behalf of such a people and as one of them could only be understood as an act of extraordinary love, a love for enemies, not just for friends.[116]

Forsyth is not, however, concerned only with distinguishing the sacrifice of Christ from other sacrifices. He also examines how sacrifice operates, and in this he sees himself as breaking new ground. According to Forsyth, the essence of sacrifice lies in obedience to God's will. He says, referring to the suffering of Christ on the cross, 'the atoning thing was not its amount or acuteness, but its obedience, its sanctity.'[117] He relates this to Hebrew sacrifice, 'The essence of all sacrifice, which is self-surrender to God, was lifted out of the Old Testament garb and symbolism, and was made a moral reality in Christ's holy obedience.'[118] What God wants to see in sacrifice is a heart inclined to keep his law. An acceptable sacrifice, that is one which brings about a restored relationship with God, is thus one that fulfils God's requirements. As he says, 'To obey is everywhere better than sacrifice.'[119] J.H. Rodgers is thus quite correct to say that for Forsyth, 'The essence of sacrifice, therefore, is faith; the total self-giving of man in response to the Holy One's grace, his provision and claim.'[120]

Forsyth therefore centres the debate about how the sacrifice of Christ brings atonement not around why blood needs to be shed for sin offerings, but on the question of the conformity to the will of God of the one who offers the sacrifice. So the discussion is located not in the precincts of ritual practice but in the arena of moral action. Forsyth thereby fuses the questions of the sacrifice of Christ with the problems of righteous living. He says, 'What a holy God requires is the due confession of His holiness before even the confession of sin,'[121] and he criticizes McLeod Campbell and Moberly for setting

---

116 Forsyth, *The Work of Christ*, p. 26.
117 Forsyth, *The Work of Christ*, p. 157.
118 Forsyth, *The Work of Christ*, p. 164.
119 Forsyth, *The Cruciality of the Cross*, p. 95. Cf. 1 Sam. 15:22. On this basis, Forsyth asserts, 'Whether no blood was shed, or every drop, was immaterial.' Forsyth, *The Cruciality of the Cross*, p. 85.
120 Rodgers, *The Theology of P.T. Forsyth*, p. 49.
121 Forsyth, *The Cruciality of the Cross*, p. 99.

their sights too low in stressing only the confession of sin.[122] This
criticism in itself displays something of Forsyth's doctrine of sin. It is
primarily a failure to be holy before it is a transgression of any law.
As such, the remedy to sin offered in sacrifice is essentially a display
of the holiness of God. So Forsyth is able to expound sacrifice in
terms of the moral order of the universe, keeping that as the central
question of atonement. He is also able to retain his emphasis on how
that moral order is to be understood in terms of actions which arise
out of faith in God, carried out in obedience to his will.

In addressing the question of how sacrifice is effective, Forsyth
gives particular attention to Lev. 17:11, 'the life of the flesh is in the
blood; and I have given it to you for making atonement for your
lives on the altar; for, as life, it is the blood that makes atonement.'
He draws two important conclusions from it. Firstly, that sacrifice is
a result of God's grace and not the cause of it. The coming of Christ
to offer sacrifice for the sin of the world was itself an act of grace
and not only the means of grace. He therefore says that those who
take the term 'propitiation' to imply that prior to the death of Christ,
God held humankind under wrath, and afterwards held them under
grace, misrepresent the grace of God.[123] And secondly, he says it is
not the death but the life poured out in the blood that is pleasing to
God, as Bishop B.F. Westcott and later Vincent Taylor argued.[124] As
such Forsyth makes it clear that he does not see sacrifice as punishment, echoing some of his remarks about judgement. He says that
'God must either punish sin or expiate it', i.e., 'He must either inflict
punishment or assume it'[125] and he chose to do the latter,[126] distancing himself again from those who view the atonement as a penal

---

122 Forsyth, *The Cruciality of the Cross*, p. 99, footnote. Forsyth also engages with
    McLeod Campbell and Moberly in *The Work of Christ* (pp. 148f) and there
    treats his own emphasis on the confession of holiness as the remedy for the
    weakness of their emphasis on the confession of sin, a point accepted by
    both Dillistone and Fiddes. Dillistone, *The Christian Understanding of Atone-
    ment*, p. 294, and Fiddes, *Past Event and Present Salvation*, p. 105. In the light
    of these remarks, it is unfortunate that Forsyth entitles one of his chapters in
    The Work of Christ, 'The Great Confessional' (pp. 141ff), with all its connota-
    tions of the confession of sin rather than the confession of holiness.
123 Forsyth, *The Cruciality of the Cross*, p. 89.
124 Vincent Taylor, *The Atonement in New Testament Teaching* (London: Epworth,
    1945), p. 187.
125 Forsyth, *The Cruciality of the Cross*, p. 98.
126 Here, Forsyth reflects Anselm's alternatives of *satisfactio* or *poena*. He is even
    content to use the term 'satisfaction' after freeing it from any lingering as-
    sociations with Anselm's legal formulation, and making it the satisfaction
    of holiness. Forsyth, *The Work of Christ*, pp. 223f.

substitution.

There are, however, two important problems with Forsyth's account of sacrifice. The first is that he gives a much reduced place to the role of the sacrificial animal itself. When he writes of the sacrifice of Christ, his primary concern is with Christ as priest, not Christ as victim. He so stresses the action of the one who offers the sacrifice that he leaves no real role for the animal that is sacrificed. He says, 'And the presentation of the victim was valuable, not because of anything in the victim, but because of the obedience and surrender of the will with which the offerer presented it.'[127] This is evidence of Forsyth's inclination towards monophysitism, seeing Jesus as God with us before he is God as one of us. For Forsyth, in Christ God was offering the sacrifice more than God being the sacrifice.[128] He says,

> Dying as man, Christ placed his whole self beside man under the judgement of God. He was beside man in court but on God's side in the issue, confessing God's holiness in judgement, and justifying His treatment of sin.'[129]

As such, Forsyth leaves too little room for the identification of Jesus by John the Baptist as, 'the Lamb of God who takes away the sins of the world' (John 1:29).

Secondly, and consequently, Forsyth gives too little attention to the death of the victim. Even the blood of Christ poured out is not so much about his death, as about his complete self-giving to the will of God.

> When we speak of the blood of Christ, then, we mean that what He did involved not simply the *effort* of His whole self (as it might be with any hero taxed to his utmost), but the *exhaustive obedience and surrender* of His total self.'[130]

When Forsyth says, 'His blood was shed in Gethsemane as truly as on Calvary; but it was on Calvary that it rose to seal all and to found for ever our peace with God,'[131] he again plays down the dis-

---

127 Forsyth, *The Work of Christ*, p. 164.
128 Alan Sell voices a concern that Forsyth has a tendency towards docetism, although this might be more properly described as monophysitism. He quotes a telling passage from a paper by Forsyth entitled 'Faith, Metaphysic and Incarnation', published in 1915, where Forsyth says, 'The inner life of Jesus could not really reveal to man the inner life of God if at his centre he was not more God than man, and doing the redeeming thing which God alone can do.' Hart, *Justice the True and Only Mercy*, p. 121. Perhaps Forsyth was overreacting to the Ritschlian tendency to underplay the deity of Christ.
129 Forsyth, *The Cruciality of the Cross*, p. 102.
130 Forsyth, *The Cruciality of the Cross*, p. 97.
131 Forsyth, *The Cruciality of the Cross*, p. 101.

tinctive place of the death of Christ for the sacrifice for the sins of the world. Forsyth even describes the death of the sacrificial victim as only 'incidental', the means by which life is separated from the body.[132] And when he says, 'whether no blood was shed, or every drop, was immaterial',[133] he gives too little attention to the teaching of the letter of Hebrews, that says, 'without the shedding of blood there is no forgiveness of sins' (Heb. 9:22). What Forsyth lacks in his doctrine of sacrifice is a strong connection between sin and death, without which the death of Christ itself is in danger of becoming extraneous. Had Forsyth made such a connection, judgement and sacrifice might also have been joined in a special bond under the single aspect of 'satisfaction' or 'justification' as he suggests. But in the form in which we have them, it might be more accurate for Forsyth to have considered a fourfold cord instead.

Overall Forsyth has many important and distinctive things to say about sacrifice. As with his treatment of judgement, he develops this account in a strikingly positive vein. He asserts the moral purpose of God as being accomplished by the holy obedience of the Son to his Father's will. He also makes powerful connections between Christ's atonement and our intercession.[134] But he is reluctant to face the significance of the death of Christ itself for the provision of sacrifice for the sin of the world, a problem we have already seen in his discussion of judgement.

C. Sanctification

The third strand of the cord is what Forsyth calls 'the regenerative aspect' or 'sanctification'. By this he means the re-creation by God of a holy people out of a sinful people. Here Forsyth is thinking not so much about what the cross of Christ has delivered us from, as

---

132 Forsyth, *The Cruciality of the Cross*, p. 89. Forsyth shows a dualistic tendency here, suggesting life exists in a purer form outside of the body. 'The blood was shed with the direct object, not of killing the animal, but of detaching and releasing the life, isolating it, as it were, from the material base of body and flesh, and presenting it in this refined state to God.' Forsyth, *The Cruciality of the Cross*, p. 89. Such Platonic thinking may also feed his tendency towards a monophysite view of the incarnation.

133 Forsyth, *The Cruciality of the Cross*, p. 85.

134 This is brought out in Forsyth's *The Soul of Prayer*: 'Our atonement with God is the pregnant be-all and end-all of Christian peace and life; and what is that atonement but the head and front of the Saviour's perpetual intercession, of the outpouring of His sin-laden soul unto death?... In this intercession our best prayer, broken, soiled, and feeble as it is, is caught up and made prayer indeed and power with God' (p. 45).

what it has delivered us to. It is about the condition of the people who have been redeemed and justified; they are to be holy to the Lord. It is this aspect which had come to dominate the, then, modern Church in its thinking about the atonement, in the form of the moral effect of Jesus on human life, repentance in the light of the cross of Christ.

This aspect of the atonement receives notably less sustained attention from Forsyth. He touches on it in many places, often in connection with a discussion of redemption, judgement or sacrifice. Where he does consider it, it is primarily to criticise what he regards as misstatements of atonement in terms of moral response.[135] He does, however, accept and affirm the important place of repentance in sanctification. This is, he says, the gateway into relationship with a holy God.

> The righteousness of God is not only holy but gracious, not only regulative and retributory, but also forgiving and restoring. It seems, indeed, in the Gospels to need no other condition of forgiveness than repentance.[136]

Repentance is thus essential to the forgiveness that yields sanctification. Forsyth does, however, have a distinctive meaning for the term, repentance.

> And the essence of repentance is not its intensity or passion but the thing confessed. It is therefore the holiness more even than the sin that holiness makes so sinful. It is the due and understanding acknowledgement of the holiness offended.'[137]

We see the positive direction in which he takes repentance to point, as we have seen in his formulations of judgement and sacrifice. Repentance is primarily about declaring God's goodness rather than admitting human sinfulness.

Not only is the meaning of repentance distinctive in the writing of Forsyth, so too is the way he brings repentance into the very work of Christ himself. He builds up his argument as follows, 'How shall I know how much repentance is deep enough? Where find a repentance wide enough to cover the sin of a guilty world?'[138] Then, after explaining what he means by repentance, he goes on to say, 'And this only a sinless Christ could really do, who was also sympathetic

---

135 E.g., 'The Cross is not there to kindle a passion of altruism but to moralize self-sacrifice, and to save it from itself by its reference to the first principle of religion – the holy.' Forsyth, *The Justification of God*, p. 199.
136 Forsyth, *The Work of Christ*, p. 188.
137 Forsyth, *The Work of Christ*, p. 189.
138 Forsyth, *The Work of Christ*, p. 189.

enough with men to do it from their side.'[139] He therefore claims that Christ not only took the part of the redeemer, but also expressed the loyal service of the redeemed; he not only gave his life as a sacrifice, but also offered the worship of the forgiven; he not only faced God's judgement, but also rejoiced in his justification. Otherwise, he says,

> That acknowledgement, that repentance, would then be outside the complete act, and would be at best a sequel to it; whereas we ought to give a real place in a complete work of reconciliation to our repentance (which some extremists say is all that is required), or to Christ's moral action on us. Do we not need to include in some way the effect in the cause, in order to give the cause its full meaning and value, i.e., its value to God.[140]

Forsyth thus wants to stress that the work of Christ is a completed work, which includes its appropriation. He says,

> Reconciliation was finished in Christ's death. Paul did not preach a gradual reconciliation. He preached what the old divines used to call the finished work. He did not preach a gradual reconciliation which was to become the reconciliation of the world only piece-meal, as men were induced to accept it, or were affected by the Gospel. He preached something done once for all – a reconciliation which is the base of every soul's reconcilement, not an invitation only.[141]

It is because he sees the repentance of humankind as intrinsic to Christ's work on the cross that Forsyth treats sanctification as an aspect of the atonement and not as a later response to it, combining past event and present experience, the objective and the subjective, as would later again be attempted by Paul Fiddes.

So where does this leave the human act of repentance? Here again, Forsyth appeals to the language of moral solidarity. The pardon of solidary sin is won by the act of solidary repentance:

> His creative regenerative action on us is a part of that same moral solidarity which also makes His acceptance of judgement stand to

---

139 Forsyth, *The Work of Christ*, p. 189. This is a point evidently missed by J.H. Rodgers, when he says of Forsyth's view of repentance, 'Christ could not, and did not, repent, which is a condition of our acceptance before God, but in his "confession" he acted in such a way as to ensure our repentance.' Rodgers, *The Theology of P.T. Forsyth*, p. 54. Rodgers may here be influenced by *The Atonement in Modern Religious Thought* where Forsyth asserts that repentance is not for Christ but for 'man' (p. 76), a position from which, he was soon to move away.

140 Forsyth, *The Work of Christ*, p. 188. Forsyth also says in *Positive Preaching and the Modern Mind*, 'The Cross *effects* the reconciliation of man and God; it does not simply announce it, or simply *prepare* for it' (p. 238).

141 Forsyth, *The Work of Christ*, p. 86.

our good, and His confession of God's holiness to be the ground of ours. The same stroke on the one Christ went upwards to God's heart and downwards to ours.[142]

So in response to the question, 'How then could He perfectly meet the conditions of salvation?' Forsyth replies,

> The answer is that our repentance was latent in that holiness of His which alone could and must create it, as the effect is really part of the cause – that part of the cause which is prolonged in a polar unity into the sequential conditions of time.[143]

Forsyth gives the same treatment to the response of faith in the plan of salvation. 'The faith which He alone has power to wake is already offered to God in the offering of all His powers and of His finished work.' So complete is the work of Christ as Forsyth describes it, that not only does the cross provide the full satisfaction for sin, it also contains everything necessary for its benefits to be applied.

> Our faith is already present in His oblation. Our sanctification is already presented in our justification. Our repentance is already acting in His confession.[145] The effect of His Cross is to draw us into a repentance which is a dying with Him, and therefore a part of the offering in His death; and then it raises us in newness of life to a fellowship of His resurrection.[146]

Both repentance and faith are thus included in the work of Christ.

The approach Forsyth takes to repentance and faith, and therefore to sanctification, is not without its problems. The first of these is with respect to what he says about the meaning of repentance. The definition Forsyth offers is in danger of taking it a long way from the change of mind and will implied by *metanoia*, in the direction of a change of opinion regarding the greatness of the holiness of God. Unless confession of the unholiness in ourselves is held together with confession of the holiness of God, the sinful tendency to belittle our own sinfulness might allow this definition to become another means of avoiding an honest acknowledgement of our guilt before the Lord.

Secondly, the stress that Forsyth lays on repentance is at the cost of a balancing emphasis on baptism.[147] To assert that repentance alone

---

142 Forsyth, *The Work of Christ*, p. 191.
143 Forsyth, *The Work of Christ*, p. 192.
144 Forsyth, *The Work of Christ*, p. 193.
145 Later Forsyth adds, ' His victory contained ours.' Forsyth, *The Work of Christ*, p. 209.
146 Forsyth, *The Work of Christ*, p. 194.
147 Baptism is by no means overlooked by Forsyth, as we shall see in chapter 7. The problem here is the lack of weight it is given in this discussion.

is needed for the forgiveness of sins is only a partial reflection of Peter's response to the question provoked by his Pentecost sermon. To the cry, 'Brothers, what should we do?' he replied, 'Repent, and be baptized every one of you in the name of Jesus Christ so that your sins may be forgiven' (Acts 2:37f). As such, Forsyth fails to give sufficient attention to the 'one baptism for the forgiveness of sins' of the Niceno-Constantinopolitan creed.[148]

Thirdly, Forsyth leaves the Holy Spirit too small a place in his doctrine of sanctification to do justice to the teaching of the New Testament.[149] For Forsyth, the work of salvation is so concentrated into the cross of Christ that he is in danger of suggesting that all that remains thereafter is to appreciate the new state into which we have been transferred. So complete is the work of Christ that our repentance and life of faith are less a joining to Christ and participation in his work than a recognition of what is already the case.[150] The role remaining to the Holy Spirit is thus essentially the educative one of bringing home to the individual and society what is already true.[151] Without a due place for the sanctifying work of the Holy Spirit, Forsyth's doctrine of atonement can hardly have the moralizing effect that he desires.

Forsyth displays many of his characteristic emphases in his discussion of sanctification. Once again, we see how he stresses atonement

---

148 Had Forsyth given baptism the prominence it demands, he might have included it in his list of what is incorporated in the cross of Christ along with repentance, faith and sanctification.

149 See 2 Thess. 2:13 ('sanctification by the Spirit'), Tit. 3:5 ('renewal by the Holy Spirit'), and 1 Pet. 1:2 ('the sanctified by the Spirit'). Gunton criticizes Forsyth for a general lack of the pneumatological dimension. Hart, *Justice the True and Only Mercy*, p. 54. There is, of course, discussion of the work of the Holy Spirit in Forsyth, especially regarding the source of the Holy Spirit being in the Cross (e.g. *The Work of Christ*, p. 218) and the role of the Holy Spirit in providing salvation with 'its continuity, its amplification and its individualization.' P.T. Forsyth, *Faith, Freedom and the Future* (London: Independent Press, 1955), p. 11. The problem lies in the lack of integration of this pneumatology into his discussion of atonement. See Rodgers, *The Theology of P.T. Forsyth*, pp. 173ff for an excellent discussion of this aspect of Forsyth's thought.

150 Alan Sell makes a similar point when he criticizes Forsyth for failing to make clear the relationship between the gift of grace as something given and something still to be received in the life of faith in Christian Community. Hart, *Justice the True and Only Mercy*, p. 122.

151 As Stanley Russell observes, Forsyth sees the Holy Spirit primarily, 'in relation to the work of the Spirit in nature, rather than in the light of being the eschatological, sanctifying gift, who draws a world back from its fallenness into completion.' Hart, *Justice the True and Only Mercy*, p. 234.

as being about the positive restoration of holiness to the moral order in God's universe, and says that it is achieved in the cross of Christ. Indeed, it might be because he has cast redemption, judgement and sacrifice in such positive terms that he has relatively little to say regarding sanctification itself. He has already said that redemption is to bring us out of slavery and into freedom, so what Forsyth sees as sanctification is already implicit in that redemption.[152] And, similarly, the vindicating aspect of judgement and the obedience at the root of sacrifice leave little scope for a further work of sanctification. But Forsyth does provide a distinctive contribution regarding how God brings holiness to his creation through the cross of Christ.

D. The Relationship between Redemption, Justification and Sanctification

Having mapped out some of the main contours of Forsyth's thought on redemption, justification and sanctification, we can now address the question with which we began this chapter. Does Forsyth accomplish the task that he set himself of co-ordinating these three elements of atonement in their mutual relationship around the central principle of perfect obedience?

The place where we find the clearest presentation of this co-ordination is in the chapter entitled, 'The Threefold Cord' in *The Work of Christ*. Here it is that Forsyth says that what furnishes this unity that he seeks is 'the perfect obedience of holy love offered amidst the conditions of sin, death and judgement,'[153] and he goes on to explain that there is another name for that perfect obedience: 'holiness'. Forsyth says, '[The holy obedience to the Holy] is the only idea which unites justification and sanctification and both with redemption. For the holiness which satisfied God and sanctifies us also destroyed the evil power in the world and its hold on us.'[154] How does this work out in Forsyth's writing?

We have already seen how Forsyth expounds the sacrifice of Christ in terms of his perfect obedience, and in that sense what it means that Christ satisfied God by his holiness. It was not the amount of blood or the degree of suffering but the conformity to the will of God that made the sacrifice of Christ acceptable to God. What we have not seen, however, is how that principle of perfect obedience is central

---

152 There is therefore little room left for his claim that 'redemption is the obverse of His regenerating and sanctifying effect on us.' Forsyth, *The Work of Christ*, p. 202.

153 Forsyth, *The Work of Christ*, p. 201.

154 Forsyth, *The Work of Christ*, p. 222.

to the other aspect of satisfaction: judgement, or of redemption or sanctification. Judgement, as Forsyth expounds it, is not essentially an act of perfect obedience, but rather the means of establishing the just rule of God in a rebellious world. It clearly depends on the obedience of Christ to the will of the Father,[155] but it is not explained in terms of that obedience. The same may also be said for redemption. Forsyth describes this as a decisive action in the past, in the death of Christ, when the kingdom of God broke into history in order to restore the world into right relationship with the King, the Creator of the universe. The perfect obedience of Christ is thus necessary for this work but not the essence of it. Nor, too, could sanctification be seen primarily as an act of the perfect obedience of Christ. It is developed instead in terms of the formation of holiness in the human race by the solidary act of Christ crucified. Clearly, all these aspects of the work of Christ are contingent upon his obedience to the will of the Father, but they cannot be seen as coming into a unity under that principle.

We must also question whether Forsyth is right to say that perfect obedience is the only idea which unites redemption, satisfaction, and sanctification. Forsyth himself suggests two other alternatives: redemption and judgement. We see the claim for the centrality of redemption in *The Work of Christ*, where, in describing the threefold cord, Forsyth says redemption is the condition of justification which is the condition of sanctification.[156] And the claim for giving judgement a pivotal role is made in *The Justification of God*, where Forsyth says, 'judgement… is the root of the whole doctrine of atonement.'[157] Since perfect obedience is itself particularly associated with the sacrificial work of Christ, Forsyth has not one but three co-ordinating principles: redemption, judgement and sacrifice, all demanding the primary place in his atonement doctrine.

Of these three competing principles, the one which promises to take Forsyth the furthest is the one he pursues the least: judgement. He speaks of 'redemptive judgement',[158] suggesting that it is judgement that brings redemption. He also says that, 'Judgement is a far greater idea than sacrifice',[159] and that, 'we have passed upward from the idea of sacrifice to the graver and more ethical idea of *judgement*',[160]

---

155 Forsyth says, 'in obedience Christ accepted the judgement holiness must pass upon sin'. Forsyth, *The Work of Christ*, p. 206.
156 Forsyth, *The Work of Christ*, p. 201.
157 Forsyth, *The Justification of God*, p. 177.
158 Forsyth, *The Justification of God*, p. 187.
159 Forsyth, *The Work of Christ*, p. 146. Compare his remark, 'judgement and not sacrifice merely'. Forsyth, *The Justification of God*, p. 176.
160 Forsyth, *The Cruciality of the Cross*, p. 98. Cf. 'Nor is the identification with us

attributing a greater significance to judgement than to sacrifice. And he speaks of 'the sanctifying effect of judgement'[161] asserting that judgement brings sanctification. These statements claim for judgement a more profound role in atonement than redemption, sacrifice or sanctification, and suggest that these other aspects of atonement may be understood under the category of judgement. But Forsyth does not develop this idea further. He does not say how it is that redemption, sacrifice and sanctification may be seen as aspects of the judgement of God. Perhaps that is because, for all its innovations, his account of the work of Christ was not sufficiently developed to support such a project.[162]

Conclusion

We have seen that P.T. Forsyth has a great deal to say about the atonement that is original and insightful. There is a pervading positive tone throughout which deflects much of the justifiable criticism leveled against less sophisticated formulations of the work of Christ and establishes it as genuinely good news. He reveals a profound knowledge and understanding of Scripture whilst carrying out minimal textual exegesis, and maintains a sense of history and eternity, the personal and the corporate. But we have to say that the attempt to unite the different aspects of atonement under the perfect obedience of Christ does not succeed. Whilst Forsyth provides reason to believe that the perfect obedience of Christ was essential to his work, he does not give sufficient evidence to justify his claim that this is the unifying principle of the doctrine as a whole. He has, however, given some indications as to how judgement might provide the unification that he sought. We shall therefore now turn in our second section to an examination of the work of Karl Barth, for whom the judgement of Jesus Christ provides the primary statement of the atonement.

---

complete till the sacrifice become judgement...' Forsyth, *Positive Preaching*, p. 248.

161 Forsyth, *The Justification of God*, p. 83.

162 Behind the often dazzling brilliance of expression lie structural fault-lines in his exposition, as we have endeavoured to point out. Professor Alan Sell exposes many other flaws in: 'P.T. Forsyth as Unsystematic Systematician' in Hart, *Justice the True and Only Mercy*, pp. 110ff.

CHAPTER 5

Karl Barth and the Judgement of Jesus Christ as the Primary Statement of Atonement

Introduction

In our first section we saw the problems that arise in treating the different elements of atonement as independent theories, images or metaphors, and the inadequacies of P.T. Forsyth's attempt to reconcile them under the principle of perfect obedience. In this second section, we will explore how Karl Barth's exposition of the judgement of Jesus Christ may be developed in such a way as to draw together the different metaphors of atonement.

Barth believed that he had so captured the essence of the work of reconciliation in terms of the judgement of God that all else he would say about the doctrine could be seen as commentaries on it. At the end of the section under the much quoted title, 'The Judge judged in our place',[1] he underlined the importance of the treatise he had just written:

> [T]his is the place for a full-stop. Many further statements may follow, but the stop indicates that this statement is complete in itself, that it comprehends all that follows, and that it can stand alone. (IV/1, p. 273)

Barth was referring to his exposition of the doctrine of reconciliation in terms of an answer to Anselm's question, 'Cur Deus homo?' which he set out as follows: '[Christ] took our place as Judge. He took our place as the judged. He was judged in our place. And he acted justly in our place' (IV/1, p. 273). Barth immediately goes on to say, 'It is important to see that we cannot add anything further to this – unless it is an Amen to indicate that what we say further has this fourfold but single answer as a pre-supposition.' He wanted there to

---

1   Barth, IV/1, pp. 211ff.

be no doubt as to the scope and significance of this part of his exposition of the doctrine of reconciliation.

Exactly how this use of judgement relates to other metaphors of atonement, however, Barth does not say. In this second section we shall examine how Barth describes the judgement of Jesus Christ in his *Church Dogmatics*, principally in Volume 4 on 'The Doctrine of Reconciliation,' and show how it may be seen as the primary metaphor of atonement, with redemption, victory and sacrifice subordinate metaphors to judgement. This is not to suggest that judgement should be given a more prominent place than reconciliation itself. Barth clearly regards reconciliation as the controlling metaphor of the doctrine of atonement and structures the fourth volume of the *Church Dogmatics* around it. However, when he comes to expound this doctrine, he does so primarily in terms of judgement.

In order to demonstrate this primary role for judgement we shall firstly consider in this chapter what Barth means by judgement, then see in Chapter 6 how judgement may be related to redemption, victory and sacrifice, and finally explore in Chapter 7 how that judgement brings salvation. We begin here with a preliminary investigation into how Barth understands judgement. In particular we shall consider how he sees judgement as taking place in the judgement of Jesus Christ and then see how this judgement relates to God's judgement at the last day. In so doing we shall note to what extent Barth agrees with Forsyth and where he differs from him, so that we may build on the work of them both in constructing the argument of this thesis.

A. The Judgement of God as the Judgement of Jesus Christ

Barth follows Calvin in expounding the doctrine of atonement in terms of the judgement of God on sin.[2] The particular way in which he applies the term 'judgement' (*Gericht*), to the work of reconciliation is determined by his characteristic christological epistemology and is undertaken with an examination of the judgement of Christ. As part of his chapter on, 'Jesus Christ, the Lord as Servant', Barth expounds what he means by the judgement of Jesus Christ for us in terms of 'The Judge judged in our place.' We shall examine this pivotal passage to see how it is that Barth understands the judgement of God as being brought to bear in the judgement of Jesus Christ, fol-

---

2   Unlike Calvin, however, Barth treats judgement almost independently of sacrifice, redemption and victory, themes that Calvin weaves together. Calvin, *Institutes*, 2.16.5-7. See also R.A. Peterson Sr., *Calvin on the Atonement*, (Ross-shire: Christian Focus Publications, 1999), pp. 126ff.

lowing Barth's own fourfold structure of the judge, the judged, the judgement, and justice.

Jesus Christ as the judge

In his introductory remarks for this section, Barth explains what judgement means in terms of the role of the judge.

> And it is to the point if we remember that the Judge is not simply or even primarily the One who pardons some (perhaps a few or perhaps none at all) and condemns the rest (perhaps many and perhaps all) – whose judgement all have to fear. Basically and decisively – and this is something we must never forget when we speak of the divine Judge – He is the One whose concern is for order and peace, who must uphold the right and prevent the wrong, so that His existence and coming and work is not in itself and as such a matter for fear, but something which indicates a favour, the existence of One who brings salvation. (IV/1, p. 217).[3]

For Barth, then, seeing Christ as judge is to see him as the one whose rightful place it is to declare what is right and good not simply as a member of the judiciary, but as the righteous ruler. To underline this definition, Barth relates his discussion of the judge to the task of the judges of the Old Testament.[4] When God raised up a judge, and empowered them by his Spirit, it was to deliver his people from their enemies by executing God's just judgement against them, as well as to administer justice amongst the people whom he redeemed. This judging was subsequently to become the work of Israel's kings, most notably King David and King Solomon. Such an understanding of the role of judge is not limited to the Old Testament. '[I]n the New Testament – a fact which was later forgotten – the coming of the Judge means basically the coming of the Redeemer and Saviour' (IV/1, p.217). Barth does not, therefore, see the work of the judge narrowly in terms of the sentencing and pardoning of the courtroom. That would reduce his task to being that of a law-enforcer rather than recognizing his position as the lawgiver. It would also suggest that there is no prior relationship between the judge and those he judges, whereas this is the coming of their true king. He is,

---

3 He puts this more succinctly in his *Dogmatics in Outline*, 'the judge is not primarily the one who rewards some and punishes others; he is the man who creates order and restores what has been destroyed.' K. Barth, *Dogmatics in Outline* (translation by G.T. Thompson, New York, Harper and Brothers, 1947/1959), p. 135.

4 Barth, IV/1, p. 217.

as Emil Brunner describes him, the 'royal judge'.[5] Such a construal of the term 'judge' means that, for Barth as for Forsyth, the judge is not simply the enforcer of some abstract law, but the one who is to promote the good of all his subjects. As such, the coming of the judge should be a cause for thanksgiving, as the psalmists declare.[6]

But if we firstly say that to call Jesus the judge is to identify him as a human ruler, we must also go further and say that when Barth describes Jesus as judge, it is to associate his work with the very work of God, the 'divine judge'. As he says, 'it is not just any judgement which He exercises and executes, but the judgement of God' (IV/1, p. 219).[7] So the Son goes into the far country in the power of the Spirit to bring the judgement of the Father. That is what makes this judgement so final, so decisive. It is 'ultimate judgement' (IV/1, p.219). There is no higher court to which appeal may be made. As such, when Barth applies the designations 'judge' or 'king' to Christ, he does so in a metaphorical fashion, as Gunton points out.[8] He is consciously carrying over the meaning from one sphere of reality, earthly rule, to another, divine rule, knowing that it must not be pressed too far. There is a uniqueness about this Messiah that requires us to transcend the language of kingship.

> The righteous king, who is at once threatened and promised in the future by the existence of the present king, is the Messiah, the king of Israel, nay the world king 'at the end of the days.'... In the *extension* of this political idea lies the picture of the human helper, comforter and lord, sent by God, who some day, at the approaching of the end of time, will realize the promise of the covenant for this people. (I/2, p. 98, my italics).

---

5   E. Brunner, *The Mediator* (translation by O. Wyon, London: Lutterworth Press, 1927/1934), p. 464. Forsyth makes a similar point when he says, 'Judgement by God is in the Bible a function of His action as king.' Forsyth, *The Justification of God*, p. 180.

6   Pss. 9, 76, 82 and 94. This is because God's judgement vindicates the righteous (Ezek. 20:36-44; Dan. 7:22; Mat. 12:36f; Rom. 2:5-11; 2 Cor. 5:10) and condemns the wicked (Exod. 12:12; Num. 33:4; Deut 32:41; 2 Chron. 24:24; Ezek 11:10f; 20:26-44; Hab. 1:12; Mal. 3:5; Mat. 12:36f; Rom 2:5-11; 2 Cor. 5:10). See also Mat. 25:31-46 and when Zec. 8:16.

7   Here Barth develops the role of Jesus as the divine judge more strongly than Calvin does, thereby minimizing the possibility of being understood as setting a vengeful Father against an obedient Son, in the way, for instance, G.W.H. Lampe understands Calvin's account, describing his portrayal of God as that of a 'hanging judge.' G.W.H. Lampe, 'Atonement: Law and Love,' in A.R. Vidler, ed. *Soundings: Essays Concerning Christian Understanding* (Cambridge: Cambridge University Press, 1962), p. 187.

8   Gunton, *The Actuality of Atonement*, pp. 109ff.

And yet it is in the language of *kingship* that we are so enabled to express the work of the incarnate Son, and to say that Jesus is the royal judge who announces and embodies the judgement of God, and by whose word we stand or fall.

So how is it that this judge, Jesus, confronts all false judges? Barth sees this firstly in terms of his spoken word. His command, 'Do not judge, so that you may not be judged. For with the judgement you make you will be judged' (Mat. 7:1f) and his condemnation of the scribes and Pharisees, who accepted the titles, 'rabbi', 'father', 'instructor' (Mat. 23:1f), are two examples he provides to show what he has in mind.[9] The word of judgement thus comes against human practices, but it does so for our good, making it clear what it means to be truly human by declaring what is excluded by that calling. As Barth says, 'We are what we are on the basis of this judgement, what we are as its hearers, i.e., we are believers or unbelievers, obedient or disobedient' (I/1, p. 161). As such, we can see how creative is the work of judgement, as Barth expounds it. The lines that are drawn between righteousness and wickedness are drawn by the creator for the well-being of his creation. And where those lines are drawn is revealed by the word of Jesus.

The judgement of Christ is also to be seen, secondly, in his action as the one who humbles himself under the judgement of God. This too is how Christ confronts the false judges, especially Judas, Israel and Pilate. His very subjection to their condemnation is itself his sovereign action as judge. For Christ to stand under their judgement is to reveal on the one hand the wickedness of humanity and on the other the graciousness of God, juxtaposing them in all their stark distinction. The judgement of God comes in contrast to the judgement of humanity in which 'man wants to be his own and his neighbour's judge' (IV/1, p. 231), which Barth identifies as the root and origin of sin. In sharp contrast to the human pride that asserted its own judgement against Christ, he himself disclosed the humility of God to stand under that judgement, as humankind refused to do. The constant justification of the self and the condemnation of others is thus exposed in all its folly. So Barth can say, 'It is by an action that we are removed from the judge's seat, by the fact that Jesus Christ did for us what we wanted to do for ourselves' (IV/1, p. 232). In the presence of the judge all such judgements are silenced, humbling and liberating people from the burdensome task of judgement which lies beyond their capabilities and setting them free to live under the wise judgement of God.

9　Barth, IV/1, p. 235.

Having seen how it is that Barth understands the role of Jesus the judge, the question arises, Why does he place this discussion under the office of Christ the high-priest (in his chapter on the Lord as servant), rather than his office as the king (in his chapter on the Servant as lord)?[10] Barth describes the three forms of the doctrine of reconciliation as: justification, sanctification and vocation, placing justification under the office of high-priest, sanctification under the office of king, and vocation[11] under the office of prophet. Justification is then interpreted in terms of the humbling of the Son of God who enters the far country to overcome the pride of humankind. But would this not instead lend itself better to an exposition of kingship in terms of humble servanthood? Then the high-priesthood of Christ could be unfolded in terms of defeating the sin of sloth by actively responding to the call into the holy presence of God, leaving the sin of falsehood still being confronted under the office of Christ the prophet who proclaims the truth. By means of this exchange in his structure of high-priesthood and kingship, Barth could have made it clearer that when he speaks of Jesus the judge, he is referring to Jesus the king.

Jesus Christ as the judged

In the second part of the exposition of, 'The Judge judged in our place', Barth portrays Christ as the one who submits himself to God's judgement. Such an assertion, Barth acknowledges, is hard to understand. He begins his account by making clear that he is not suggesting Jesus himself has done anything wrong or ceased to be the one who lives righteously and judges justly. It is instead to say that he takes upon himself the wrongdoing of others by choosing to shoulder responsibility for their sin. So Barth says Jesus

> [G]ives Himself (like a *rara avis*) to the fellowship of those who are guilty of [disputing, evil-doing and enmity against God], and not only that, but He makes their evil case His own. He is above this fellowship and confronts it and judges it and condemns it in that He takes it upon Himself to be the bearer and Representative, to be responsible for this case, to expose Himself to the accusation and sentence which must inevitably come upon us in this case. (IV/1, p. 236)

---

10   Barth prefers the terms 'the Lord as servant' and 'the Servant as lord' to the traditional categories of the high-priestly and kingly offices of Christ. He finds them more precise and more comprehensive, since they overcome the divide between the person and work of Christ. Barth, IV/1, p. 135.
11   Barth, IV/1, p. 147.

So Jesus came under the judgement of God as a consequence of his fellowship with sinful humanity and his choice to take upon himself the burden of their sin. Barth acknowledges his debt to Luther for this point, accepting his assertion that Christ was willing to stand as 'the greatest transgressor, murderer, adulterer, thief, rebel, blasphemer etc. that ever was or could be in all the world.'[12] 'Making their evil case His own' is thus located in voluntary action subsequent to his birth, by which he chose not to enjoy the blessings belonging to his own sinlessness, but instead to take the curse belonging to the sinfulness of those amongst whom he lived.

But that is not to say that this decision was only subsequent to the decision of the Son to humble himself and go into the far country at his Father's behest. The decision to take human flesh was the decision to take mortal flesh because it was as such sinful flesh, as opposed to the immortal, sinless flesh of his resurrection body. Writing of the humanity that the Word assumed, Barth says,

> Flesh is the concrete form of human nature marked by Adam's fall, the concrete form of that entire world which, when seen in the light of Christ's death on the cross, must be regarded as the old world already past and gone, the form of the destroyed nature and existence of man as they have to be reconciled to God. (I/2, p. 151)[13]

But that decision to take sinful flesh, Barth says, then needed to be ratified and reinforced by the self-identification of Jesus with sinners, even tax-collectors and prostitutes, in order to make explicit what was otherwise only implicit. Here Barth diverges somewhat from Forsyth, for whom the emphasis is on the taking of sinful flesh rather than any subsequent identification with sinners. However, both agree that Christ was incarnate of sinful flesh and thereby give the incarnation an integral and decisive place in understanding the atonement.

---

12 M. Luther, *Commentary on the Epistle to the Galatians* (translation by P.S. Watson, London: James Clarke and Co., 1535, 1953), p. 269. See Barth, IV/1, p. 238.

13 Barth notes that theologians up to and including the Reformers tended to be reserved on such a point, not wishing to undermine the assertion that Christ was sinless. He acknowledges his debt to Gottfried Menken and Edward Irving amongst others for having established such a position (I/2, p. 153). Professor T.F. Torrance traces this view back to the Greek fathers, and especially Irenaeus. T.F. Torrance, *Karl Barth, Biblical and Evangelical Theologian* (Edinburgh: T. & T. Clark, 1990), p. 202. For a fuller discussion of the questions raised by this point, see Kelly Kapic, 'The Son's Assumption of a Human Nature: A Call for Clarity', *International Journal of Systematic Theology*, (2001), vol. 3, no. 2, pp. 154ff.

In asserting that Christ chose to shoulder the burden of human sin, Barth describes him as the representative of the human race. By this he means that Christ should not be regarded as someone unconnected with us who is doing something to us from outside, but instead that he stands in relation to sinful humanity as the one who bears our sin. So Barth says,

> He represents us in that which we truly are. That He represents us in it does not mean that we are not in it, but that we truly are, our being in sin, is taken over by Him, that He is responsible for it in divine power, that it is taken from us with divine authority, and forgiven. But although He takes it over, and is responsible for it and it is forgiven us, it is still our being in sin. (IV/1, p. 241)

Barth further elaborates on this point in his discussion of the resurrection,

> For the fact that God has given Himself in His Son to suffer the divine judgement on us men does not mean that it is not executed on us but that it is executed on us in full earnest and in all its reality – really and definitely because He Himself took our place in it. That Jesus Christ died for us does not mean, therefore, that we do not have to die, but that we have died in and with Him, that as the people we were we have been done away with and destroyed, that we are no longer there and have no more future. (IV/1, p. 295)[14]

Here, Barth's use of the term 'judge' serves to illuminate his meaning, since such a royal judge is a representative of the people. The destiny of this one person carries the destiny of them all; any victories or defeats for this judge are victories or defeats for all his people. He is their champion. Barth is thereby able to expand on how it is that an action which we cannot accomplish nor even contribute to ourselves, namely purification from sin, is achieved by Christ not apart from us, but by standing with us and for us.

In this emphasis on representation Barth is not seeking to avoid using the terminology of substitution,[15] as Forsyth is inclined to do. Indeed, he places great emphasis on it, at one point answering the question 'What has in fact taken place in Jesus Christ?' with the reply, 'We will first give the general answer that there has taken

---

14   This is very much in line with Forsyth's view of Christ's solidary action for us. Indeed, Barth uses the adjective, *'solidarisch'* (Barth, IV/1, p. 264, German edition) translated by G.W. Bromiley as the noun, 'solidarity' (IV/1, p. 240), to describe the relationship between Jesus Christ and sinful humanity.

15   This situation is complicated by the fact that the German word *'Stellvertreter'* may be translated 'representative' or 'substitute'. G.W. Bromiley himself notes this ambiguity in his preface (IV/1, p. vii) and generally translates it

place in Him the effective self-substitution [*selbsteinsatz*][16] of God for us sinful men' (IV/1, p. 550). Barth sees this as a repeated theme of the Gospels, but perhaps his clearest example is in the trial of Jesus when Pilate releases Barabbas. Barth puts it thus,

> The Jesus who was condemned to be crucified in the place of Barabbas (Mark 15:6-15) stands on the one side, and Barabbas who was pardoned at the expense of Jesus stands on the other; for he was not crucified, nor did he really contribute to his own liberation which came about when sentence was pronounced on that other. (IV/1, p. 230)

Jesus exchanged his own position as the obedient Son of God for that of this disobedient son of Adam. But as representative of sinful humanity standing under the judgement of God, he bore not just this one man's sin, but the sin of the world, allowing it to take its course to death in him. So Barth says,

> It was to fulfil this judgement on sin that the Son of God as man took our place as sinners. He fulfils it – the man in our place – by completing our work in the omnipotence of the divine Son, by treading the way of sinners to its bitter end in death, in destruction, in the limitless anguish of separation from God, by delivering up sinful man and sin in His own person to the non-being which is properly theirs, the non-being, the nothingness to which man has fallen victim as a sinner and towards which he relentlessly hastens. (IV/1, p. 253).

The judgement of God in Jesus Christ is thus to be understood essentially as the judgement of the sin of all in the one who was without sin but who took it upon himself to be the one great sinner and to be judged in the place of sinners.

Jesus Christ undergoing judgement

Here, Barth turns his attention more directly to the biblical testimony to the passion of Jesus Christ in order to elucidate what it means that he suffered judgement for us. The action of Christ in willingly submitting to the judgement of God is rooted into its historical context as the time and space in which God acted decisively to judge the world

---

as 'representative'. At times he translates '*für uns*' as 'substitute' (e.g., IV/1, p. 230 of the English edition, p. 252 of the German edition) although that may simply mean 'for us' in the sense of 'on our behalf', as our representative, rather than 'in our place', as our substitute. As we will see, however, Barth's use of the concept of substitution is not dependent on the translation of either of these terms.

16 Literally 'self-insertion'.

in Christ. Here it is that Barth makes it clear that he is not purely discussing theoretical concepts. He is considering instead how it is that the life, death and resurrection of Jesus Christ have their saving effect. It is the passion and death of Jesus Christ that destroy sin and overcome death, not our ideas about them. It is his active, humble obedience to the Father that fulfils his calling to be the saviour of the world, not our intellectual understanding of what he has achieved. It is therefore a saving work that is effective even if our conceptual grasp of it is weak or muddled. Important as concepts are for the exposition of what it is that Christ achieved, we must be clear that we are saved by the work of Christ and not by our ideas about it.

It is in this section that Barth points out that it is not the willingness of Christ to suffer, nor the severity of the pain he endured nor even the redemptive effect of his death that makes his death so decisive, since others may be seen as dying such a death. The significance of this death lies in the person who dies. As Barth says, 'it is the eternal God Himself who has given Himself in His Son to be man, and as man to take upon Himself this human passion' (IV/1, p. 246).

The form that judgement takes is not so much revealed in the arrest and trials of Jesus Christ but in the sentence of death and especially the crucifixion itself under which he condescends to go. It is here that Barth makes one of his most crucial contributions to the doctrine of reconciliation. He locates the moment of judgement in the moment of death, something which, as we have seen, Forsyth is reluctant to do. In his discussion of anthropology, Barth says, 'Death, as it actually encounters us men, is the sign of God's judgement on us' (III/2, p. 596).[17] Barth thus brings together death and judgement, seeing them not so much as two sequential elements of the last things, but as inseparable occurrences, since it is the shadow of judgement that falls upon the living in death. As such, death is not to be seen as something essential to the constitution of human being,[18] but rather as something resulting from human sinfulness.

---

17 In his *Credo* Barth says, 'In itself, indeed, the death of a man, as confirmed and sealed by his burial, is still less to be understood as acquittal, sacrifice and victory than above as judgement.' K. Barth, *Credo* (translation by J. Strathearn McNab, London: Hodder and Stoughton, 1935/1936), p. 91.

18 We should note here that Barth also wants to give a positive assessment to the value of death in providing a limited time span (III/2, p. 557), distinguishing it from the second death, which is corruptive and unnatural (III/2, p. 637). However, Barth is not clear here whether that would be true of a world without sin; it might only be a blessing in the sense that it brings an end to suffering in a sinful world, rather than actually being part of God's good creation. It is highly significant in this regard that prior to the sin of

As Barth says, 'our death is intrinsically connected with our sin and guilt' (III/2, p. 600), and he cites in support Rom. 5:12 ('death came through sin'); Rom. 6:23 ('the wages of sin is death'); Rom. 8:13 ('if you live according to the flesh you will die') and Jas. 1:15 ('sin, when it is fully grown, gives birth to death'). Barth, then, sees death as the stark and unavoidable evidence that we live under the judgement of God. And when Jesus died, he submitted to that judgement of God, the judgement on sin that results in death.[20]

Seeing death itself in terms of judgement has important implications for Barth's understanding of atonement. It means that for Christ to succumb to death is for him to succumb to judgement. Barth is explicit about this, 'He suffered death as the judgement of God' (III/2, p. 600). It was the judgement of an 'alien burden' (III/2, p. 628), but it was judgement nevertheless. So it was not the degree of pain endured, or the amount of blood shed that makes the passion of Christ effective in expiating sin; it was the very death itself. The significance of his death as judgement does not, therefore, rest on whether it was a judicial death or a painful death or even a godforsaken death. These things are decisive for illuminating what

---

Adam and Eve, they were, it seems, permitted to eat of the tree of life (Gen. 2:16f); only after their sin was that possibility prohibited (Gen. 3:22-24). And, of course, there is to be no death or mourning in heaven (Rev. 21:4). Together, these observations suggest that where there is no sin, there is no death. This need not require that earthly life be of infinite duration, since limited time span is possible without death, as Enoch (Gen. 5:24), Elijah (2 Kgs. 2:11) and the resurrected Christ testify (Luke 24:51; Acts 1:9). So we do not accept Barth's affirmation of death in God's good creation. Interestingly, Professor Douglas Farrow of McGill University sees Barth's positive evaluation of death as a lapse into natural theology. D. Farrow, 'Robert Jenson's *Systematic Theology*: Three Responses', *International Journal of Systematic Theology* (1999), vol. 1, no. 1, p. 92.

19   Hans Küng wrestles with the question that this raises about the obvious fact that people do not all die when they sin, and makes this reply: 'God spares the sinner... He does not allow him to carry out his work of destruction to its conclusions. He wishes to give him time to repent.' Hans Küng, *Justification: The Doctrine of Karl Barth and a Catholic Reflection* (translation by T. Collins, E.E. Tolk and D. Grandskou, London: Burns and Oates, 1957/1964), p. 148. This does, of course, raise the problem of why in God's providence some enjoy longer periods of mercy than others, but it does maintain the biblical witness to the God who has no pleasure in the death of the wicked (Ezek. 18:23) without minimizing the destructive effects of that wickedness.

20   Barth also draws attention to how the New Testament treatment of the death of Christ is mostly directly or indirectly in connection to sin, citing John 1:29; 6:51, Rom. 4:25; 5:9; Gal. 1:4; 1 Cor. 15:32 Cor. 5:15, Acts 20:28; Heb. 9:28; 1 Pet. 2:24 and 3:18.

kind of judgement he was under, but they are not required in order to establish his death as one under the judgement of God. Death is always to be seen as the judgement of God. Barth is thereby able to make the closest possible connection between Christ's death on the cross and the atonement, something which, in the end, Forsyth failed to do.

But, we must ask, What did that death of Christ actually achieve, since clearly death itself has not been eliminated? Barth replies that it achieves reconciliation with God, the conversion of the world from a state of enmity with God to a state of friendship with God, which rescues human beings from the path to death and destruction and delivers them onto the path of life.

> The sin and sins of man form the disruptive factor within creation which makes necessary the atonement, the new peace with God, the restoration of the covenant with a view to the glory of God and the redemption and salvation of man as the work of God's free mercy. (IV/1, p. 252)

To live now that this judgement has taken place is to inhabit a world in which we may know God with us again, by the presence of his Spirit poured out at Pentecost. And to die now that judgement has come to pass may be to fall into the hands of God who is for us and not against us. It means not to fall into the abyss, but to fall asleep and to awake in the glorious presence of the Lord.

Here Barth makes it clear that, in speaking of reconciliation, he has in mind the restoration of a relationship that has broken down.[21] Barth thereby makes the covenant between God and humankind the framework within which reconciliation is to be understood. 'In [Christ]', says Barth, 'the covenant which God has faithfully kept and man has broken is renewed and restored...as He fulfils His judgement on us all' (IV/1, p. 251). This covenant is 'the presupposition of reconciliation' (IV/1, pp. 22ff), for without it, there would be no relationship to be repaired. So atonement is, for Barth, a profoundly relational matter, concerned with the creatures with whom God has a covenant relationship, albeit a fractured relationship. It is therefore an act of mercy within the covenant of grace by which the presence of God is brought to bear to restore his relationship with his people. Barth, like Forsyth, thus casts judgement in a positive light as the means of bringing about restoration to the relationship between God and humankind. Judgement is thus for Barth, as for Forsyth, an act of grace, rather than an act which merely creates the

---

21 The German word translated, 'reconciliation', *Versöhnung*, may also be translated 'atonement', since both words speak of two separated parties being brought together.

possibility of grace.[22]

The gracious action by which God restored the covenant that humankind had broken by their sin and could not repair was to carry out the demands of that covenant in such a way as to fulfill its demands and at the same time to restore his covenant partner.

> [I]t needed nothing less than God Himself to remedy the corruption of our being and ourselves, to restore order between Himself as Creator and the world as His creation, to set up and maintain again the covenant broken by man, to carry it through against man for the sake of man, and in that was to save man from destruction. (IV/1, p. 251)

God's way was not to withdraw the threat of judgement that hung over his creation, but to carry it out so that the world may be purged and purified. The very wrath of God that is aroused by human sin is therefore brought into the service of those against whom it is directed, another point that is reminiscent of Forsyth.[23] As such we see that the judgement of God against his covenant-partners is an action of a friend and not an enemy. It is the work of a God who is, as Barth never tires of saying, *'pro nobis'* and who alone is able to turn the human race from enemies into friends.

It is within this covenantal understanding of judgement that Barth introduces the subject of punishment. Barth is conscious of how little the term is used in relation to atonement by the New Testament authors, and how its influence primarily stems from Isa. 53.[24] He justifies the continuing use of the term in the doctrine of reconciliation by saying that our sin calls down God's wrath to bring the sinner to destruction, something that should be understood as punishment for sin. Since Christ has made our sinful situation his own, it would be true to say that he suffered our punishment. 'We can say that He

---

22 As Barth puts it, the 'binding order' of grace and judgement, 'consists in the fact that God's will is to keep man in grace, or to lead him to it, by means of judgement' (IV/2, p. 773).

23 Forsyth spoke of how God managed 'to make sin further the purpose it seemed to foil.' Forsyth, *The Cruciality of the Cross*, p. 100.

24 The Old Testament scholar John Goldingay takes issue with Barth here, denying that there is a link between atonement and punishment in Isa. 53:5, 6, 10-12. J. Goldingay ed. *Atonement Today* (London: SPCK, 1995), p. 8. However, Barth's position is supported by many other Old Testament sscholars, including J.L. McKenzie, Claus Westermann and John D.W. Watts. J.L. McKenzie, *Second Isaiah* (New York: Doubleday, 1968), p. 133; C. Westermann, *Isaiah 40-66: A Commentary* (Old Testament Library, London: SCM Press, 1969), p. 263 and J.D.W. Watts, *Isaiah 34-44* (Word Biblical Commentaries vol. 25, Texas: Word, 1987), p. 231.

fulfils this judgement by suffering the punishment which we have all brought on ourselves' (IV/1, p. 253).[25] This is the manner in which the wrath of God against sin is encountered as an 'alien form' of God's being (IV/1, p. 490), as an aspect of his 'fatherly chastisement' (II/2, p. 748) that is seen in the punishment of his unruly children.[26] But this punishment of God is no fit of rage. It is the natural expression of God's covenantal love in response to rejection by those he loves and who depend on him totally for their well-being. Barth does not, however, want punishment to become a major focus of this doctrine, as some followers of Anselm have made it, whether in terms of Christ's suffering delivering us from future suffering, or of his punishment satisfying the wrath of God. The punishment he suffered does indeed deliver us from the punishment we deserve, but this is not to be seen as the mechanism by which we are freed from our sin. Punishment is, for Barth, a consequence of a judgement that yields condemnation, not a process that must be undergone in its own right. Barth thereby distinguishes his position from that of penal substitution, not by denying that either penalty or substitution have a place in the doctrine of reconciliation, but by reassessing what that place is. It is not so much that Jesus bore the punishment that we deserved in order to save us from it, but that Jesus bore the judgement of God against sin as the representative sinner and thereby delivered us from the punishment which that judgement justly demanded.

Jesus Christ the just

In this fourth section, Barth turns his attention to the character of Christ, who is the judge judged in our place. What does it mean to say that he is the justice or righteousness of God revealed in these end times? What was it about Christ in his life on earth that made him the just man who was judged for the unjust? Barth here points to his obedience to the Father, and in doing so follows Calvin closely.[27]

---

25 Paul Fiddes is therefore misleading when he says, 'Barth, then rejects any idea that Christ atones for our sin by bearing a punishment in our place.' Fiddes, *Past Event and Present Salvation*, p. 143.

26 Cf. 'The father has to punish his children. He institutes certain laws, the children disobey; they must be punished, or, using the more dignified term, judged.' Forsyth, *The Work of Christ*, p. 119. Barth and Forsyth here distance themselves from Ritschl, who saw wrath as unworthy of a God of love and grace. A. Ritschl, *A Critical History of the Christian Doctrine of Justification and Reconciliation* (translation by J.S. Black, Edinburgh: Edmonston and Douglas, 1872), pp. 198ff.

27 'When it is asked then how Christ, by abolishing sin, removed the enmi

It is this which makes Jesus righteous and distinguishes him from the disobedient unrighteous people amongst whom he lived. It is this which rendered him sinless and kept him from undergoing the condemnation of God on his own account, and displayed the very righteousness of God instead.

> Jesus Christ was obedient in that He willed to take our place as sinners and did, in fact, take our place. When we speak of the sinlessness of Jesus we must always think concretely about this. It did not consist in an abstract and absolute purity, goodness and virtue. It consisted in His actual freedom from sin itself, from the basis of all sins. That is why He was not a transgressor and committed no sins. That is why He could take on Himself and deliver up to death the sins of other men. (IV/1, p. 258)[28]

This discussion of the obedience of Christ casts fresh light on how it is that Barth sees him as bringing about reconciliation with God. His obedient life was what came to the rescue of disobedient human lives. Where Adam had rebelled against God's command and fallen into the way of death, Jesus had accepted God's command and chosen the way of life. For Christ, entering the jaws of death was not a consequence of succumbing to temptation, but itself an act of obedience to the will of God for the well-being of his creatures to deliver them from the consequences of their falling into temptation. Barth puts it in this way:

> In their place and for their sake, instead of committing fresh sin, He returned to the place from which they had fallen into sin, the place which belongs to the creature in relation to God. In so doing, in His own person, He reversed the fall in their place and for their sake. He acted justly in that He did not refuse to do what they would not do. (IV/1, p. 259)[29]

Where Adam had exalted his will over the will of God in pride, Jesus humbled himself under the will of God to come to our aid. Where Adam failed to live out his calling to be the image of God,

---

ty between God and us, and purchased a righteousness which made him favourable and kind to us, it may be answered generally, that he accomplished this by the whole course of his obedience.' Calvin, *Institutes*, 2.16.5.

28 In seeing Christ's righteousness in his obedience to his Father, and in the active construal of that righteousness, Barth again echoes Forsyth. E.g., Forsyth, *The Work of Christ*, p. 164.

29 Here we see the influence of Irenaeus and the recapitulation in Jesus of past sinful action in his own sinless action in order to save the world. Vernon White reasserts the importance of this aspect of the atonement in his recent work, *Atonement and Incarnation* (Cambridge: Cambridge University Press, 1991), especially pp. 51-68.

Jesus committed himself unreservedly to fully being that image in the world. And where Adam hid behind falsehood, Jesus unashamedly proclaimed the truth even at the cost of his own life. It was in this way that human disobedience was undone, that the fall which results from pride was reversed, that the misery which follows sloth was converted into joy, and that the condemnation which issues from falsehood was turned to vindication.

In saying this, Barth in no way diminishes the sense in which Jesus lived life in complete freedom. His obedience to the Father is exactly the manner in which he lived freely. That is how Barth understands freedom.

> In obedience man lives and acts in freedom. He is true to his own nature as the creature of God, the creature who is appointed in its own decisions to follow and correspond to the decisions of God, to follow and correspond to the decisions of God in its decisions which are its own. (IV/1, pp. 257f)

To all the evil insinuations that freedom is to be found in rejection of the command of God, Barth replies that freedom is only to be lost in such sinful action and inaction. It was in his constant attention to the command of God and continual obedience to the will of God that Christ lives and judges in perfect freedom.

This free obedience in which Jesus acted justly is not only the means by which he faced the judgement of God against sin, it is also the form of his penitence as the one great sinner responding to the light of that judgement. Barth sees the beginning of Christ's penitence in the baptism of Jesus by John, and it was thus that he 'fulfilled all righteousness' (Mat. 3:15).[30] The fasting in the wilderness that follows his baptism is seen by Barth as a further act of penitence, with the temptations of the devil being understood in terms of ceasing to repent for other people. The first temptation is thus understood in this context as being to break his fast, the second, not to acknowledge God as the Lord, and the third, to put God to the test.[31] The passion of Christ, and especially his anguished prayer in Gethsemane, is again seen in terms of the penitence of Christ.

> He does not reserve His future obedience. He does not abandon His status as a penitent. He does not cease to allow that God is in the right, even against Himself. He does not try to anticipate His justification by Him in any form, or to determine it Himself. He does not think of trying to be judge in His own cause and in God's cause. (IV/1, p. 270)

---

30   Barth, IV/1, p. 259.
31   Barth, IV/1, pp. 261ff. Jesus is understood here as 'a great sinner repenting' (IV/1, p. 261).

This total surrender to the will of his Father is thus not only the act of the sinless one but also the act of the one great sinner who, as a friend of sinners, takes his place alongside them and puts himself in the position of the penitent. It is in this sense that Barth would say that Christ repented for sinful humanity.[32]

This obedience to the will of the Father is not something to be assessed by human judges. It is instead declared in the Father's own assessment on the Son delivered in his raising him from the dead. 'To sum up,' says Barth, 'the resurrection of Jesus Christ is the great verdict of God, the fulfilment and proclamation of God's decision concerning the event of the cross' (IV/1, p. 309). The resurrection is thus conceived as another aspect of the judgement of God. It is his divine verdict. In the first place, this refers to the justification of God himself who willed and planned this judgement as creator and covenant partner to show his own righteousness in dealing with the sin of the world. In the second place, it is the verdict on Jesus Christ himself, that he had been fully obedient, both actively and passively, and that his life had been truly pleasing to the Father. This is his beloved Son in whom he is well pleased. And in the third place, it refers to the effectiveness of the death of Christ for sinners, that the judgement which had come against Jesus as the representative of sinful humanity had yielded salvation for them. To feel the force of this astonishing outcome, Barth speculates that the coming of Jesus Christ as judge might have been to announce and implement a judgement of final destruction. 'The judgement executed on Him in the place of all might have meant the end of all things' (IV/1, p. 294). Only when this dreadful negative possibility is faced in all its seriousness can we see clearly the positive outcome demonstrated in the resurrection of Jesus Christ from the dead. It is an act of unimaginable grace and mercy undertaken by the Father through the Spirit. If it had not been foretold, it could not have been foreseen. In this way Barth is able to give the resurrection the decisive place it commands in the Gospel accounts,[33] without making

---

32 So Barth, like Forsyth, wants to assert that Christ not only made atonement available, but also participated in the new situation which resulted from that atonement to make it a finished work of reconciliation. Barth is, however, more successful than Forsyth in making his case by virtue of the fact that he grounds his argument in the historical events of Jesus life, rather than in a deduction from the inability of sinful humanity to offer satisfactory penance. In David Ford's phrase, it is because Barth does not 'look for the meaning in God outside of the story' of Jesus Christ that he is able to make his case for the repentance of Christ so compellingly. D.F. Ford, *Barth and God's Story* (Frankfurt: Verlag Peter Lang, 1985), p. 39.

33 Something we found lacking in Forsyth.

it an inevitable sequel to the cross, or allowing it to loom so large as to obscure the central significance of the crucifixion itself. It is instead the indispensable evidence that the judgement of almighty God has fallen on Jesus Christ and revealed his perfect righteousness.

In the light of such an understanding of the resurrection, we may now see how Barth understands justification as arising out of judgement. It is firstly that God himself is revealed as the one who acts justly, not letting sin go unpunished or excusing it, but bringing it down to death in the death of Christ. And it means, secondly, that human beings are set free from sin and made right before God because in Jesus Christ their rebellion has culminated in their death. The judgement of Jesus Christ is thus the justification of God and the justification of humankind. Judgement is therefore not seen as something preliminary to justification but the very action in which justification takes place. It is in this sense that both God and humankind are affected by this judgement. It is not that both sides equally need reconciling to each other; only the world needs reconciling to God. But it is in this judgement of Jesus Christ that both the covenant partners are restored in their mutual relationship. In this judgement, God is justified in pardoning human sin and sinners are justified by having their sin so pardoned, removing what destroyed communion between God and humankind, and thereby bringing about reconciliation.

So to speak of justification in terms of the imputation of the righteousness of Christ, as the Reformers did, does not go far enough for Barth.

> It cannot in any sense be an improper justification of man which has its basis in this happening. Otherwise how could it be a perfect happening, and how could the love of God for man realized in it be a perfect love? Rather, the alien righteousness which has been effected not in and by us but in the sacrifice of Jesus Christ does become and is always ours, so that in Him we are no longer unrighteous but righteous before God, we are the children of God, we have the forgiveness of our sins, peace with God, access to Him and freedom for Him. (IV/1, p. 283)

Something concrete has actually taken place in this judgement of Jesus Christ that brings about a real and lasting justification of sinful human beings. It is not an 'as if' we are righteous, but simply an 'as' we are righteous.[34] Barth can claim such an ontological change because of the way he sees Christ representing humankind. As he

---

34 This too is anticipated in Forsyth. 'We are justified only as we are incorporate (not clothed) in the perfect righteousness of Christ'. Forsyth, *The Work of Christ*, p. 215.

explains, 'Negatively, the justification of sinful man before God means a basic turning away from his wrong and from himself as the doer of it. Positively, it means his basic turning to God' (IV/1, p. 556). He thus sees a real and effective repentance having taken place in the judgement of Jesus Christ that actually turns the human race from rebellion to service, from wrong to right, from godlessness to godliness. As such, the justification of sinners can be said to have come about in the judgement of Jesus Christ.

Barth acknowledges that this situation of a world already judged and justified is not what we see with our natural eyes.

> That we live as righteous men is not an immanent determination of our existence and cannot therefore be conceived. It is not in our existence that man has acquired this future. Looking at ourselves we should have to regard this future as that of the man of tomorrow as just as unreal and impossible as the fact that that man of yesterday is our past. (IV/1, pp. 554f)

The continuing problem of sin is an inescapable daily reality. Pride, sloth and falsehood still mar lives. And yet in Christ we have undergone judgement for these very things and been justified by God. Barth asserts that both of these statements are true. The same judgement that reveals that we are sinners and also makes us justified sinners.[35] But Barth wants to steer our attention away from ourselves and our own works and to turn them to Jesus Christ and his works. So he goes on to say,

> In Jesus Christ, the very man who as such is the eternal Son of the eternal Father, this future man, the new and righteous man, lives in an unassailable reality. In Him I am already the one who will be this righteous man, to the extent that I once was this man. (IV/1, 555)

Here again, Barth wants to stress that not only does Jesus do away with sin, he also actively introduces righteousness. Looking at ourselves will certainly not reveal an unambiguous movement from darkness to light and from death to life. But in looking at Jesus and the judgement that he has undergone, these things may indeed be seen, so that the righteousness of God is disclosed by him as something that has already come to pass.

Before moving on to the question of future judgement, let us summarise what we have found Barth to mean by the term 'judgement'.

---

35 'For by the same judgement of God he is a sinner and yet a justified sinner, lost and yet saved, a victim to death and yet raised again from death to life' (IV/1, p. 593). Here, Barth echoes Luther who described the saints as *'simul iustus et peccator'* in his Lectures on Romans. Luther, *Werke*, (Weimer: Böhlau, 1515-16/1938), vol. 56, 272.3-21.

There are two main strands to his usage: firstly, judgement is the action of God to restore justice under the covenant of grace. For Barth, the work of Jesus Christ in reconciling the world to God is an action of God the judge in the person of his Son, the Messiah. It is thus the righteousness of God that is being brought to bear on a rebellious world in this judgement. As such, this reconciling work is to be seen in the context of the providence of God over the world he created and sustains, in which goodness is vindicated and evil is condemned, not simply for their own sake, but for the well-being, the salvation, of his creation.[36] Judgement is therefore to be seen positively as the means by which the justice of God is established on earth.

Secondly, judgement for Barth is the verdict of condemnation on those who breach the covenant. Judgement is not only the restoration of covenantal order when God the judge is present, but also the condemnation of humanity in transgressing the covenant. So judgement is used to mean not only the process of judging but also the outcome of it, not only the discernment but also the denunciation. As Barth says, 'the incarnation of the Word means the judgement, the judgement of rejection and condemnation which is passed on all flesh' (IV/1, p. 220), and those who will be their own judges are, 'judged and rejected and condemned by God as wrongdoers' (IV/1, p. 221). That is the state in which humanity finds itself in the presence of the judge, and that is the state into which the judge willingly placed himself so that that he may bear that judgement in our place. These two aspects of the term 'judgement' are brought into close proximity by Barth's use of covenant. To be the judge is to be the one who implements covenant justice, and to be the judged is to be the one who bears the penalty for transgressing that covenant. Both uses of judgement are therefore often to be found in the same context.[37] By developing this dual use of the term *'Gericht'*, mirrored in the English word 'judgement' and in the Hebrew *'din'* and Greek *'krisis'* of the Bible, Barth is able to retain the negative connotations with which the term is commonly associated but also to broaden it to include the more positive aspects of the implementation of justice, as we have seen Forsyth did before him.[38]

---

36 Barth defines salvation in terms of the 'fulfilment of being' (IV/1, p. 8), so well-being is a state of salvation.

37 For example: 'What took place is that the Son of God fulfilled the righteous judgement on us men by Himself taking our place as man and in our place undergoing the judgement under which we had passed' (IV/1, p. 222).

38 Indeed, Barth uses the phrase 'redemptive judgement' (*heilsames Gericht*), (IV/1, p. 247), which might be better translated, 'saving judgement', expressions Forsyth also used. Forsyth, *The Justification of God*, pp. 187 and 170.

B. The Judgement of God at the Last Day

Although Barth places great emphasis on the judgement that has already taken place in the past judgement of Jesus Christ, he is quite clear that we await a day of judgement that is yet to come. He sees all the prophetic declarations of judgement as finding fulfilment in this future day of judgement, and not only in the past passion of Christ; each of these, 'attest the judgement, the day of the Lord, which will be accompanied and followed by salvation' (IV/1, p. 279).

Barth, like Forsyth, wants to make that judgement an inescapable present reality and not merely some threatened future event. So he says, 'The judgement seat of Christ, before which we obviously do not stand here and now, has already been set up, and whether we have done, do or will do good or evil has already been decided from it' (II/2, p. 633), echoing Forsyth's remark, 'We are all standing before the judgement seat of Christ. And one day we shall know it.'[39] That last judgement will be a time of great humiliation as we realize the terrible seriousness of sin. He says, 'We will all be ashamed before Him then as those who are compared with Jesus and measured and therefore shamed by Him' (IV/2, p. 387). So Jesus' endurance of shame, and all humanity in him, does not mean that we shall not be ashamed, just as the penitence of Jesus does not eliminate the need for the penitence of the sinner. Instead it makes possible the response that is appropriate to our condition and should serve to prompt us to repent. But that shame is, for Christians at least, a shame that heralds forgiveness not final condemnation, so this future judgement of Jesus Christ should instill a sense of hope, the hope 'of the dawn of eternal light' (IV/3.2, p. 934). Barth indicates that the extent of that hope should not be narrowly conceived, for he also says,

> What will finally be at issue in the coming of Jesus Christ to the last judgement of the quick and the dead, in the resurrection of the flesh and the manifestation of the life everlasting, will be not merely the consummation but the universality of the renewal which has come here and now. (IV/3.2, p. 675)

Christians therefore find themselves presently in a situation in which they enjoy a liberation to prophetic witness to good news for all the earth.

However, it has to be said, Barth gives the judgement still to come only a relatively minor role. By so concentrating the judgement of God in the past judgement of Jesus Christ, Barth, like Forsyth, has left Christ little judging still to do. The judgement at the last day serves largely as an appendix to the judgement that has already

---

39   Forsyth, *The Justification of God*, p. 187.

come to pass, reversing the biblical emphasis on the final judgement as the great assize.[40] Perhaps Barth would have restored something of this balance had he produced his fifth volume on, 'The Doctrine of Redemption', in which he was to expound the last things. But the way in which Barth has constructed his account of the judgement of God in terms of the judgement of Christ means there is little scope for such a development.

That is not to say, however, that Barth evades the question of who shall ultimately be vindicated and who shall be condemned. He addresses the subject most directly in his discussion of election. It is here that Barth examines how Jesus Christ is the electing God and the elected man, and says,

> In the eternal election of the one man Jesus of Nazareth, God makes Himself the covenant-partner of the sinful man who has fallen away from Him and therefore fallen a victim to death according to His just judgement. The purpose of the election of this one man is God's will to save this lost man and to make him a participant of the glory of eternal life in His kingdom by taking his place in the person of this one man, by taking to Himself man's misery in Him, by making it His own concern, by clothing him in return with His own righteousness, blessedness and power. (II/2, p. 205)

The election of Christ is thus an election to judgement on behalf of 'sinful man' in order to bring salvation to him. But who is this elect sinful man? Is it the whole of humanity, or just some portion of it? Generally speaking, the elect is, for Barth, an ever growing community which will in the end embrace all humanity. As he says, 'The elect man is chosen in order that the circle of election... [should] grow and expand and extend' (II/2, p. 419).[41] 'Included in His election there is, therefore, this "other" election, the election of the many (from whom none is excluded) whom the electing God meets on this way' (II/2, p. 195). In the end, Barth says, all are elect in Christ.

It is not only election that encompasses all of humanity; so too does reprobation. This too is developed christologically by Barth, who says that Jesus is not only the electing God and the elected man,

---

40   Matthew's Gospel is especially clear about the sobering prospect of the final day of judgement. Jesus warned his disciples in a series of disturbing parables about the danger of not being ready when he comes again to judge the world and so being shut out of the kingdom of heaven and left weeping and gnashing teeth outside (Mat. 24 and 25).

41   This is a similar assertion to one made by Forsyth: 'From the non-elect in one stage comes the elect for the next. And so on, in an ascending series of elects, till the whole human lump is refined, till all are brought in – the very worst and most intractable last, since freedom may not be forced. There is all eternity to do it.' Forsyth, *The Justification of God*, p. 161.

he is also the rejected one.

> The man rejected by God is the man who, because of his sin and guilt, is denied and repudiated by the righteous judgement and sentence of God, and transferred to the utterly untenable condition of Satan and his kingdom. He is the man abandoned to eternal perdition. He is the man whom this befits, and who has to suffer that which befits him, because he has challenged and drawn upon himself the destructive hostility of God. To be the rejected of God is the threat whose fulfilment would be the inevitable lot of every single human life. And it is this threat which in the election of Jesus Christ is diverted to Him, the One, and in that way averted from others. (II/2, p. 346)

Stated like this, the rejection of Jesus Christ is made the essence of the gospel. It is as the rejected one that Christ took the rejection which we have called down upon ourselves and turned it into a passing rejection, one that has passed in the rejection of Jesus Christ.

But election and reprobation are not to be seen as equal partners in a theological system. It is God's electing purposes that are to be regarded as primary and decisive, because that is how they are in Jesus Christ. Since his election triumphs over his reprobation, our election will in the end be victorious over our reprobation. In his discussion of the election of the individual, Barth says:

> It is just because man may genuinely and legitimately be an "individual"[42] before God that if he wills to be this apart from God it can only be *per nefas* and to his own ruin. The "individual" man who desires and undertakes this posits and conducts himself as the man who is rejected by God from all eternity. It can only be man's own godless choice that wills to be this "individual," the man who is isolated in relation to God. He therefore chooses the possibility which is excluded by the divine election. For this isolation is not intended for man in the divine election of grace (in Jesus Christ). On the contrary, it is a satanic possibility which is excluded and destroyed. (II/2, p. 316)

And regarding double predestination, Barth explains:

> If the teachers of predestination were right when they spoke always of duality, of election and reprobation, of predestination to salvation and perdition, to life or death, then we may say already that in the election of Jesus Christ which is the eternal will of God, God has ascribed to man the former, election, salvation and life; and to Himself He has ascribed the latter, reprobation, perdition and death. (II/2, pp. 162f)

So Barth claims that the rejection of Jesus Christ makes it impos-

---

42   Barth sets the word 'individual' in quotation marks to draw attention to the fact that he regards such a use of the term as a corruption of its proper usage since it brings it too close to 'individualism' with all its connotations of godlessness (II/2, p. 318).

sible for others to be rejected.

> [T]here is only one Rejected, the Bearer of all man's sins and guilt and their ensuing punishment, and this One is Jesus Christ. Those who undertake the attempt [to be counted among the rejected] may indeed lie – but can only lie – against the divine election of grace. (II/2, 346)

He also says, 'There is no one who is not raised and exalted with Him to true humanity' (IV/2, p. 271), 'There is not one whose sin is not forgiven in Him, whose death is not a death which has been put to death in Him' (p. IV/1, p. 630), and those who are not Christians do not 'lack Jesus Christ and in Him the being of man reconciled to God' (IV/1, p. 93).[43] He even takes the case of Judas Iscariot, and concludes that, 'His election excels and outshines and controls and directs his rejection: not just partly, but wholly; not just relatively, but absolutely' (II/2, p. 504). Although Barth regards the question of the final destiny of Judas as one that 'can only be left unanswered' (II/2, p. 476), he indicates that his own view is that in the end even Judas Iscariot '*the* great sinner of the New Testament' (II/2, p. 461), is included amongst those who stand to benefit from the judgement of Jesus Christ. For Barth, to be rejected, to be reprobate, is always to be in an untenable and transient position because that is how it has been rendered by Jesus Christ.

In saying these things, Barth comes very close to eliminating the possibility of final rejection, and on the basis of these remarks he has been described as a universalist from the time of the first publication of his views on election, both by some who are sympathetic to such a position themselves[44] and by others who are not.[45] Emil Brunner is

---

43   Barth also says, 'Christ lives in Christians, as He also lives in non-Christians, as the Mediator, Head and Representative of all as new and true Adam' (IV/3.2, p. 604) but clarifies what he has in mind by saying that there is also a form in which Christ only lives in Christians: as the Holy Spirit. But if that is not the form in which he inhabits the non-Christian, in what sense can Barth say he lives in them as mediator, head and representative?

44   The Catholic scholar, Hans von Balthasar, says, 'it is clear from Barth's presentation of the doctrine of election that universal salvation is not only possible but inevitable. The only definitive reality is grace, and any condemnatory judgement has to be merely provisional.' H.U. von Balthasar, *The Theology of Karl Barth* (translation by J. Drury, New York, Chicago, San Francisco: Holt, Rinehart and Winston, 1971), p. 163. George Hunsinger also see Barth's position as tending strongly in the direction of universalism, and rejoices that such a position should be so eloquently re-established following its demise after Athanasius. G. Hunsinger, *How to Read Karl Barth* (Oxford: Oxford University Press, 1991), pp. 106, 108 and 130-135.

45   Cornelius van Til is one of the first such, although he goes too far when he

one such who expresses his concern eloquently:

> What does this statement, 'that Jesus is the only rejected person', mean for the situation of humanity? Evidently this: that there is no possibility of condemnation... The decision has already been made in Jesus Christ – for all humanity. Whether they know it or not, believe it or not, is not so important. They are like people who seem to be perishing in a stormy sea. But in reality they are not in a sea in which one can drown, but in shallow waters, in which it is impossible to drown. Only they do not know it.[46]

Wolfhart Pannenberg presses the case further:

> Paul certainly says that sin dies only with the death of sinners and that this has happened already for believers because of the linking of their death to the fate of Christ (Rom. 7:4). But by ascribing to the event of Christ's death what Paul describes as the work of baptism, Barth has raised the question whether the final result is not the total disappearance of our independent humanity.[47]

Such criticisms of Barth on this issue are far-reaching, with immensely important implications for the significance of the judgement of Jesus Christ.

Barth himself, however, was not unaware of these problems and wanted to distance himself from an unambiguously universalist position.[48] He recognized that we cannot say with certainty that all humanity is saved and accepts that, 'Nowhere does the New Testament say

---

says that, 'For men to depend upon the Jesus Christ of Barth is to depend upon being ourselves inherently righteous.' C. van Til, *Westminster Theological Journal* (1955), p. 181. Others include Robert Jenson, Dorothee Sölle and G.W. Bromiley. R.W. Jenson, *Alpha and Omega: A Study in the Theology of Karl Barth* (New York: Thomas Nelson, 1963), D. Sölle, *Christ the Representative* (London: SCM Press, 1967), p. 90, and G.W. Bromiley, *Introduction to the Theology of Karl Barth* (Edinburgh: T. & T. Clark, 1979), p. 97.

46   E. Brunner, *The Christian Doctrine of God* (translation by O. Wyon, London: Lutterworth Press, 1949), pp. 348-351.

47   W. Pannenberg, *Systematic Theology* vol. 2 (translation by G.W. Bromiley, Grand Rapids: Eerdmans, 1991/1994), p. 431.

48   It should be said, however, that he did not repudiate universalism unequivocally. In a reply to a question about his teaching on universalism, he said, 'I do not teach it, but I also do not not teach it.' Quoted by Eberhard Jüngel, *Karl Barth: A Theological Legacy* (Philadelphia: Westminster Press, 1986), pp. 44f.

that the world is saved,[49] nor can we say it without doing violence to the New Testament' (II/2, p. 423). He acknowledges that in John's Gospel, only those given to the Son by the Father are received by him. In, 'The Condemnation of Man', he asks, 'Can we count upon it or not that this threat will not finally be executed, that the sword will not fall, that man's condemnation will not be pronounced, that the sick man and even the sick Christian will not die and be lost rather than be raised and delivered from the dead and live?' (IV/3.1, p. 477). Barth's reply is twofold. Firstly, he says that if there is no final condemnation, that must be seen as an 'unexpected work of grace' (IV/3.1, p. 477). It is not something that we can count on in advance because it is not something that we can see revealed in the judgement of Jesus Christ. 'No such postulate can be made even though we appeal to the cross and resurrection of Jesus Christ' (IV/3.1, p. 477). The second part of his reply is that there is no reason why we must forbid ourselves the possibility of believing that this ultimate threat might in the end be withdrawn. So he says we may still,

> [H]ope and pray cautiously and yet distinctly that in spite of everything which may seem quite conclusively to proclaim the opposite, His compassion should not fail, and that in accordance with His mercy which is "new every morning" He "will not cast off for ever" (Lam. 3:22f, 31). (IV/3.1, p. 478)

So we see that Barth is aware that the proclamation of judgement fully borne for all humanity in Jesus Christ elicits a confidence in a universal reconciliation that goes beyond a biblical mandate. We have, however, already seen several passages in which Barth makes statements about election and reprobation that foster just such confidence. There is thus a tension in Barth's position between his formulation of the doctrine of election and his faithfulness to the biblical witness, both of which are fundamental to his work in the *Church*

---

49   This point is disputable, since texts like Acts 3:21 (which speaks of 'universal restoration'), Rom. 11:32 ('For God has imprisoned all in disobedience so that he may be merciful to all'); 1 Cor. 15:25 ('For [Christ] must reign until he had put all his enemies under his feet'); Eph. 1:10 (the plan 'to gather up all things in [Christ]'); Phil. 2:10 ('so that at the name of Jesus every knee should bend'); Col. 1:20 ('through [Christ] God was pleased to reconcile to himself all things'); and 1 Tim. 4:10 ('…God, who is the saviour of all, especially of those who believe'), may be interpreted as having that meaning. As we have already seen, however, Barth's general point is well taken, especially in the light of other New Testament teaching, eg. Mat. 10:32-33; 11:20-24; 12:37; 13:24-30, 47-50; 21:33-41; 22:1-13; 24:45-51; 25:1-13, 14-30, 31-46; Rom. 2:5; 2 Thess. 1:9-10; Heb. 10:26-28; 2 Pet. 2:4,9; 3:7, Jude 6-7 and 15.

Dogmatics. He indicates the direction in which this might be resolved when he says in a telling remark, 'Even though theological consistency might seem to lead our thoughts and utterances most clearly in this direction [of universal salvation], we must not arrogate to ourselves that which can be given and received only as a free gift' (IV/3.1, p. 477). So if his formulation of the doctrine of election suggests universal salvation, as in places it does, it demands revision so that the possibility of not receiving the saving gift is readmitted. We must therefore return to aspects of what Barth has said about the outcome of the last judgement to identify remarks that need modifying in the light of these considerations.[50]

Firstly, if we cannot say with confidence that all humanity has already stood under the judgement of God in Christ so that now their judgement is a matter of the past, we must return to the question of the extent and effectiveness of election in Christ Jesus. In order to do so, we take the summary of Barth's view of election provided by Professor John Webster:

> [I]n election, God "does not say No but Yes" (II/2, p. 28). And so we do not here face an inscrutable divine decision, but rather the unbroken continuity between God's enactment of His own life in Jesus Christ and his disposing of his creatures to life and blessedness.[51]

So to be elect is to be promised salvation. If we cannot safely say that all humanity can look forward to such an outcome then it is either because not all are elect in Him, or that it is ultimately possible to resist that election, which would call into question the significance of election. Barth himself indicates a preference for reopening the question of whether all people are elect in Christ. He says, 'it is not legitimate to make the limitless many of the election in Jesus Christ the totality of all men' (II/2, p. 423). So if we are to reinstate the terrible possibility of a future judgement which will not yield salvation for all because some stand outside of Christ and his past saving judgement, then it is by readmitting the possibility that not everyone is elect in Christ.[52]

---

50 Since the doctrine of election is so fundamental to Barth's theology, the ramifications of these modifications will be too numerous for us to consider in this thesis.

51 J. Webster, *Barth's Ethics of Reconciliation* (Cambridge: Cambridge University Press, 1995), p. 48.

52 It is by re-examining Barth's doctrine of election that Colin Gunton argues accusations of universalism are to be seen as unfounded. He says 'It is failure to understand that election is about God that has led to fruitless arguments about Barth's alleged universalism.' Gunton, *Theology Through the Theologians*, p. 97.

Who, then, is elect in Christ and already judged in him? It is a question that Barth himself addresses in terms of the elect community, a
community understood in terms of both Israel and the Church.

> Israel is the people of the Jews which resists its election; the Church
> is the gathering of Jews and Gentiles called on the ground of its
> election...We cannot, therefore, call the Jews the "rejected" and the
> Church the "elected" community. The object of election is
> neither Israel for itself nor the Church for itself, but both together
> in their unity. (II/2, p. 199)

Later, he elaborates on what he means as follows.

> The specific service for which Israel is determined within the whole
> of the elected community is to reflect the judgement from which
> God has rescued man and which He wills to endure Himself in the
> person of Jesus of Nazareth. (II/2, p. 206)

And he says,

> The service for which the Church as the perfect form of the one
> elected community is determined, whether Israel obeys its elec-
> tion or not, consists always in the fact that it is the reflection of the
> mercy in which God turns His glory to man. (II/2, p. 210)

There are thus central places in God's electing purposes for both
Israel and the Church, but it is to the Church that we must primarily
turn to see the positive form of God's elect community.

This brings us to the second modification required in Barth's
account. He wants to claim that this election of the Church is to be
understood not so much in terms of salvation as the mediation of
salvation through the proclamation of the divine revelation of God
in Christ Jesus. He says,

> As the Church is elected, called and gathered from among Jews
> and Gentiles, the task laid upon it consists in the proclamation
> of its knowledge of the judgement that has overtaken man in the
> death of Jesus, in witness to the goodwill, readiness and honour of
> God with respect to man accepted and received by Him in Jesus
> Christ. (II/2, p. 210)

There is, therefore, a universalising tendency in the way Barth
describes the work of the Church. By making the purpose of its election primarily one of vocation to declare God's salvation, Barth is
again in danger of suggesting that there is no significant and lasting
distinction between those who do acknowledge Jesus as Messiah and
Lord, and those who do not.[53] Even if we accept that God might, in

---

53   There is a danger here that God's revelation in Christ is being allowed to re-
     place God's salvation through Christ in Barth's scheme. As such, McGrath
     has a point when he says that Barth makes so much of the educative role of
     the Church as to bring it strikingly close to that given it by Ritschl. A.E. Mc

his infinite mercy, withdraw the final threat of destruction, this cannot form part of the gospel proclamation itself. The work of the elect community must be more than that of witness to a universal future salvation. It must include a positive and urgent call to take hold of that salvation by responding in faith to the judgement of Jesus Christ rather than facing final judgement unprepared.[54]

Likewise, Barth's doctrine of the election of the individual, which follows from his doctrine of the election of the community, requires modification. He says,

> There are no predestined families and no predestined nations – even the Israelite nation is simply the first (transitory) form of the community – nor is there a predestined humanity. There are only predestined men – predestined in Christ and by way of the community. It is individuals who are chosen and not the totality of men. And God seeks, calls, blesses and sanctifies the many, the totality, the natural and historical groups and humanity itself, in and through the individual. (II/2, p. 313)

Again, the tendency to extend the election of the individual to all individuals must be resisted. If the possibility of final condemnation is not to be removed, we cannot claim that everyone will in the end be found among the elect. The election of the individual cannot only be seen as testimony to salvation, but also as a warning of perdition; not only a constant reassurance, but also a continual call to flee from the wrath to come.

Thirdly, in the light of these modifications, we must also reconsider how Barth treats the need for a human response to the work of Christ. In his stress on the completeness of the reconciling work of Christ, Barth seems to obscure the need for a human response. As G.C. Berkouwer says, 'In Barth's theology the triumph of grace makes vague the seriousness of the human decision, just as the kerugma [sic.] is threatened with becoming a mere pronouncement without any vital exhortation.'[55] So complete is the work of Christ, not only in bringing about the possibility of reconciliation but also in repenting and being baptized in the place of sinful humanity, that the call to repent and be baptized may now be robbed of its urgency. In his affirmation that we have been reconciled to God, Barth leaves little place for the call to 'be reconciled to God' (2 Cor. 5:20). And

---

Grath, *The Making of Modern German Christology* (Leicester: Apollos, 1994), p. 140.

54 How one should respond to the judgement of Christ we will consider in Chapter 7.

55 G.C. Berkouwer, *The Triumph of Grace in the Theology of Karl Barth* (translation by H.R. Boer, London: Paternoster Press, 1956), p. 279.

so great is the place accorded to the past judgement of sin in the judgement of Jesus Christ that there is little scope left for the Word and Spirit to convict of sin and bring human beings to repentance in readiness for the judgement that is to come.

Here again, Barth is not unaware of the danger of imbalance. He acknowledges that we have to appropriate the forgiveness that Christ has procured before we can meaningfully speak of reconciliation. He says, 'We have not received forgiveness, nor are we acquitted and justified in God's judgement, if we do not acknowledge and confess our sin' (II/2, p. 756). But so great is his emphasis on the grace of God in Christ that such a statement is not permitted a formative role in his theology. Barth does not want reconciliation with God to depend upon the response of the sinner. As a result, the continuing intercessory role of the ascended Christ and the recreating work of the Holy Spirit in the Church and the world have little place in Barth's salvation history.[56] If the proclamation of the gospel is to become more than a declaration of what has already come to pass, and if the forgiveness of sins is to be seen as something which is freely offered to humanity but needs to be received for reconciliation to come about, then much more must be made of this human response. Proclamation of the judgement of Jesus Christ must retain the element of warning that to fall into the hands of the living God is not a prospect that all should welcome.[57]

Conclusion

Barth's discussion of judgement is enormously rich and illuminating, involving both the process of judging and its verdict. It is developed metaphorically in terms of the just and justifying rule of God determined to bring about righteousness and salvation by restoring the covenant of grace that was broken by human sin. The glory of God and the rebellion of humanity are treated with great seriousness, and the means of reconciliation between these covenant partners explained in terms of the justifying words and actions of the judge. Many of the ideas we have seen in Forsyth are developed more fully here and the connection between judgement and death,

---

56   Gunton also criticizes Barth for allowing the doctrines of the Holy Spirit and the ascension to play 'little structural part' in his discussion of salvation. C. Gunton, 'Salvation', in John Webster ed., *The Cambridge Companion to Karl Barth* (Cambridge: Cambridge University Press, 2000), p. 157.

57   Cf. '[U]nless you repent, you will perish as they did' (Luke 13:3 and 5); 'Repent, therefore, and turn to God so that your sins may be wiped out' (Acts 3:19). See also 2 Pet. 3:7.

missing in Forsyth, is made and expounded in a way that renders Barth's the more satisfactory account. We shall therefore take what Barth has unfolded here as the basis for our own meaning of the term 'judgement', allowing for the modifications of the extent of salvation and the necessity of response. If in the end, the Lord in his compassion extends his mercy more broadly, that should remain as an unanticipated possibility. In the meanwhile, Christians must proclaim the coming of the judgement of almighty God against all ungodliness and call upon everyone who hears to turn away from every form of wickedness and come to Jesus, on whom the judgement of God has already fallen.

CHAPTER 6

Judgement as the Paradigmatic Metaphor of the Doctrine of Atonement

Introduction

Having seen how Karl Barth develops the doctrine of reconciliation in terms of the judgement of Jesus Christ we turn to a consideration of how that exposition may be related to that of other metaphors of atonement. In this chapter we shall take in turn victory, redemption and sacrifice and see how they may be related to the judgement of God as expounded in the previous chapter. In each case we shall begin by examining how Barth understands these metaphors of atonement as, 'other lines of approximation', (IV/1, p. 274) to the whole truth of this saving work, before relating them to judgement. Since he does not directly address the question of how the metaphors may be seen in relationship to each other, we shall here be developing Barth's work in new ways. By so doing, we come to the heart of our thesis: that the doctrine of atonement may be best understood by treating victory, redemption and sacrifice as subordinate metaphors to that of judgement.

A. Victory

When Barth mentions the military metaphor as one of the alternative images the New Testament provides for understanding the work of Christ, he gives a brief elaboration of what he has in mind. He cites Mark 3:27, ('no-one can enter a strong man's house and plunder his property without first tying up the strong man'), Col. 1:13 ('[The Father] has rescued us from the power of darkness and transferred us into the kingdom of his beloved Son') and, more tentatively, Eph. 6:11f (on the armour of God), as biblical evidence for claiming that the atonement may be seen in terms of a military metaphor. He also notes how the Eastern Church and Luther have described the work of Christ as a victory over death and the devil. Barth is quick to point out, however, that he does not see this military metaphor as a suitable basis for a systematic presentation of the doctrine of reconciliation. He even prefaces his remarks by saying, 'There is perhaps also a military view' (IV/1, p. 274), introducing an element of doubt about its place here, although he concludes that it should be included in an overall exposition. The question is, if this is to be included as an element of the doctrine of reconciliation, what is the place that it should occupy?

In his fuller elaboration of this aspect of the work of Christ in the section, 'Jesus is Victor',[1] in Chapter XVI, 'Jesus Christ, the true Witness', Barth suggests how this might be, when he considers the third aspect of the work of reconciliation, revelation, which complements the first two: justification and sanctification. Here it is that Barth examines the prophetic office of Christ and what bearing this has on the doctrine of atonement. He begins by explaining what he means when he calls Jesus a prophet. He has in mind,

> [O]ne to whom it is given to see and to understand the doing of the will of God on earth, and who is also charged to declare, expound and explain, and thus to mediate, his understanding, thus enabling others to participate in what takes place. (IV/3.1, p. 180)

As such, Christ is to be seen in continuity with the biblical prophets. For him, as for them, we are to regard the title as designating a work which centres on the uncompromising proclamation of the word of God, whether it is welcome or not.[2] But that is not to say that Jesus Christ is just one more such prophet. The particular sense in which he is a prophet transcends what is to be seen in other prophets. Barth here draws attention to John's Gospel,[3] where John the Baptist bears witness to the far greater work of Jesus,[4] and Jesus himself claims the testimony of the Old Testament Scriptures as pointing

---

1   Barth acknowledges his debt to J.C. Blumhardt for this phrase (IV/3.1, p. 168), who in turn explains that he learned it from an exorcism of Gottliebin Dittus during which the words, *'Jesus ist Sieger!'*, were spoken by her sister, Katherina, and taken by Blumhardt to be a cry of surrender through her lips by a self-confessed angel of Satan. Barth is content to take up the phrase himself not on the basis of this event, since he regards experience as an unreliable guide to Christian theology, but because of the New Testament evidence to support it, and he mentions: John 16:33; Rom. 8:37; 1 Cor. 15:54, 57; 2 Cor. 2:14; Col. 2:15, 2 Tim. 1:10, Heb. 2:14; 1 John 5:4; Rev. 5:5; 6:2; 11:15 and 19:11f. This is a considerably greater list than that he provides on IV/1, p. 274, and indeed, than Gustaf Aulén adduces to support his case for *Christus Victor*, and perhaps helps to explain why it is that he shows no further sign of questioning the place of victory as an image of reconciliation.

2   He, like them, would meet resistance; 'the prophecy of Jesus Christ taking place in relation to an opposition and challenge on the part of the world' (IV/3.1, p. 171).

3   Barth, IV/3.1, p. 233.

4   John 1:30 and 3:28-31.

to a prophetic work only realized in himself.[5] The word of Jesus is thus another prophetic word but one with a unique and unparalleled place in salvation history. He alone is the way to the Father. He alone has the words of eternal life.[6] He alone is able to bring a rebellious people back to God.

By setting the victory of Christ in the context of prophecy, Barth establishes that he is concerned here with the epistemology of reconciliation or, as he puts it, 'knowing the atonement' (IV/3.1, p. 180). It is thus essentially a matter of making manifest what is real but hidden. This mediatory aspect of the atonement is to bring to realization what Christ has done in justifying and sanctifying the world. Against the blessings of the restored covenant between God and humankind remains the curse of evil asserting itself against the completed atoning work of Christ. The light has dawned but the darkness remains and has yet to be banished. So Barth summarizes the prophetic task of Christ by saying that,

[A]s the world is told, not merely what is resolved concerning it, but what has already been done for it, for its total renewal and transformation; as it is thus given news concerning itself, it has to decide whether it will accept this information or not. (IV/3.1, p. 186)

So this aspect of reconciliation is not merely a matter of acquiring some new knowledge which we previously lacked. Barth is referring to knowledge in the biblical sense of the verbs *yada* and *ginōskō* i.e. as something which involves the whole person, mind, heart and will, encountering an alien history and being drawn into it and transformed by it.

Having set the context, Barth begins to describe the battle waged by Jesus the prophet, showing none of his earlier hesitancy in using a military metaphor. He begins by insisting that this is truly a battle, and one which Christ initiates. He is 'the Aggressor' (IV/3.1, p. 239), who declares war and comes into the world to conduct a campaign which brings the kingdom of God against its enemies. By the very act of becoming man, Barth sees the Son of God presenting himself as the warrior going into battle.[7] Jesus brought a sword upon the earth,[8] a sword which, Barth says, he wielded 'against sin, death and the devil' (IV/3.1, p. 238), three of Luther's tyrants. This battle is then to be understood as raging throughout his life and especially in the prophetic ministry of Christ. Barth wants to ground the atone-

---

5   John 5:39, 45f and 8:56.
6   John 14:6 and 6:68.
7   Barth himself used the term 'warrior' of Christ (IV/3.1, p. 212).
8   Mat. 10:34.

ment in the life and work of Jesus Christ himself, and not in some
ideal which may be abstracted from it.[9] As such we see that Barth,
like Aulén, has this '*Christus Victor*'[10] motif rest on the whole life and
ministry of Jesus Christ, and not just his death and resurrection.

So how is this battle joined? According to Barth, along several
lines:

> In general, [Christ] conducts it quite simply but powerfully by see-
> ing, addressing and treating the world, i.e., humanity as such, each
> individual man, and the whole creaturely world which shares the
> existence, activity and destiny of man, from a standpoint which is
> incomparable in critical force, namely, as the world which is rec-
> onciled to God, which is delivered from destruction, which in His
> person is loved by God and loves Him in return. (IV/3.1, p. 239)

The military metaphor is here subverted. Far from a description of
conquest in which the forces of evil are faced on their own terms and
subdued by a greater display of force, the campaign of Jesus Christ
is portrayed in terms of the triumph of good over evil, of perfect love
casting out fear. The double-edged sword of the word of God is not
so much a weapon of destruction as a tool of liberation. Barth goes
on to explain,

> [T]he attack is that of the love of the Father and the Son. It is the
> attack of the grace of God. It is the attack of His affirmation of the
> world, of His generous, self-giving to it, of His intervention for its
> salvation, of His pledging and guaranteeing of its life. (IV/3.1, p.
> 240)

So, as George Hunsinger says of Barth's treatment of the atonement, 'The politics of God thus reveals itself as the politics of non-
violent love.'[11] However hostile the world might have become
towards God, it remains his creation and the object of his love. When
Christ comes to reclaim it for his Father in the power of the Spirit, he
does so as its friend and not its enemy.

The battle as Barth describes it is essentially a battle of words in
which the Word of God comes against all contradictory words. This
occurs, firstly and negatively, in that this Word puts all contrary
words into the past tense, as words that can no longer be treated as
valid. God has established his kingdom on earth and thereby disem-
powered all rival kingdoms. Human beings may continue to justify

---

9   'It must be stated expressly and considered with great precision that in this
    equation [of Jesus the high-priest and king as also the prophet] we have the
    description of a history' (IV/3.2, p. 165).
10 Barth uses this phrase in IV/3.1, pp. 197 and 216.
11 G. Hunsinger, 'The Politics of the Non-Violent God', *Scottish Journal of Theol-
    ogy*, vol. 51, no., 1 (1998), p. 72.

themselves in their own eyes, but that has been rendered both futile and unnecessary now that Jesus Christ has brought us justification in the eyes of God. And people may go on seeking sanctification through their own self-improvement, but Jesus Christ has now introduced sanctification through his own elevation to the right hand side of the Father, and seated all those in him in the heavenly places. All anxiety, worrying and quarrelling on the one hand and hopeless resignation on the other are disallowed in this new era, since their basis has now been removed by Christ. This word of Jesus is thus not merely a call to ethical behaviour, although that will follow from it.[12] It is instead a word that asserts the authority of God decisively against all rivals. As Barth puts it, 'All the realisms supposedly asserted against [the Word of God spoken in Jesus Christ] are themselves shown to be illusions on this basis' (IV/3.1, p. 249).

Secondly and positively, the prophetic word of Jesus declares that a new era has begun. There is now the 'presence of the new man' (IV/3.1, p. 246).[13] Barth declares that this newness is to be found in the restored relationship with God brought about by the justifying and sanctifying action of Christ. At last, human beings are free to be themselves as children of their heavenly Father. This is not a call to be humbled before their God, but a declaration that, in Christ, they have been humbled before their God. It is therefore a call to give thanks for the discovery that a new world has begun in the midst of the old. Humankind has been set free to rejoice. The basis for human relationships has been re-established on this covenant relationship with God. The last things, towards which creation has been directed by its Creator, have been disclosed and initiated in the course of human history.

It is only at this point that Barth wants to say who that enemy is that the Word of God comes against. Even here he is reluctant to do so, and begins by only naming the territory occupied by this enemy.

---

12 'The Word of grace in not the Word of divine morality in conflict with human immorality. Only indirectly, secondarily and incidentally does it say of the being and attitude in which man finds himself engulfed that it is evil or bad or at least imperfect and in need of correction' (IV/3.1, p. 242).

13 Barth brings these two aspects of the victory of God together when he says, 'There can be no trifling with the establishment of the kingdom of God and the deliverance and reconciliation of the world as proclaimed to it in the Word of Jesus. To the continuance of its history in the first form there is presented a command to halt behind which there is a corresponding and no less imperious command to advance. This aeon is at an end. The world and its relationships and orders, can have a future only in the new aeon determined by the deliverance and reconciliation accomplished and revealed and the lordship of God established and proclaimed within it' (IV/3.1, p. 241).

'All things considered, we do well to speak only of "something in man" which is attacked and forced on to the defensive' (IV/3.1, p. 251). The Word of God is thus directed at human beings not because they are themselves the enemy to be defeated but because that is where the enemy is entrenched. This word is therefore still a word of grace to the human race. But it is to human ears that the word comes, for it is there that the enemy may be confronted.

Having specified the location of this enemy, Barth goes further in identifying who that enemy is. And he does so negatively, 'Since', as he says, 'its being is supremely non-being, we cannot do it the undeserved honour of a positive definition' (IV/3.1, p. 252).[14] He then names the enemy as, 'that which resists the grace attested in this Word' (IV/3.1, p. 252) and goes on to explain not so much who that enemy is as what it does. This enemy opposes all that God proposes for the well-being of his creatures, such as freedom, gratitude and love and therefore tries to resist the Word of God in three ways. Firstly, by asserting the reality of its own opposition, by acting as if there is a continuing place for pride, sloth and falsehood in the world from which they have been eliminated by Jesus Christ. Secondly by speaking a word contradicting the word of Christ, suggesting that human pride, sloth and falsehood have a valid place and that no substantial alterations to the *status quo* are required. And thirdly there is the even more sinister self-defence in the establishment of counterfeit Christianity. As Barth says, '[This enemy] may establish Christian communities and establish Christian worship and preaching and theology in a work which looks as though it is supremely concerned with grace and its Word', but it is, in fact 'the church of the antichrist' (IV/3.1, p. 258). The word that it proclaims constantly affirms people in the state in which they find themselves and refuses to disturb them from it. Barth does not name any particular examples, perhaps in deference to his own concern to leave all such judging to Christ, but this and later

---

14 Only occasionally is the devil named as the 'resisting element' (Barth, IV/3.1, pp. 260 and 270ff). Gustaf Wingren, amongst others, have complained that Barth gives too little attention to the devil. Barth was aware of such criticism and responded by saying that he believes in the existence and work of the devil but, following the example of the New Testament authors, did not wish to say much about him. Barth, IV/3.1, p. 260.

15 Barth returns to the subject of the church of the antichrist and speaks of the Bible being 'suppressed and falsified', of 'corrupt traditions and liturgy and practice', and of 'dreadful preaching' but of occasional 'strange resurrections and revivals of the true Church in the midst of the false' when the word of God rings out (IV/3.1, p. 268).

remarks[15] suggest that he is not limiting his attention to Christian sects such as the Jehovah's Witnesses and the Mormons, but also considering Roman Catholic, Liberal Protestant and perhaps even Evangelical congregations too.

Yet, for all these cunning strategies, the battle must not be regarded as one between equals. Jesus comes against these hostile forces as victoriously as light comes against darkness. Barth makes this point repeatedly.

[T]he light is wholly and utterly light and darkness is no more than darkness, having no light, dynamic or authority of its own, existing and known only in virtue of its opposite, having only the substance and significance still left to it by this opposite' (IV/3.1, p. 239).

Barth later explains,

[T]here can be no question of an equality between the two factors which here confront and conflict with one another, but that their encounter can be understood and described only as that of a greatly superior and a greatly inferior, and therefore a struggle concerning the issue of which there can be no doubt… From the very outset it is clear and certain what will be the result of His ministry and rule, namely, that His right and might will triumph in opposition to the resistance and challenge offered to him, removing the challenge and destroying the resistance. (IV/3.1, p. 172)[16]

In the end, the darkness cannot master the light; it can only be mastered by it.

And yet, the darkness still persists. As Barth says,

That [reconciliation] applies to all in this two-fold sense [the declaration of reconciliation and the resistance to that declaration] means that as the light of life *shines* in the darkness, the world and all men come within reach of its beams, but as it shines in the *darkness*, the world and all men are still in the sphere of darkness. (IV/3.1, p. 191)

The metaphor of light dispelling darkness is thus used by Barth not only to assert the certainty of final triumph, but also to take seriously the hostility of the enemy against which this triumph comes. He does not wish to minimize the seriousness of the threat of the forces of evil in the present time, only to draw attention to the decisive victory over this enemy which has taken place and which will

---

16 He also says, 'This light which streams into the world is still the eternal light which cannot be vanquished or extinguished' (IV/3.1, p. 167).

one day be made known.[17] Barth acknowledges that to speak of a victory which is not yet consummated can be profoundly unsettling.

> Even in our strongest faith in Jesus Christ, are we not helpless in the face of supreme indifference, of the constant jugglery of worldviews, and finally and above all of the dreadful possibility of mock Christianity, of the church of the Antichrist? (IV/3.1, p. 262)

In view of this present ambiguity, we must ask, On what can faith in Christ's victory be securely built? As expected, Barth replies to his own question christologically.

> To know [Christ] as the living One, the Risen from the dead, is to receive and have at once, from the very outset, basic, direct and unconditional certainty of the final victory which is still awaited but which comes relentlessly and irresistibly. (IV/3.1, p. 263)[18]

He also says, 'It means the constant increase of light in darkness' (IV/3.1, p. 263), not referring to some form of historical progress, but to the victory of knowledge over ignorance.[19] Barth wants to distinguish this relentless progress both from any identification with the mission of the Church or with personal growth in faith, since these again draw attention away from the subject of Christian mission and the object of Christian faith: Jesus Christ. So he says, 'Generally speaking it is an unconditional certainty of victory in the fact that it

---

17   This point goes some way to responding to the criticism often made against Barth's view of evil as nothingness, *das Nichtige*, which he is developing here. When he speaks of evil as non-being, as darkness in comparison to the light of God, he is not dismissing its terrible effects. When he says the enemy is not a creature of God, 'but only a devastating interposition between Him and the world, which can be addressed only as nothingness' (IV/3.1, p. 267) he is not suggesting it does not exist, only that it is utterly contrary to God who alone is the basis of all being and in whose rejection can only lie oblivion. Berkouwer therefore goes too far when he says Barth, 'robs the revelation about demons of its *concrete character*', and encourages, 'the denial of the activity of the dethroned powers post Christum, concerning which the whole New Testament testifies.' Berkouwer, *The Triumph of Grace*, pp. 239 and 377.

18   We must therefore disagree with the conclusion reached by Grant, following Donald Bloesch, that for Barth, 'atonement is finally a matter of the revelation of the grace of God in Christ, rather than something actually effected in the concrete reality of Christ.' Grant, 'The Abandonment of Atonement', *Kings Theological Review*, 9 (1986), p. 2. Barth makes the atonement nothing more nor less than the concrete reality achieved by Christ, and his prophetic work is to make this atonement known.

19   'For in relation to Jesus Christ [history] has a definite *telos* and direction in which it cannot result in defeat or stalemate but only in the triumph of knowledge over ignorance' (IV/3.1, p. 197).

is clearly based on the unconditional superiority of Jesus Christ to His opponent, to the resisting element in man' (IV/3.1, p. 266).

Before we come to relate this aspect of atonement to that of the judgement of Jesus Christ, we must make two comments. Firstly, by expounding the victory of Christ chiefly in terms of the demand to acknowledge his triumph, Barth portrays Jesus as a prophet who does not suffer. The opposition to his word may exist, but it can do him no injury. Since this prophetic work is so much identified with a triumphant Christ, Barth suggests that, despite the subtlety of the enemy, he inflicts no wounds on Christ. The humanity of Jesus, and his reliance on the Spirit, are here hardly to be seen. Even where he is compared with other prophets, it is to describe the great gulf that separates them. The mediatorial role of Christ is thus allowed to be identified much more with a divine than a human victory.[20]

Secondly, we must question whether Barth is right to treat the victory of Jesus under his office as prophet rather than as king. If we are to associate certain actions more particularly with one aspect of the threefold office of Christ, then victory more naturally fits under kingship than prophecy.[21] To lead God's people into victory over God's enemies is more a kingly work than a prophetic one. Barth himself appears to acknowledge this when, in his exposition of the prophetic work of Christ, he describes the victory of Christ in terms of the kingly categories of rule and lordship.[22] He also indicates this understanding when he describes exorcisms and raising the dead as 'military actions' (IV/2, p. 232) in his discussion of the work of, 'The Royal Man'. Whilst the roles of prophet and earthly ruler can be combined, as we see in Moses, if we are to attribute certain actions to these different offices, victory should be considered under the office of king.

---

20 Gunton, who is critical of Barth for his failure to give the humanity of Christ sufficient weight in his doctrine of reconciliation, seeks to correct this imbalance by relating soteriology to a more fully incarnational christology. Gunton, 'Salvation', in Webster, ed., *The Cambridge Companion to Karl Barth* p. 157 for an example of the criticism of Barth, and Gunton, *Yesterday and Today*, pp. 129ff for his constructive proposals.

21 Hunsinger points out that T.F. Torrance, who, like Barth, identifies the prophetic work of Christ with the proclamation of the cross, treats the breaking of the bondage to sin under the kingly office of Christ. Hunsinger, 'The Politics of the Non-Violent God', *Scottish Journal of Theology*, vol. 51, no. 1 (1998), p. 74.

22 Barth, IV/3.1, p. 172.

The victory of Christ as God's judgement against his enemies and for his covenant people

Now that we have seen how Barth understands victory, we may begin to compare it with what he says about judgement. Two questions will be of particular interest to us here. What relationship may be seen between the two? And how much of the doctrine of atonement can victory express in comparison to judgement?

We address the first of these questions by noticing that the victory Barth describes is a victory for the Word of God. It is this Word which comes against all other words that would oppose it by unresponse, contradiction or mimicry. As such, this Word comes as a word of judgement that exposes the true state of all contrary words and condemns them as falsehood. To say, as we have seen Barth does, that the prophetic word of Jesus puts all other words into the past tense and initiates a new era, is to say that his word judges these other words.

This connection between victory and judgement is made more strongly in Barth's description of Jesus the judge in terms of Old Testament judges and kings. The judge is the warrior king, the champion, who actively pursues the well-being of his people, creating and sustaining a society of justice and peace.[23] When God delivered the Hebrews from Egypt through the ten plagues and the drowning of the Egyptian army at the Red Sea, it was an act of judgement. The tenth plague in particular is described as the Lord's judgement on the gods of Egypt,

> For I will pass through the land of Egypt, and I will strike down every firstborn in the land of Egypt, both human beings and animals; on all the gods of Egypt I will execute my judgements: I am the Lord. (Exod 12:12)[24]

And God's victory over the Egyptian army in their destruction in the Red Sea (Exod. 14) recalls the judgement of God in the engulfing water of the flood.[25]

The conquest of the promised land is also seen as a victory that results from the judgement of God on his enemies. In Deut. 9:4-6, Moses tells the Israelites:

---

23 This point would have come out even more strongly had Barth treated victory as an aspect of the kingship of Christ, as we suggested he should.

24 A similar point is made in Num. 33:4, that the Israelites left Egypt boldly while the Egyptians buried their firstborn as, 'The Lord executed judgements even against their gods.'

25 See R.A. Cole, *Exodus*, Tyndale Old Testament Commentaries (Leicester: Inter-Varsity Press, 1973), p. 122.

When the Lord your God thrusts [the peoples inhabiting the promised land] out before you, do not say to yourself, 'It is because of
my righteousness that the Lord has brought me in to occupy this
land'; it is rather because of the wickedness of these nations that
the Lord is dispossessing them before you.[26]

Indeed, the lengthy delay in receipt of land promised to the
descendents of Abraham is foretold to him with this explanation,
'for the iniquity of the Amorites is not yet complete' (Gen. 15:16).
The gracious gift of land promised to the redeemed people of Israel
is only one side of the story. The other is that the wickedness of its
previous inhabitants had provoked the Lord to anger over several
generations, and Israel's victories over them are to be understood as
God's judgement upon them.

The reversal of fortunes that Israel endured when they were disobedient to their covenantal obligations is also expressed as a judgement revealed in victory, this time as a victory for their enemies. As
the author of the book of Judges explains, after the death of Joshua,

They abandoned the Lord, and worshipped Baal and the Astartes.
So the anger of the Lord was kindled against Israel, and he gave
them over to plunderers who plundered them, and he sold them
into the power of their enemies all around, so that they could no
longer withstand their enemies. (Jdg. 2:13f)

The exile is another example of God's judgement on his sinful people being executed in defeat by their enemies. As Jeremiah
prophesies of Jerusalem,

Your wealth and your treasures I will give as plunder, without
price, for all your sins, throughout all your territory. I will make
you serve your enemies in a land that you do not know, for in my
anger a fire is kindled that shall burn forever. (Jer. 15:13f)[27]

So both the defeats and the victories of Israel are to be understood
in terms of judgement, with the victor in each case acting as the
mediator of the judgement of God.

We find further evidence of victory as the judgement of God when
we look more closely at the life of Christ, especially in connection
with moments of conflict associated with the devil and his demons.
When Jesus is confronted by the words of temptation from Satan in
the wilderness (Mat. 4:1ff; Luke 4:1ff), from the lips of Simon Peter
(Mat. 16:22) and, more implicitly, in Gethsemane and Golgotha, Jesus
responds with contradiction.[28] The words of the devil are not merely
resisted but exposed for their error and refuted. In other words, they

---

26   Cf. Num. 33:50-53; Deut. 7:1-6,16; 12:2-3 and 18:9-12.
27   See also Isa. 63:10; Jer. 17:4; 18:12-17; 19:7-9 and 21:3-7.
28   Barth, IV/1, pp. 260-264.

are judged. As Barth says in his consideration of the temptation of Jesus in the garden of Gethsemane,

> And Satan, the evil one, and the world ruled by him, and the *hamartōloi* as his agents and instruments? Is it not clear that in the prayer prayed in this hour the 'prince of this world' is judged (John 16:11), 'cast out' (John 12:31)? 'He hath nothing in me.' (IV/1, p. 272)

We notice here that the prince of this world is judged as he is cast out. The moment of judgement is the moment when the devil is defeated and driven out. It was in his death, the sign of judgement, that Jesus, 'disarmed the rulers and authorities and made a public example of them, triumphing over them' (Col. 2:15) in order that he, 'might destroy the one who has the power of death, that is the devil' (Heb. 2:14). When Jesus judged the sin of the world by bearing that judgement in himself, he thereby triumphed over the prince of this world and the whole dominion of darkness.[29]

Having begun to consider how victory may be related to judgement, we now turn to our second question regarding the extent to which victory can illuminate the doctrine of atonement in comparison to judgement. We have seen that it can speak of the defeat of the forces of evil through the life, death and resurrection of Jesus Christ, but can it also help us understand the wider work of salvation? There are several limitations here. The first is that victory does not lend itself to an understanding of the incarnation, as we have seen judgement does. Both in Barth's 'Jesus is Victor' and in Aulén's *'Christus Victor'* there tends to be a preoccupation with the divine vanquishing of enemies, but only a relatively minor place for the human victory of Christ over sin and death. The second problem is that a victory in itself may only be evidence of military superiority, not moral superiority. The image of victory needs to be associated with that of the judgement of a righteous ruler if it is to be delivered from suggesting that this is yet another conquest by a tyrant. Thirdly, in the use of the military metaphor there is a tendency to so emphasise the triumph of the cross that the suffering of Christ is obscured. It is an invincible Jesus who is the prophet of deliverance for Barth and a conquering Christ who defeats the evil powers of the world in Aulén. Fourthly, it says nothing about the state of those in whose favour the victory is won. That this is a victory for people who them-

---

29 The benefits of this victory are therefore not limited to human beings. It is for the salvation of the whole cosmos because judgement is universal in extent. As Barth says, 'He will triumph in judgement upon the cosmos, He who is now vanquished by the cosmos.' (III/2, p. 501)

selves merit only defeat because of their sin is not in evidence. As a result, whilst it may say something about the representative role of Christ, victory can say nothing about the substitutionary aspect of his work nor the forgiveness of sin and of the justification that secures reconciliation to God for those on whose behalf he acted. So, whilst the language of victory can shed important light onto our understanding of the cross it is rather narrowly focused in comparison to judgement and needs to be associated with other metaphors of atonement if it is to be a reliable guide. We therefore concur with Barth that victory is not a suitable image for working out the doctrine of reconciliation. However, by treating victory as judgement on God's enemies, it is possible to make clear that this is a triumph of good over evil, through which the justice and peace of God are brought to earth.

B. Redemption

When Barth mentions redemption as another New Testament image for reconciliation after his discussion of 'The Judge judged in our place', he does so in terms of the financial language of the payment of ransom. He acknowledges that it might be possible to develop these ideas to provide a framework for the doctrine of reconciliation, but he regards such an approach as 'not very profitable' (IV/1, p. 274), especially in light of the 'relatively slender' (IV/1, p. 274) place it is given in the New Testament.[30] So he does not attempt to address such questions as the value of the ransom or when and to whom it is paid. Very significantly, though, he does suggest that this redemptive aspect might be used in a 'subsidiary manner to clarify the matter to ourselves and others' (IV/1, p. 274). But how that might be worked out, he does not say. Indeed, Barth does not have a great deal to say about redemption. Much more might have been expected in volume V of the *Church Dogmatics*, which was to be devoted to the doctrine of redemption, had it been written. He does, however make remarks at different points in his *Dogmatics* which may usefully be drawn together here.

Barth sees redemption essentially in terms of a state of existence to be experienced in the future as a result of the work of Christ in the past. When he mentions redemption in discussion of reconciliation, Barth is generally describing the future state of blessing of those who enjoy the full measure of the benefits of Christ's reconciling work. So he says, 'In the New Testament redemption is from the stand-

---

30   The passages to which he here makes reference are: Mark 10:45; 1 Pet. 1:18; Tit. 2:14; Rom. 3:24 , Gal. 3:13 and 4:5.

point of revelation or reconciliation the future consummating act of God which has still to come' (I/1, p. 409). Barth also remarks, 'Yet the fact remains that the consummating revelation of Jesus Christ and its redemptive work have not yet taken place' (IV/3.2, p. 917), 'His prophetic work is thus reconciliation in its transition to consummation in redemption' (IV/3.1, p. 263), and he speaks of the 'still awaited redemption of the world reconciled in Him' (IV/3.1, p. 343). Redemption is thus the future goal towards which the atonement is directed. So it is not something that can be witnessed in all its splendour at present; it is instead something that must still be awaited in the future.

And yet redemption is also something which has already occurred.

> What has taken place in Jesus Christ is the removal from the world of the curse under which it has arbitrarily placed itself, its redemption from the bondage in which – piling one sin upon another, heaping guilt on guilt, adding always to its own misery – it seemed inextricably to have entangled itself, the ending of its campaign against its Creator which inevitably brought it into internecine and inner conflict. (IV/3.2, pp. 660f)

This past redemption has taken place in Christ when he overcame sin and the bondage, guilt and curse that follow in its train. It is a redemption that has come to pass in his saving work that centred on the cross, where he fully entered into the misery and hopelessness of sinful humanity. By entering our slavery Christ has broken our bonds, and this is something that has already taken place.[31]

The redemption awaited in the future is so firmly grounded in the redemption that has taken place in the past that we can speak of the awaited redemption as something that has already occurred. Comparisons with redemption by the payment of ransom, by military victory that liberates prisoners of war, and by a pardon that releases convicts from the punishment for their crime can serve to clarify this point. In each case, there may be a delay between the action that secures release and the experience of freedom. But in that interim period, knowledge of what has taken place is a sound basis on which to build hope for the future. So we may also speak with confidence about the redemption that is yet to come because of the redemption that has taken place already.

Barth sees this redemption more in terms of an outcome than as a process. In a particularly illuminating remark, Barth describes redemption as,

---

31 Cf. 'Christ redeemed us from the curse of the law by becoming a curse for us' (Gal. 3:13).

[T]he making eternal of [the world's] temporal life, the transcending of its this-worldly, the investing of its corruptible with incorruption, the clothing of its humanity in divine glory, the perfecting of its creation by the new creation of its form in peace with God and therefore in and with itself. (IV/3.1, p. 315)

How this paradisic state is obtained he does not say, at least not in terms of redemption. Barth has already said what he wanted to about that in his discussion of the judgement of Jesus Christ and it does not need to be supplemented by his description of redemption. It is only to be considered, as we have seen, in a 'subsidiary manner' (IV/1, p. 274). In Barth's view, redemption is not so much an aspect of the reconciling act of Christ in his passion, death and resurrection, as an inevitable consequence of it. So we may say that as victory is, for Barth, primarily about what takes place after reconciliation in order to implement that reconciliation, redemption is about the final destination secured by that reconciliation.

But who is this redeemer that brings about such a great redemption? It is, in the first place, God the creator who is our redeemer. Writing of God the Redeemer, Barth says, 'He who has made man and reconciled him to Himself, encounters him in His Word in order that He may be his entire future, fulfilling and consummating what is promised in His creative and reconciling work' (I/2, p. 875). The work of redemption cannot in the end be separated from the work of creation. Only the God who made the heavens and the earth possesses the knowledge and power required to recover his creation from the crisis into which it has fallen. As we have seen, Forsyth makes a similar point when he says, 'Redemption of the world is only possible because of His part in its creation, who took the responsibility of creating because he knew He possessed the power to redeem and retrieve whatever creation might come to.'[32] We cannot properly understand the work of God the redeemer in isolation from that of God the creator. Only the God who made the world could redeem it

But the redeemer is not only the creator of the world, he is also the king of the universe. Barth says, redemption is, 'granting life in His perfect kingdom to His creatures' (II/1, p. 514). To be redeemed is to enter the full-orbed experience of the kingdom of God and to receive the blessings of his kingly favour. This is an astonishingly generous act and all the more remarkable when we remember that it is the One whose rule and judgement has been rejected by his subjects that so graciously confers the benefits of his just and gentle rule on his undeserving people. Such is the humble service that God offers to his rebellious creatures.

---

32 Forsyth, *The Justification of God*, p. 32.

As the action of the king, redemption is closely associated with the triumphant or victorious aspect of atonement. It is about releasing people from the snares of the devil. Christ brings about this redemption as a mighty conqueror, not by taking up weapons of destruction, but by overwhelming the powers of evil with his love. It was through his unlimited self-giving that Christ has redeemed us from our slavery to sin by becoming sin for us. He wore our shackles so that they might be undone and he paid our debt so that we might be unburdened from it and set free, which again echoes Forsyth.[33]

And, finally, redemption is about the restoration of the creation so marred by sin and evil. 'Redemption means the resurrection of the flesh. It means eternal life as deliverance from eternal death' (II/2, p. 78). This redemption is no mere return to an old life, wonderful as that deliverance might be; it is the commencement of a whole new life. It is not only the end of captivity it is also the beginning of true freedom. The redemption achieved by Christ goes even beyond the forgiveness of sins to the healing and perfecting of creation.[34]

Taken together, these observations provide us a basis for comparison with what Barth says about reconciliation in terms of judgement, and for assessing to what extent redemption may serve as a vehicle for understanding the full breadth of God's saving work.

The redemption by Christ as the liberation of his covenant people brought about through judgement

We notice, in the first place, that the use of redemption as a metaphor of atonement is very closely associated with that of victory. Prisoners of war may be redeemed as a result of military conquest as were Lot and his family by Abram, and slaves may be set free from their bondage by the defeat of those who enslave them, as the Hebrews were through the ten plagues and through the drowning of the Egyptian army.[35] So, by making Christ the royal judge, Barth also suggests how redemption might be related to judgement. We may see redemption as the liberation of his covenant people brought

---

33 'We are redeemed *from* the ban of sin's magic circle by the only One who has the secret of the unseen powers; we are joined with the sin-destroying death of Christ.' Forsyth, *The Work of Christ*, p. 217.

34 Cf. Rom. 8:22 and 23.

35 It is only when the strong man has been bound by someone stronger that his goods can be plundered (Mark 8:27). We have also seen that Aulén and Dillistone treat victory and redemption almost synonymously. It is indeed hard to separate redemption from victory since the two are so closely intertwined.

about through judgement.

In the case of the redemption of the Hebrews from slavery in Egypt, we notice that redemption came by way of judgement on their enemies. After the first confrontation with Pharaoh, Moses received the promise, 'I am the Lord, and I will free you from the burdens of the Egyptians and deliver you from slavery to them. I will redeem you with an outstretched arm and with mighty acts of judgement' (Exod. 6:6). J.P. Hyatt comments on this verse, 'God's acts will be punishment for the enemies of Israel, but salvation and deliverance for Israel; they will in the end create a condition of justice.'[36] The judgement of God, which reveals itself as punishment on the enemies of Israel, also manifests itself as the means of liberation for the people of God. So we may say, borrowing a phrase from Forsyth, that this was a 'redemptive judgement'.[37]

If the imagery of redemption is developed in a more financial rather than military direction, as Irenaeus, Tertullian and Origen proposed, that too may be understood in terms of judgement. The day when the payment is due is a day of reckoning and therefore a day of judgement, when all debts are cleared and all accounts settled. When Barth affirms in his *Dogmatics in Outline* what he briefly mentions in his *Church Dogmatics* that the New Testament writers speak of Jesus making a ransom payment, he does so in judicial terms. He says that this redemption, 'is a legal concept which describes the ransoming of a slave',[38] transforming someone's status in law. As such Barth here draws attention to the connection between redemption and judgement in the case when redemption is construed in financial terms.

This association between redemption and judgement is further reinforced when we remember that the moment when the redemption of the world occurred was when Christ died, and that death is the sign of the judgement of God. It was in his death that he gave his life as a ransom for many. It was by undergoing the judgement of God that Christ redeemed his kinsmen. He hung on the cross under the condemnation of God in order to vindicate his people, thus paying the ransom that set them free. It was by undergoing judgement for us that Jesus Christ redeemed his elect and delivered them from their slavery to sin. The redemption Christ achieved, then, may be seen as what comes about for those in whose favour judgement is made.

But how much of the saving work of Christ may be understood

36   J.P. Hyatt, *Exodus*, The New Century Bible Commentary (London: Clarendon Press, 1980), p. 94.
37   Forsyth, *The Justification of God*, p. 187.
38   Barth, *Dogmatics in Outline*, p. 121.

from the metaphor of redemption, and how does that compare to that understood from the metaphor of judgement? It is highly evocative about the liberation of captives to sin and death by the Creator of the world which restores them into the full joy of the kingdom of God. It can also illuminate the prior relationship between redeemer and redeemed, the helplessness of those who needed redemption, and the benefits of being redeemed. But there are certain important limitations to redemption as a metaphor of atonement. The first is that it is unable to speak of the unworthiness of those who needed redemption. They were not merely the hapless victims of an oppressive ruler, like the Hebrews in Egypt, or those who had fallen into a financial crisis through personal tragedy, like Naomi and Ruth. The redemption wrought by Christ was for the benefit of those who had, both actively and passively, placed themselves under the realm of the devil in their rebellion against God and stood under the condemnatory judgement of God.[39] Secondly, it cannot explain how redemption comes about; it can only talk about the transformation that it brings to pass. Redemption as the release of captives by military conquest relies on the metaphor of victory to express how this liberation comes about, and redemption as the payment of a ransom does not bear scrutiny as a mechanism of atonement for it cannot say how much and to whom the ransom was paid. Nor, thirdly, does it have a place for the resurrection of Jesus Christ from the dead, as we have seen judgement does. The ransom could have been paid that sets the world free from its bondage to decay without Christ rising from the dead or returning to his Father in heaven. And, fourthly, it can give no account of the requirement to respond to this redemption. So complete is the work done by the redeemer that nothing more can be expected of the redeemed other than to offer praise and thanksgiving for what has been achieved for them. No repentance or baptism is required. So the language of redemption, as that of victory, does not lend itself to a full development of the atoning work of Christ, as Barth observes. It needs to be seen in the light of other aspects of that work, especially that of victory and of the judgement of Jesus Christ.

C. Sacrifice

When Barth discusses the alternative viewpoints to that of judgement for descriptions of atonement, he devotes the great majority of

---

39 As Forsyth puts it, 'And as a race we are not even stray sheep, or wandering prodigals merely; we are rebels taken with weapons in our hands.' Forsyth, *Positive Preaching*, p. 38.

his attention to the imagery of sacrifice.[40] He acknowledges that it is given considerable exposure in the New Testament, especially in the Epistle to the Hebrews and in the Johannine and Pauline writings. He even goes so far as to accept that, with regard to the doctrine of reconciliation, 'it would be quite possible to put our whole presentation within the framework of this standpoint' (IV/1, p. 274). He explains his choice to work out the exposition in forensic rather than cultic language by making two observations. Firstly, that it would make a complex subject still harder to grasp by describing it in cultic terms which are now rather remote,[41] and, secondly, we are able to see the matter, 'more distinctly and more comprehensively' (IV/1, p. 275) in terms of, 'the Judge judged in our place'. Barth then restates what he has been saying in sacrificial terms, not to add anything to his account so far, but to say the same things in other language in order to confirm its accuracy and completeness. In the process, Barth gives some important indications as to how sacrifice and judgement might be related as metaphors of atonement.

Barth begins by taking his phrase, 'Jesus Christ took our place as our Judge' and rephrasing it as, 'He is the Priest who represents us' (IV/1, p. 275). To a people burdened by sin and in need of propitiation and of instruction in the law of the Lord comes a priest who can bring them to their God through the mediatorial work of sacrifice and by the proclamation of the word of the Lord. In saying that, Barth does not wish to subsume the work of Christ under the Old Testament priestly office. What Christ does goes far beyond anything performed by Aaron and his descendants. As Barth puts it, 'The image indicates the fact. But the fact is greater and more powerful than the image. It necessarily transcends it' (IV/1, p. 275). After all, Christ does not need to offer sacrifices for himself, neither does he need to offer sacrifice repeatedly, and nor does he need to have any successor. The priestly work of Christ has been foreshadowed but it has not been foreseen. As such, Barth is using the cultic language in a consciously metaphorical fashion.

Barth then goes on to explain how the work of Christ may be described more specifically as that of the high-priest who, like the judge he had described earlier, takes the place of humankind and

---

40   There is, however, less discussion of the topic elsewhere in his *Church Dogmatics*, in contrast to the subject of Jesus as victor about which Barth has so much to say in IV/3.1.

41   Barth is directing his comment at the Old Testament usage of the term. As such, Frances Young would not object to this remark, although she would want to point to more contemporary usages of the term 'sacrifice'. Young, *Sacrifice and the Death of Christ*, pp. 101ff.

fulfils an office representatively on their behalf. Here, as in the expositions of the judgement and victory of Christ, a new era is introduced by the re-establishment of the broken covenant. Jesus takes this action on behalf of a people incapable of taking it for themselves in order to humble them so as to save them. In this cultic language Barth is therefore again able to describe the negative putting away of sin and the positive introduction of righteous relationship just as he could of Christ the judge.

Next, Barth restates what he had previously expounded as the second and third points of, 'The Judge judged in our place' as Jesus Christ the one who was judged in our place, by saying, 'He gave Himself to be offered up as a sacrifice to take away our sins' (IV/1, p. 277). Here he introduces the aspect of the sacrificial work of Christ that sets it apart from all comparison, even with Melchizedek. What Jesus offered was himself. It is Jesus Christ who is the lamb of God that takes away the sin of the world, who is offered up as our passover, and whose blood seals the new covenant.[42] And it is because this is a perfect self-offering that its effect is eternal, as Heb. 9:12 proclaims. As such, the whole sacrificial system finds its fulfilment and completion in Christ. By stressing these discontinuities with Old Testament sacrifice, Barth reissues a warning which we have already heard from Forsyth, that to interpret the sacrifice of Christ in terms of the general religious practice of making offerings, as Young, Dillistone and many others have done, is to seriously distort our understanding of the sacrifice of Christ. All such approaches are in danger of fostering a religious self-sacrifice which is, 'the most perfect kind of self-glorification' (IV/1, p. 263). But whereas Forsyth makes that point by rejecting heroic interpretations of the death of Christ favoured by the Liberal Protestants, Barth does so by direct appeal to Scripture, a difference of approach that we have witnessed before.[43] So Barth is able to express with considerable force that the sacrifice of Christ is not another example of something with which we are already familiar, but an event the like of which has never been seen before and need never be repeated again.

It is at this point that Barth stops to ask, What, then, do we mean by sacrifice? He begins by saying it is a term that is to be understood from its relationship to sin. As such, he makes it clear that he has in

---

42   Barth draws attention to 1 Cor. 5:7 (Christ as passover lamb) and Exod. 24:8 (the sacrificial blood sprinkled over the people seals the Sinai covenant). Barth, IV/1, p. 277.

43   See their arguments for asserting that Christ was penitent for us in Chapter 5, section A, on *Jesus Christ the Just*, where again only Barth makes direct appeal to the Scriptures.

mind sin and guilt offerings, not thank-offerings or fellowship offerings, which, as Frances Young points out, are also aspects of cultic
activity.[44] Barth is considering the doctrine of reconciliation and as
such is only concerned here with the restoring of the broken covenant relationship. So Barth says that sacrifice is, 'an attempt to deal
with this discord' (IV/1, p. 277) between humankind and God, and
explains,

> Offerings are substitutes for what [sinful man] really ought to
> render to God, but never does do, and never will. They are gifts
> from the sphere of his most treasured possessions which represent
> or express his will to obey, which symbolize the life which has not
> in fact been offered to God. (IV/1, p. 278)

By making these offerings, acknowledgement is made of an obligation to God and of guilt with regard to a failure to discharge it. So
it speaks of restoring a prior relationship rather than an attempt to
create something entirely new. At times, sacrifice in Israel lapsed into
being empty rituals, attempts to manipulate God, or to massage a
sinful conscience rather than have it purified, and it thereby invoked
the chastisement of the prophets and psalmists.[45] But, Barth says, it
could never entirely lose its characteristic expression of a God-given
provision to restore covenant relationship after breaches from the
human side.

Sacrifices cannot, therefore, satisfy God as if they properly com-
pensated him for what he is owed.

> On the contrary, it is a question of attesting the Godhead as God-
> head by an action which does not conform in the very least to His
> goodness or claim to satisfy Him, by a gift which does not even
> remotely correspond to the Giver, and of which He does not stand
> in the slightest need; of attesting Him as the Lord, to whom man
> owes everything, to whom he owes himself with everything that he
> is and has, to whom he owes it to give the glory which belongs to
> Him in the sphere of our humanity, the glory which He can receive
> if we do the best we can in His service. (II/1, 218)

The countless ways in which we fail to love the Lord our God with
all our heart, soul, mind and strength are by no means redressed
by the offering of a sacrifice. It can only acknowledge that this defi-
cit cannot be rectified and that we stand in need of mercy. But that
is precisely what sacrifices do. They admit the failure to live a life
pleasing to God and the impossibility of restoring what has been

---

44 Young, *Sacrifice and the Death of Christ*, pp. 29f and 61ff. Here too Barth ech-
    oes Forsyth in *The Work of Christ*, pp. 11ff.
45 Barth cites a number of examples: Amos 5:21f, Isa. 1:10f; Jer. 7:21f and Psa.
    40:7f; 50:13f and 51:18f. Barth, IV/1, p. 278.

lost, but come to God expressing humble penitence, asking for his forgiveness and renewing the promise of living in obedience to the Lord our God.[46]

Barth then addresses the problem of how sacrifice counteracts sin. He notes that the writer of Hebrews makes it clear that in sacrifices there is only a 'reminder of sin' (Heb. 10:3).[47] The blood of bulls and goats cannot take sin away.[48] The Old Testament sacrificial system could do no more than bring about a partial and temporary reconciliation with God. They were of no avail in the case of deliberate sins, and did not ensure that Israel was spared all punishment for sin. So Barth says, 'It is only a substitute for what has to happen when the people and individuals who are obedient to God are set aside in order to make way for the new individuals and the new people' (IV/1, p. 279). Only in Jesus Christ do we see how it is that sacrifice can take away sin. Here Barth comes to the heart of the meaning of sacrifice,

> God wills and demands the man himself, to make an end of him, so that the new man may have air and space for a new life. He wills and demands that he go through death to life. He wills and demands that as the man of sin he should abandon his life, that his blood as this man should finally be shed and fall to the ground and be lost, that as this man he should go up in flames and smoke. That is the meaning and end of sacrifice. (IV/1, p. 280)

Barth's christological epistemology makes for particular clarity and incisiveness at this point. Debates about the significance of the shedding of blood are given a decisive turn when Barth points out that the blood shed is that of 'the man of sin'. And questions of obedience to the divine command are given due weight but not allowed to obscure the centrality of the death of the victim. The significance of sacrifice is that sin is brought to death, where it ends. As such, we can see that Old Testament sacrifices could do no more than promise this occurrence, and that in Christ this sacrifice has been fulfilled by the only pure and spotless man who ever lived. None other was worthy to offer a sacrifice acceptable to God.

But Barth wants to go further. This sacrifice is not only made by man and of man, but also by God and of God. '[I]t is God Himself who not only demands but makes the offering' (IV/1, 280). This is how it is that the sacrifice brings about what Barth describes as 'real

---

46   As such, sacrifices must be offered freely and thankfully. 'A sacrifice offered in dread and constraint is not, in the biblical sense, a real sacrifice. Sacrifice and thanks are only what is offered gladly' (II/1, p. 219).

47   Barth, IV/1, p. 278.

48   Heb. 10:4.

satisfaction' (IV/1, p. 281). It is God satisfying God. This should not be taken to suggest that human beings cannot satisfy God as human beings, but as a reminder of how incapable people are to satisfy God in their sinful state, and of how fully involved God was and is in the work of reconciliation. God did not passively accept an offering made by his creatures but actively came among his people to offer sacrifice with them and for them.

Lastly, Barth takes the phrase 'Jesus Christ was just in our place' from his judicial exposition and repeats it as, 'He has made a perfect sacrifice' (IV/1, p. 281). By this Barth means that Christ has fulfilled the will of God, and thereby offered a sacrifice acceptable to him which has secured peace with God. Barth finds New Testament evidence to support this remark in the Fourth Gospel. 'Jesus knew that all was now fulfilled' (19:28) and said from the cross, 'It is finished' (19:30), which Barth sees not as a despairing cry but as God's own perspective on the crucifixion: that this is a perfect sacrifice completed. Here it is that two differing and apparently unrelated strands of prophecy find fulfilment. Firstly, that the man of sin is dead, showing that sin has led to death; the wicked have been cut off from the land of the living.[49] And secondly, more positively, God has received the offering he desires, that of a 'broken and contrite heart' (Psa. 51:17). A righteous man has at last been found who has obeyed the law of the Lord. The two lines of prophecy are combined in that the life of disobedience has been brought to an end by a life of obedience. Of particular importance to Barth here is the exposition of Psa. 40:6-8 in Heb. 10:5ff,

> Consequently, when Christ came into the world, he said, 'Sacrifices and offerings you have not desired, but a body you have prepared for me; in burnt offerings and sin offerings you have taken no pleasure. Then I said, "See, God, I have come to do your will, O God" (in the scroll of the book it is written of me).'

When the author goes on to say, 'He abolishes the first to establish the second' (Heb. 10:9), Barth draws out the decisive change that has taken place. He says of God that,

> In the person of His Son there has taken place the event towards which the history of the old covenant was only moving, which it only indicated from afar – the rendering of obedience, humility and penitence and in this way the conversion of man to God, and in this conversion the setting aside, the death, of the old rebellious man and the birth of a new man whose will is one with His. (IV/1, p. 282)

The event that stands at the fulcrum of this momentous transition

---

49   Psa. 37:28, 34 and 38, and Prov. 2:22.

is the sacrifice that brings reconciliation. This expiation of sin has removed the hostility between humankind and God and allowed this decisive *rapprochement*. This is what was achieved in the sacrifice of Christ. In his perfect obedience, an offering has been made that has brought about purification of sinful flesh and the restoration of relationship between humankind and God which issues from it.

It is at this point that Barth introduces the substitutionary aspect of the sacrificial work of Christ. Where Christ the priest acted representatively, Christ the victim died vicariously. It was because of his death that those on whose behalf he died may live. He says, 'In Him there takes place that which we need but which we cannot do or bring about for ourselves' (IV/1, p. 282). It is thus with regard to Christ as the Lamb of God that we are able to see that he died in our stead. But Barth also points out that the sacrificial victim died as a representative. He says that in this sacrificial death God willed,

> [T]o accept the perfect sacrifice, the righteousness of Jesus Christ as our righteousness, our sacrifice, and therefore as the finished work of reconciliation. Not only as though we had brought this sacrifice, but as the sacrifice which we have brought. Not only as though the righteousness of Jesus Christ were ours, but as the righteousness which we have achieved. Not only as though the work of reconciliation finished in Him were our work, but really as the work which we have achieved. (IV/1, 282f)

This is how Barth describes in sacrificial terms what he has said about justification in terms of judgement. Indeed he brings that judicial metaphor into his discussion of how it is that Christ bore the sin of the world as a sacrifice:

> [God] shows Himself to be pure and holy and sinless by not refusing in [Christ] to become the greatest of all sinners, achieving the penitence and conversion which is demanded of sinners, undertaking the bitter reality of being the accused and condemned and judged and executed man of sin, in order that when He Himself has been this man no other man can or need be, in order that in place of this man, another man who is pleasing to God, the man of obedience, may have space and air and be able to live. (IV/1, 281).

By means of both cultic and judicial images, Barth is able to say that it is not only an imputation of a righteousness not our own, but an actual making good of sinful humanity. The sacrifice of Christ as our representative is our sacrifice; his death is our death.

But we must say, as we found in his judicial account, Barth again leaves too little scope here for human response. The sacrifice of Christ for the sins of the whole world has brought God's forgiveness to us, but we are now called to receive that gracious gift by repentance, baptism and living in obedience to the word of the Lord by the enabling of his Spirit. This possibility has been created by this sacrificial work and in no sense by any work independent of Christ, but it now needs to be received by faith. There must be a death to our sinful lives which echoes the death in his, and an obedience in our rebellious lives that responds to the obedience of his. This does not and cannot add to the work of Christ, but it is the evidence of the efficaciousness of the atoning sacrifice that he has offered for us.

Sacrifice as God's judgement on sin revealed in death

Having briefly surveyed how Barth understands sacrifice, we are now in a position to make comparisons between this account and what he has already said about the work of Christ in terms of judgement. We ask again two questions: How can sacrifice be understood in relation to judgement? And to what extent can sacrifice help us understand the full breadth of Christ's atoning work?

In order to address the first of these questions we notice how Barth himself indicates these two metaphors may be related to each other. One remark he makes is of particular interest here: 'In sacrifice Israel – fallible, sinful and unfaithful Israel – is summoned to bow beneath the divine judgement, but also to hold to the divine grace' (IV/1, p. 278). Sacrifice is here described in terms of a submission to God's judgement, making the cultic offering an expression of God's righteous condemnation of sin. Where Barth goes on to say that sacrifice is, 'also to hold to the divine grace', it need not be interpreted as something standing in contrast to judgement, since judgement is itself an expression of God's grace and mercy, in the vindication of righteousness and the upholding of justice. Taking these two aspects together, we may press further what Barth says and assert that to offer sacrifice for sin and to be sacrificed for sin is to undergo the judgement of God. The former aspect is to be identified with the positive judgement of God's vindication of righteousness in obediently offering a sacrifice, and the second with the negative judgement of God's condemnation of wickedness in the death of the sacrificial victim. So we may say, taking up a suggestion from Barth, that sacrifice is God's judgement on sin.[50]

Barth is not alone in proposing that there is a connection between sacrifice and judgement. Colin Gunton notes that in his account of the institution of the Lord's Supper, 'Paul links sacrifice with judgement', and says of the Letter to the Hebrews, 'it is as sacrifice that

---

50   In saying that, we are taking sacrifice to mean sin and guilt offerings, as Barth assumes.

Christ is judge'.[51] P.T. Forsyth does not so much suggest a particular connection between the two concepts but certainly regards judgement as operating at a deeper level when he describes judgement as a 'greater idea than sacrifice',[52] and calls the transition from sacrificial language to judicial a move to a 'graver and more ethical idea'[53] than sacrifice. But what Barth points to here is a specific manner in which these two metaphors may be related. Sacrifice may be viewed as a form of judgement. As such, he not only indicates that they are expressing something of the same theological truth, but suggests that, in judgement, we have the more profound insight, in terms of which sacrifice for sin may be understood.

This connection between sacrifice and judgement may also be seen, again, in the account of the Exodus. It was through the offering of the passover lamb that the Hebrews were spared from God's judgement on the first-born males. Immediately following the requirement for this sacrifice, Moses and Aaron are told, 'For I will pass through the land of Egypt that night and strike down every firstborn in the land of Egypt, both human beings and animals; on all the gods of Egypt I will execute my judgements: I am the Lord' (Exod. 12:12). Only where there was blood on the door-posts and lintels was the household spared by the destroyer.[54] Neither the national identity of the Hebrews nor their individual holiness was sufficient to secure God's vindication. The passover lamb, prefiguring the Christ who would come to bear the sin of the world,[55] was required to die so

---

51 Gunton, *The Actuality of Atonement*, pp. 197 and 154.
52 Forsyth, *The Work of Christ*, p. 146.
53 Forsyth, *The Justification of God*, p. 83.
54 'For the Lord will pass through to strike down the Egyptians; when he sees the blood on the lintel and door posts, the Lord will pass over that door and will not allow the destroyer to enter your house to strike you down' (Exod. 12:23).
55 This relationship between the passover and the work of Christ may be seen from the Last Supper narratives and in the Fourth Gospel where we have the comment during the trial of Jesus before Pilate, 'Now it was the day of Preparation for the Passover; and it was about noon' (19:14), mention of the branch of hyssop (19:29) and that Jesus' legs were not broken (19:36). It is also apparent in Paul's remark, 'For our paschal lamb, Christ, has been sacrificed' (1 Cor. 5:7). Martin Hengel, following Joachim Jeremias in taking the Last Supper to have been a passover meal, reinforces the importance of this association when he says, 'It was not primarily their own theological reflections, but above all the interpretative sayings of Jesus at the Last Supper which showed them how to understand the death properly.' Martin Hengel, *The Atonement: The Origins of the Doctrine in the New Testament*, (translation by J. Bowden, London: SCM Press, 1980/1981), p. 73. Jeremias also regards

that the firstborn and their household may live.[56] So we may say that the judgement of the Lord was visited on every house in Egypt that passover night. Either it fell on the firstborn sons and male animals, or it fell on the passover lamb. Only where the pascal lamb had been slain were the people and their flocks spared, because in their case the judgement of God has already fallen there. On that night, judgement resulted in the death of the firstborn or the offering of a sacrifice for sin, but everyone underwent God's judgement.[57]

The basis for asserting such a relationship between sacrifice and judgement lies again in the interpretation of death. Since death is the sign of judgement, and since sacrifice for sin demands death – an obedient life is not enough, only an obedient death can take away sin – we may say that sacrifice is God's judgement on sin revealed in death. The Old Testament scholar Professor Gerhard von Rad draws attention to this connection between sacrifice and death with regard to the need for sin and guilt offerings and for the effect of these offerings. He firstly explains what it means for a sinner to 'bear guilt' by saying:

> It means, in an ambivalent way, both to 'incur guilt' and to 'bear one's punishment,' in the sense that the agent is abandoned to the evil which he has occasioned. What this means for him was clear. Since man has in himself no powers of defence against the evil, and is unable to free himself from its embraces and pollution by any heroic moral action of his own, he inevitably becomes its prey.[58]

---

the eucharistic words of Jesus as crucial to seeing how his death would have been understood by his disciples. He summarizes their meaning as follows: '*his death is the vicarious death of the suffering servant, which atones for the sins of the 'many', the peoples of the world, which ushers in the beginning of the final salvation and which effects the new covenant with God.*' Joachim Jeremias, *The Eucharistic Words of Jesus*, New Testament Library, (translation by Norman Perrin, London, SCM Press, 1964/1966), p. 231.

56 Thereafter, the firstborn belonged to the Lord and should be redeemed (Exod. 13:13ff, Num. 18:15) or given to his service, as Samuel (1 Sam. 1:28) and Jesus (Luke 2:22f) were. See Talbert, *Reading Luke*, p. 36.

57 Some scholars question whether the death of the passover lamb is directly associated with forgiveness of sin. Frances Young, for instance, sees it only as an aversion sacrifice, which brings protection from the destroyer whom she identifies as the devil. Young, *Sacrifice and the Death of Christ*, p. 66. But the question remains as to how this sacrifice secures such protection. Is it not by bringing about purification from the sin that leads to death? Leon Morris argues that by the end of the Old Testament era, all sacrifices were understood to have expiatory power, and quotes the Midrash and Josephus where they explain the effect of the blood of the passover in terms of the forgiveness of sin. Morris, *The Apostolic Preaching of the Cross*, pp. 131f.

58 Gerhard von Rad, *Old Testament Theology*, vol. 1 (translation by D.M.G. Stalker, London: SCM Press, 1957/1975), p. 268.

He then goes on to discuss how the death of the sacrificial victim benefits the sinner. Drawing on Lev. 17:11 ('For the life of the flesh is in the blood; and I have given it to you for making atonement for your lives on the altar; for, as life, it is the blood that makes atonement') and the rituals on the Day of Atonement (Lev. 16), he says,

> What was effected in expiation was that in both cases, with persons and objects alike, Jahweh removed the baneful influence of the act. He broke the nexus of sin and calamity; and this was as a rule by way of channelling the baneful influence of the evil into an animal which died vicariously for the man (or for the cultic object).[59]

These two ideas are brought together in the Letter to the Hebrews, where we read that for those who, 'willfully persist in sin after receiving the knowledge of the truth, there no longer remains a sacrifice for sins, but a fearful prospect of judgement' (Heb. 10:26f), showing that sacrifice delivers from judgement but only if its benefits are received.

To make a sacrifice for sin, therefore, is to come into the holy presence of God the judge bringing an offering. The humble, obedient attitude of the one who makes the offering and the purity of that which is offered are both submitted to God's judgement. It is a moment of reckoning. This is particularly clear in the work of the High Priest on the Day of Atonement. If Aaron or his successors entered the holy of holies without the young bull for a sin offering for himself and a ram for a burnt offering, dressed in the garments the Lord decreed, burning incense, he would die.[60] In the presence of the Lord, all that is ungodly is destroyed and all that is righteous and good is transfigured so that its glory is revealed. Whilst Jesus was seen in something of his own sinless glory on the mount of transfiguration, it was as a sinner and the representative of sinners he brought the sin of the world under the judgement of God so that it could be destroyed. And it was in his death that the sin of the world was taken away, because it was then that Christ brought sin under the judgement of God where it was condemned and destroyed.

Turning to our second question, we now ask how whether sacrifice can illuminate the doctrine of atonement as broadly as judgement. In comparison with victory and redemption, it certainly encompasses a very wide range of its meaning. Sacrifice can provide language to articulate the incarnation, the freely chosen life of obedience to the Lord, the representative and substitutionary death that bears away sin and introduces righteousness, reconciling us to God. But it does have important limitations. Firstly, it is unable to speak sufficiently

---

59   Von Rad, *Old Testament Theology*, vol. 1, p. 271.
60   Lev. 16:2-13.

seriously of reconciliation as being the work of the creator and ruler of the universe. A priest can only speak the word of God and bring reconciliation with God as an intermediary, not as their author or source. He operates within a covenant framework that is graciously given to him by God but has no part in issuing the commands that are to be obeyed or in prescribing how infringements of them should be treated. What can be said of Jesus as judge with regard to being the originator of God's commands cannot be said of Jesus as high priest. Secondly, and consequently, whilst sacrificial vocabulary may be able to express the bearing of human sin, it cannot also elucidate what that sin is. The death of the victim only reveals that a life has been terminated, but it cannot say why that death was required or what it signifies. We must turn to the judicial categories of sin as disobedience to God's command and death as God's verdict on sin in order to do that. And thirdly, sacrifice cannot go on to speak of resurrection, ascension and sovereign rule, as we have seen that judgement can.[61] Although at times he alludes to the sense of the new life introduced by sacrifice,[62] Barth cannot say where that is to be found in sacrificial imagery. Nor can Young,[63] Dillistone or Fiddes. Gunton positively asserts that sacrifice should not to be expected to cover all aspects of the work of Christ, speaking as it does principally about his life and death, but that is to be understood as evidence for treating it as a metaphor, not a theory of atonement.[64] This is, however, an important limitation to the use of this cultic metaphor. Whereas resurrection is, from the perspective of judgement, God's verdict on the judge who was judged, from the perspective of sacrifice, it can only be seen as a new state made possible by a sacrifice which has been made. Sacrifice is, therefore, less capable than judgement of expound-

---

61 It is significant in this regard that Professor F.F. Bruce comments on the Epistle to the Hebrews, 'It is because of his concentration on the priestly aspect of Christ's work that our author has so little to say of His death and exaltation, but so little of His Resurrection.' F.F. Bruce, *The Epistle to the Hebrews*, The New London Commentaries on the New Testament (London: Marshall, Morgan and Scott, 1964) p. lvi.

62 He speaks of the death of, 'the old rebellious man and the birth of a new man whose will is one with His' (IV/1, p. 282), but by so doing departs from the sacrificial metaphor with which he had been operating.

63 On the rare occasions when resurrection is mentioned, it is through the image of victory, not sacrifice. For instance, Young says that for Christians in the early Church, 'Christ's work was understood as life deliberately challenging death and conquering it in the resurrection, as good deliberately challenging evil and triumphing, as light deliberately challenging darkness and dispelling it.' Young, *Sacrifice and the Death of Christ*, p. 77.

64 Gunton, *The Actuality of Atonement*, p. 123.

ing the full extent of the work of Christ. Indeed, sacrificial language
needs to be interpreted from within a judicial context, for only in
the light of the law of God and the punishment for transgressions of
them can its meaning be understood. That is why it cannot be separated from forensic imagery, as is commonly pointed out. Without it,
the connection between God's just rule and humble service is lost.
We must therefore call into question Barth's assertion about sacrifice
that 'it would be quite possible to put our whole presentation within
the framework of this standpoint' (IV/1, p. 274). Judgement is not
only the more comprehensible metaphor,[65] it is also, as he had earlier
said, the more comprehensive.[66]

D. Judgement as Paradigmatic Metaphor

Now that we have looked at victory, redemption and sacrifice as
metaphors of atonement and at their relationship to judgement, we
may begin to draw conclusions from our findings.

We recall, firstly, that it is possible to relate victory, redemption
and sacrifice to judgement. The victory of Christ may be seen as
God's judgement against his enemies and for his covenant people,
his redemption as the liberation of his kinsfolk brought about by
that judgement, and his sacrifice as God's judgement on sin revealed
in death. In other words, victory, redemption and sacrifice may be
understood not only in relation to judgement, but in terms of judgement. They may be regarded as forms of judgement, whether it be in
the condemnation of sin and evil or the vindication of the righteous
elect. Victory, redemption and sacrifice could indeed be described
as metaphors of judgement, since each of them is able to illuminate
some aspect or aspects of judgement in language normally used in
another context. Victory expresses the judgement of God on god-
less tyranny; redemption, the liberation by God's judgement of those
held under the thrall of that tyranny; and sacrifice, the costliness of
undergoing that holy and purifying judgement. Each, therefore,
articulates some aspects of judgement, which expresses the atoning
work of Christ.

Secondly, we notice that judgement as we described it in our previous chapter is capable of spanning a very large part of the work
of Christ. It can speak lucidly about the righteous ruler of the world

---

65 Not least because the movement from Christ the priest to Christ the victim
    involves a move from a man to a lamb, which introduces a degree of com-
    plexity that is not found so sharply in the transition from being the judge to
    being judged.

66 Barth IV/1, p. 275.

taking sinful human flesh, living obediently to the will of God, revealing human sin, taking that sin upon himself as representative and substitute and bringing it to death, making sinful human beings righteous, reconciling the world to God, rising from the dead with all the elect in him, and ascending into the presence of God from where he offers intercession for us in preparation for final judgement. This is a significantly broader presentation of the work of Christ than that which is offered by victory, redemption or even sacrifice.

We also observe, thirdly, that what can be said here of judgement cannot equally be said of victory, redemption or sacrifice. The other atonement metaphors cannot all be seen in terms of any one of these. The metaphor which is most promising in this regard is sacrifice, as Frances Young, Colin Gunton, Stephen Sykes, John Moses and Ian Bradley suggest, as we saw in Chapter 2. Sacrifice is closely related to victory and redemption in the New Testament, as we saw in Chapter 3; on occasions both victory and redemption are expressed in terms of sacrifice.[67] But how may judgement be understood in terms of sacrifice? We have seen that sacrifice is unable to illuminate the resurrection, so there are aspects of atonement of which sacrifice cannot speak. And whilst it is certainly possible to expound judgement without reference to sacrifice, as we have seen in Chapter 5, it is not possible to expound sacrifice without reference to judicial categories. What sacrifice cannot do, victory and redemption, with their much narrower scope, are certainly unable to do. It is only judgement that can span the gospel message sufficiently and operate with such depth as to provide a basis from which to understand these other metaphors in their relationship to the work of Christ.

Taking these three observations together, we conclude that judgement should be seen as the paradigmatic metaphor of atonement. By this we mean that judgement is the metaphor that so fully and profoundly expresses the atonement that the other metaphors should be treated as subordinate to it. Judgement provides the pattern to which other metaphors may be compared and to which they can be related. That is not to say that judgement is able to contain all that is said by these other metaphors of atonement. Victory, redemption and sacrifice offer insights that are not to be found in judgement. For instance, the personal sense of triumph of good over evil expressed in victory, the healing from the ravages of sin found in redemption, and the costliness of the self-giving required in sacrifice are at most only implicit in judgement. So we agree with Barth in saying that we need all these metaphors or we shall, 'miss certain definite insights'

---

67   Redemption is said to come by sacrifice in Heb. 9:12 and 1 Pet. 1:18,19, and victory is said to come by sacrifice in Rev. 12:11.

(IV/1, p. 273).[68] And nor is this to claim that judgement, or even all these metaphors between them, are able to articulate the whole story of salvation. For instance, none of them adequately captures the importance of the Creator himself being the saviour, although all of them would make some reference to it.[69] But it is to say that judgement should be treated as the primary metaphor of atonement with the other metaphors subordinate to it.

Seeing judgement as the paradigmatic metaphor has important implications for the problem we earlier identified in presentations of the doctrine of reconciliation and on the evangelistic preaching that draws on it. It is our contention that much of the current weakness of the proclamation of atonement lies in the concentration on one aspect of the work of Christ to the exclusion of all others or in the presentation of several aspects of reconciliation which appear unrelated to each other. If it is possible to take judgement as the primary metaphor of the atonement as we suggest, the proclamation of salvation may justifiably centre on that image, not to the exclusion of the others but as their organising principle. Those who preach and teach on how it is that God has reconciled the world to himself may concentrate on expounding the work of God the merciful judge that has been brought to bear in the gracious judgement of Jesus Christ, that is now being worked out in history of the world by the Holy Spirit, and will finally be disclosed at the last day.

This does not mean that other atonement metaphors may be disregarded. The New Testament clearly bears witness to several different metaphors of atonement as we have seen. The question is, what place should they be given in relation to each other? Our contention is that judgement demands primary place amongst them and that the other metaphors should be seen in relation to judgement. Victory is what Christ achieved in his judgement, redemption is the libera-

---

68 Barth also says in his discussion of reconciliation in *Dogmatics in Outline,* 'Let me add that no doctrine of this central mystery can exhaustively and precisely grasp and express the extent to which God has intervened for us here. Do not confuse my theory of the atonement with the thing itself. All theories of reconciliation can be but pointers.' Barth, *Dogmatics in Outline,* p. 116. It is surprising that he here uses the term 'theory' in view of his metaphorical usage of judgement, victory, redemption and sacrifice, but his point is clear nevertheless.

69 This should not surprise us since, in the Bible, it is only God who creates. I am indebted to Stephen Holmes of King's College, London, for this point. We must therefore say that what we propose fits none of the seven possible ways for relating the different images of atonement as proposed by John McIntyre and considered in Chapter 2, section G.

tion of those set free by this judgement and the death of the sacrificial victim is the sign of God's judgement on sin. These relationships are not to be found in any particular New Testament text, but rather from a broader consideration of how these metaphors are used in the Bible. It is on this basis that we claim that the victory, redemption and sacrifice of Christ can be used to illustrate aspects of this saving work, but that judgement should be treated as the paradigmatic metaphor of atonement.

Conclusion

Our consideration of victory, redemption and sacrifice as metaphors of atonement and their comparison to that of judgement has yielded some important findings. We have seen that judgement has been developed in such a sophisticated and comprehensive way by Karl Barth that, with the amendments proposed in the previous chapter, we may see it as the paradigmatic metaphor of atonement, with victory, redemption and sacrifice as subordinate metaphors to it. This has important implications for the presentation of the gospel, since it allows those who proclaim its message to give their primary attention to the judicial metaphor, and to relate other metaphors to that. It also has important implications for what response should be called for in the light of that gospel message. It is to this subject that we shall turn in our next chapter

CHAPTER 7

Responding to the Gracious
Judgement of God

Introduction

If we are right in saying that judgement is the paradigmatic metaphor of atonement we would expect there to be implications for how
those who hear the gospel message should respond to it. What is
called for by the proclamation of God's merciful judgement should
itself be understandable in terms of that judgement. In this chapter
we shall explore what these implications might be. We shall do so by
considering four of the New Testament responses expressing faith in
Christ through which God's grace is received as his word is heard
and believed: repentance, baptism, eucharist and holiness, and consider how each of these is related to God's judgement.

A. Repentance as accepting God's condemnation of sin and
vindication of Christ

In the frequent biblical references to repentance, the call to repent
is often explicitly related to the threat of God's judgement. Ezekiel
warned the House of Israel that, faced with the imminent judgement
of God, sinful people should repent of their wickedness,[1] and Paul
told the Athenians that in view of the coming judgement they must
repent.[2] It was by repenting that they would receive forgiveness
of sins and thus be able to stand under God's exacting judgement
because their wrongdoings were no longer held against them. The
work of Christ thus demands a decisive rejection of godlessness and
an obedience to Christ in the life of faith. On the other hand, if sinful people hear this warning of God's coming judgement and refuse
to repent, judgement will be the more severe, as Jesus declared to
Chorazin, Bethsaida and Capernaum.[3] So the call to repent is made

---

1   'Therefore I will judge you, O House of Israel, all of you according to your
     ways, says the Lord God. Repent and turn away from all your transgres-
     sions; otherwise iniquity will be your ruin' (Ezek. 18:30).
2   Acts 17:30f.
3   Mat. 11:20-24 and parallel in Luke 10:13-15.

in the light of the coming judgement of God. Sinful ways need to be rejected and the way of Christ embraced.

The turning from sin and the turning to Christ that are involved in repentance are themselves both related to the judgement of God. Firstly, the turning away from the sinful life in response to the work of Christ and the prompting of the Spirit, is a recognition that sinful life has been condemned in him. As Barth puts it,

> It follows that I am seriously alarmed at myself, that I am radically and heartily sorry for my condition, that I can no longer boast of myself and my thoughts and my words and works and especially my heart, but can only be ashamed of them, that I can think of myself and my acts only with remorse and penitence. (IV/1, p. 771)

There must be no evading this painful realization that the judgement of Christ reveals our failure to live rightly.[4] Our thoughts, words and deeds all testify against us and invite God's judgement upon us. We must therefore be unsettled from any quiet serenity about our own state before God as we hear what Christ proclaimed and realize that his death was a death for us. There must be a personal engagement with the judgement that has come upon Christ and a realization that this is the judgement which we deserve.

This first aspect of repentance is not only the moment when the sinner turns from sin, it is also the moment when the sinner discovers what sin is. For it is only in the light of the reconciliation brought about by Christ that sin can be recognized for what it is and receive a proper rejection. As Barth explains 'What we may more or less know apart from forgiveness is perhaps defect, error or vice. But to know sin as sin, as our rebellion against God, as our transgression of His command, we must know its forgiveness' (II/2, p. 768).[5] True repent-

---

4   Even in this context, though, Barth is rightly concerned not to lose the sense of Christian hope grounded in the grace of God. He says, 'As he bears that deep wound and accepts that bitter pain of penitence, he will hope for the grace of God and in that hope he will be at bottom a cheerful man' (IV/1, p. 775).

5   'Only when we know Jesus Christ do we really know that man is the man of sin and what sin is and what it means for man' (IV/1, p. 389). So Barth rejects the traditional view that a knowledge of sin must precede a knowledge of salvation in Christ which, he says, is found in 'the dogmatics of all ages, Churches and movements' (IV/1, p. 359). Colin Gunton follows the same ordering as Barth, and draws attention to the biblical support for such an approach. 'Paul speaks of sin only in the light of the gospel of Jesus Christ, Genesis only as the prelude to the call of Abraham and his descendants. And it is with Abraham that we begin an account of how it is that the historical and social shape of redemption corresponds to that which it seeks to amend.' C.E. Gunton, *The Christian Faith* (Oxford: Blackwell, 2002), p. 68.

ance can, therefore, only take place in recognition that we have taken our stand against God and been living a life displeasing to him, and as such brought ourselves under the condemnatory judgement of God. And that is what has been decisively revealed in the judgement proclaimed and endured by Jesus Christ.

On this basis, Barth specifies what this sin is that must be rejected in the light of the judgement of Christ. It is the pride which so contrasts the humble obedience of the Son of God, the sloth which resists the active exaltation of the Son of Man, and the falsehood which seeks to mask the glory of the mediator. This pride is a grasping after divinity, a wanting to be lord rather than submit to the Lord, 'a concrete form of what a more general definition rightly calls the disobedience of man and Christianity rightly and more precisely calls the unbelief of man' (IV/1, p. 414).[6] The very attempt to help ourselves out of the futility into which this plunges us is another expression of that same pride that brought about our fall. Pride is then followed by sloth, 'evil inaction' (IV/2, p. 403), which issues from the evil action of pride. Rather than face the pain of admitting our folly, there is an inclination to avoid such a disturbance even if that means continuing to live in great pain and distress. The resulting damage to ourselves, to those close to us and to the wider world is accepted as a price worth paying for the maintenance of the status quo. This too is an expression of unbelief in God and disobedience to God's call.[7] Lastly, there is falsehood. This is the self-deception that evades the seriousness of what has gone wrong with our lives and which seeks to persuade ourselves and others that we are basically all right.[8] This falsehood does not manifest itself in a flat denial that anything is wrong, but rather in sophisticated arguments that bring reassurance that we are fundamentally good and only occasionally make mistakes. It accepts the truth that something is wrong and then subtly subverts it into untruth by minimizing its significance. So it

---

6   Barth enlarges on his remarks here when he explains that, following John's Gospel (e.g. 3:18, 36; 5:23; 12:48) 'unbelief is the sin' and '[d]isobedience springs up necessarily and irresistibly from the bitter root of unbelief' (IV/1, p. 414) It is essentially because we do not trust God that we do not obey him.
7   Barth here adds that unbelief and disobedience lead to ingratitude (see IV/2, pp. 405-407). Rather than answering the call to come back to God and enjoy the good gifts he lavishes upon us, we are suspicious of God's intentions and prone to think that he denies us what is good and permits us what is evil. So where there should be the sound of praise, there is the sound of cursing.
8   'The falsehood of man is the great enemy which resists the divine promise declared in the prophetic work of Jesus Christ' (IV/1, p. 434).

is that the evils of pride and sloth are disguised under an attractive and versatile mask. These three basic sins as Barth develops them can speak of wrong thoughts, words and deeds, of negligence, weakness and our own deliberate fault. Taken together they provide a powerful framework for understanding sin without trivializing it or underestimating its many guises and camouflages.[9]

Repentance from such insidious and ingrained sin cannot be the matter of one moment only, however important one moment may be in decisively turning from it, and so Christians will continue to live a life that invites God's condemnatory judgement. Current sinful practices will not all be immediately broken and the continuing temptation to sin will not always be resisted. So repentance will be needed repeatedly.[10] As Professor James Denney says,

> Repentance is not the act of an instant, in which the sinner passes from death to life, it is the habit of a lifetime, in which he assimilates ever more perfectly the mind of Christ in relation to sin – his sorrow, his confession of God's righteousness in judging it as he does, his unreserved submission to everything in which God's reaction against it comes home to him.[11]

Sin and death may have been defeated but they have not been eliminated. We cannot continue in sin as if nothing has happened, and yet we cannot stop sinning. There should be some evidence of

---

9   By replacing 'ambition' with 'sloth' in Calvin's trilogy of 'ambition, pride and ingratitude' (which, he says, all spring from infidelity, *Institutes*, 2.1.4), Barth is able to articulate not only the sinful overreaching of humanity's true place in God's creation, but also the sinful underestimation of who God has created people to be. As such, Barth is better able than Calvin to meet the objection raised by Valerie Saiving Goldstein that sin is too often identified with the more male tendency to pride, thus overlooking the more female tendency to, 'the underdevelopment or negation of the self.' V. Saiving Goldstein 'The human situation: A feminine view', *Journal of Religion*, vol. 40, (1960), pp. 108f.

10   Barth also says, 'For although that removing and destruction and putting to death has come to me it has not taken place in me. When I believe in Jesus Christ and see what has come to me in Him, I still find myself in my pride and my fall. In this respect there is no sense in trying to imagine that my history coincides with that of Jesus Christ and that sin and death in me have no more further power over me' (IV/1, p. 771). And so he says repentance, 'does not have to effect once only, but continually, which does not determine his attitude only occasionally, but is everywhere present as a muffled undertone' (IV/1, p. 772).

11   James Denney, *The Christian Doctrine of Reconciliation* (Carlisle: Paternoster, 1918/1959) p. 328f.

12   Barth comments on 2 Cor. 7:8-11 that Paul saw true repentance in response to his previous letter as being evident in 'carefulness... clearing themselves...

change,[12] but it will always be ambiguous. Even after the apostle Paul has assured believers that they are already seated with Christ in the heavenly realms (Eph. 2:6) he still has to beg them to lead a life worthy of this calling (Eph. 4:1). We should therefore not look for our assurance of salvation in our moral change, but in Christ alone. The deliberate turning from sin which is required in repentance is never accompanied by a complete purity of life, no matter how much it may be desired or how real its occurrence in Christ. As such, repentance will always mean not only a recognition that judgement is now something in the past in Christ Jesus, but also that it is a reality of the present, that my life now falls short of the glory of God and needs his forgiveness and renewal.

Such penitence should not be understood in terms of an individual judgement only, but also as a corporate judgement, for Christ did not just die for the sins of individuals but for the sins of the world.[13] We are completely immersed in a sinful culture and perform our sinful actions and inactions from within that context. It is not only I but also the society in which I live that call down God's righteous judgement. So it is not enough to acknowledge that I have sinned and brought myself under God's condemnation; there must also be a realization that the society in which I live has sinned and come under God's condemnation. It is therefore important not only to repent of our own sins but also for those of the communities we inhabit, as we see in the examples of Ezra, Nehemiah and Daniel.[14]

But repentance is not to be regarded only in terms of the condemnation of sin; it is also a vindication of God's righteousness. It is as much a turning to Christ as it is a turning away from sin. This positive aspect of repentance was identified by P.T. Forsyth,[15] although for him it was to be stressed over that of the admission of sinfulness rather than balanced against it. Barth gives both equal weight. He says, 'True penitence will show itself as such in the fact that man will not rest in what he was and still is and has to accept and confess, but will resolutely turn to what he will be and already is' (IV/1, p. 594).[16]

---

indignation... fear... longing and zeal' (IV/1, pp. 361f). See also the discussion of justification in Chapter 5.

13 1 John 2:2.
14 Ezra 9:5-15; Neh. 1:4-11 and Dan. 9:3-19.
15 See Chapter 4, section C.
16 As Barth also says, 'This divine judgement will demand a subjection and sheer obedience (and find them in faith) in which man must resolutely turn his back on his own being, in which he finds the old man still there and the new man not yet present, and sets his face equally resolutely to his being in Jesus Christ in which the former is dead and the latter lives' (IV/1, p. 98).

Christ both declares that we have fallen into a sinful state and delivers us from it as we turn to him. The judgement revealed in the condemnation of sin is also made known in the vindication of righteousness. Both are to be found in the same judgement of Christ to which the Spirit calls our attention so that a real *mortificatio* and *vivificatio* take place simultaneously.[17] The gospel proclamation must therefore invite a turning to Christ as strongly as a turning from sin. To emphasize turning from sin alone is to invite introspection and despair, whereas calling people to Christ and away from sin is to breathe hope in the same breath as the declaration of guilt. Thus it is to accept not only God's condemnation of sinful people, but also his vindication of Jesus Christ and all who are in him.

This again may be taken too far if it is allowed to suggest that the turning to Christ is itself complete in a moment. Just as the judgement that condemns sin is not just a one-off judgement, so also the judgement that exalts Christ and recognizes that he is Lord is not just momentary but a continual exaltation and glorification.

> We say too much if we try to deduce from my restoration as it has taken place in Jesus Christ that it has taken place in me, that before God and man and myself I can boast of a right which is under my own name, which has come into my own possession, and of a life which I can live and enjoy as my own life. On this side, too, there is no sense in imagining that my history coincides with that of Jesus Christ (IV/1, p. 773).

There is no scope for triumphalism here. Although Christ has died and risen for us, and we in him, we have much more dying and rising still to do. We must not lose sight of what Christ has done for us, and yet we must neither expect to see the full fruition of it in the present. This aspect of repentance also has to be ongoing.

The turning to Christ, like the turning from sin, also has a corporate dimension, although this is harder to specify. Some biblical texts speak of the benefit that accrue to a believer's spouse, to their children and to the city where they live.[18] But one of Ezekiel's prophecies suggests that we should not press this too far. He warns that even the presence of Noah, Daniel and Job would not be sufficient to save their own children or a sinful land from the judgement of

---

17 See IV/1, pp. 772 and 774.

18 See 1 Cor. 7:14 ('For the unbelieving husband is made holy through his wife, and the unbelieving wife is made holy through her husband. Otherwise, your children would be unclean, but as it is, they are holy.'), Gen. 18 (where Abraham pleads for the city of Sodom to be delivered from God's judgement on the basis of even ten righteous people) and Jer. 5:1 (about the search for one righteous person on whose account Jerusalem may be pardoned).

God.[19] Dietrich Bonhoeffer is amongst those who have wrestled with this problem. He concludes, 'How in particular cases it is possible to imagine a collective person as being accepted or rejected on his own account is something that remains obscure.'[20] Whilst we may and must say that there is a corporate dimension to the vindication of Christ when anyone turns to him, we should therefore not be too prescriptive about the exact extent of that vindication.

What shall we say, then, of those who do not repent at hearing the gospel of God's merciful judgement? Some, as we have just seen, may be covered by the repentance of spouse, parents or fellow citizens. But can we confidently say that all will receive mercy and find that the judgement revealed in Jesus Christ is a judgement that he has borne for them and is now in the past? If we resist Barth's attempt to include every one amongst the elect we must say, No, and make more prominent the dreadful possibility of dying in sin under God's condemnation and facing destruction under his just wrath. The judgement of God borne by Christ may then be seen as a judgement that will come to us all unless we repent.

When the gospel is proclaimed that Jesus Christ the judge has been judged in our place, those who hear this good news are compelled to make a decision. They must decide whether or not they believe what they have heard.[21] Is it actually true that Jesus Christ is the judge, divine and human, and that he has indeed not only declared his judgement against us but also accepted condemnation in our stead? If someone believes that this has indeed come to pass then a response is demanded. There should be a sense of grief over past and present sin that warranted such a death, a gratitude that such love has been expressed to me and to us by the God whom we have so grievously offended, and a growing recognition that I cannot go on living as I have but must live under Christ as Lord and love as I have been loved. Such a person thus repents and is forgiven their sin. On the other hand, there may be a response which is essentially unbelief, in which this judgement is not recognized to be God's judgement but is regarded as an unnecessarily bleak view of me and the society in which I live. In this case there will be a profound ingratitude for what Christ has done, and a resistance to his claims to be Lord of my life, rather than an obedience to his word. Such a person does not

19 Ezek. 14:12-20.
20 Dietrich Bonhoeffer, *Sanctorum Communio* (translation by R. Gregor Smith, London: Collins, 1927/1963), p. 198.
21 It is therefore a question of faith or the lack of it. As Barth says, 'We are what we are on the basis of this judgement, what we are as its hearers, i.e., we are believers or unbelievers, obedient or disobedient' (I/1, p. 161).

repent and remains in their sin. As we are warned in John's Gospel, 'Those who believe in [Christ] are not condemned; but those who do not believe are condemned already, because they have not believed in the name of the only Son of God' (John 3:18).[22] There remains condemnation for those who do not repent at the preaching of Christ,[23] just as there is salvation for all who truly turn to him.[24]

The call to repent, then, carries great weight. Someone hearing this gospel of God's gracious judgement may either accept this judgement as God's judgement, or reject it in favour of their own judgement, the very thing that Barth describes as the root of all sin.[25] Either there is a turning from the sin of unbelief, disobedience and ingratitude and a turning to Christ, or there is a hardening in that sin and a further distancing from Christ. The same message may therefore be for one person a moment of liberation when they repent of their sin and escape judgement, and for another a moment when they are confirmed in their sin and sealed under judgement. In other words, when the gospel is proclaimed, a judgement takes place amongst all who hear. As P.T. Forsyth puts it, preachers of the gospel, 'are adding to the judgement of some as well as to the salvation of others.'[26] This is, of course, a derivative and a provisional judgement, since it does no more and no less than present the claims of Christ the judge, and it may not be the last opportunity someone is given to turn from their sin and follow Christ. But it is a moment of judgement nevertheless. And those who accept God's judgement by the prompting of the Spirit, repent and find God's forgiveness of their sin and reconciliation with God, whilst those who do not accept his judgement and resist the gracious invitation only add to their sin and remain at enmity with God.[27]

---

22 See also John 3:36; 5:23 and 12:48.
23 See Luke 14:12-24; Heb. 10:26-31 and Rom. 8:13.
24 See John 3:14-16; 10:9; Acts 2:21; 16:31 and Rom. 10:13.
25 'All sin has its root and origin in the fact that man wants to be his own judge' (IV/1, p. 220).
26 P.T. Forsyth, *The Soul of Prayer*, p. 72.
27 In this connection we recall that Jesus warned that the slave who beat other slaves and got drunk although he knew what his master wanted would receive a more severe beating than the slave who did the same things not knowing what his master wanted (Luke 12:42-47). We also recall that the writer of the Letter to the Hebrew asks, 'how can we escape if we neglect so great a salvation' (Heb. 2:3)?

B. Baptism as passing through the waters of judgement in the name of the Lord

The second aspect of response to hearing the gospel message that we need to consider is baptism. After Peter's Pentecost sermon, he told his hearers, 'Repent, and be baptized every one of you in the name of Jesus so that your sins may be forgiven; and you will receive the gift of the Holy Spirit' (Acts 2:38). If the call to repentance has so many associations with judgement, what about the call to be baptized?

In both Matthew's and Luke's Gospels, the baptism of Jesus by John the Baptist is introduced in the context of judgement. John's baptism was to prepare a proper reception for the arrival of the Christ, by calling people to lay aside all those wicked practices which dishonour him and to display instead the fruits of righteousness which give him the praise that is his due. It was a baptism of repentance in preparation for the coming of the kingdom of God and the judgement that would inevitably entail. So when the Pharisees and Sadducees came to John, he castigated them, 'You brood of vipers! Who warned you to flee from the wrath to come?' and said, 'Even now the axe is lying at the root of the trees; every tree therefore that does not bear good fruit is cut down and thrown into the fire.'[28] In view of the coming of Christ, John called everyone to repent and be baptized so that they might be forgiven and be ready for his arrival.

John the Baptist then goes on to explain that the baptism which Jesus himself will offer is even more decisively about judgement:

> I baptize you with water for repentance, but one who is more powerful than I is coming after me; I am not worthy to carry his sandals. He will baptize you with the Holy Spirit and fire. His winnowing fork is in his hand, and he will clear his threshing floor and will gather his wheat into the granary; but the chaff he will burn with unquenchable fire.[29]

Water, fire and winnowing forks are all Old Testament symbols of judgement. Water was the means of God's judgement in the flood,[30] and fire consuming stubble and the winnowing fork sifting grain were used by the prophets to warn of God's judgement.[31] All three express both the sense of evaluation (will it float? will it be consumed? will it survive the wind?), and vindication or condemnation (being saved or lost) that the judgement of God entails. This is brought out

---

28 Mat. 3:7 and 10, cp. Luke 3:7 and 9.

29 Mat. 3:11,12, cp. Luke 3:15-17

30 Gen. 6-9.

31 Joel 2:5 and Mal. 4:1 (the arrogant and evildoers as stubble to be consumed by fire) and Jer. 15:7; 51:2 (the winnowing fork judging Jerusalem and then Babylon).

explicitly in the case of water in the parallel made between baptism and the flood in 1 Pet. 3:20-22, a parallel which assumes baptism by immersion.[32] Noah and seven members of his family (benefiting from his righteousness) were 'saved through water' (v. 20). The flood which engulfed and overwhelmed the wicked was unable to harm these eight people because Noah trusted in the word of God, heeded the warning he was given, and took his family and the animals into the place of safety that God had designed. They were then able to pass through the waters of judgement unharmed.

To be baptized with the baptism of Jesus is to submit to judgement. It is an event in which the candidate, and with them the congregation that witnesses their baptism, faces the crisis into which the world and they themselves within it have fallen, and acknowledges that the condemnation and wrath of God which should justly come upon them. As Barth comments:

> More strictly than the baptism in the Jordan, with the strictness with which only one was baptized there, baptism can now mean subjection and unconditional surrender to this judgement, the judgement of the Lamb of God which took away the sin of the world, but which in so doing took away every excuse, so that in face of it there is no possibility whatever of declaring any liberty for further sin, or compulsion thereto. Before His judgement seat we must all be made manifest (2 Cor. 5:10). The baptizing community and those baptized by it stand together before this seat. (IV/4, p. 79)

Colin Gunton draws out this same connection when he says, 'The baptism of Jesus was his undergoing the judgement of God proclaimed by John against Israel,' and 'To be baptized is to undergo judgement, by accepting the work of Christ in our stead.'[33] As such, baptism is a very serious and sober matter, which should not be undertaken proudly or lightly. Confronted with the word of God, there can be no excuses, only a humble declaration of guilt before the Lord and a plea for his mercy.

And yet baptism is also a moment of great hopefulness because this condemnation is that which has already been borne for us by Christ. He who himself freely submitted to this judgement and was baptized with sinners as representative sinner has taken upon himself the wrath of God that we incur. So the word which confronts sinners with the error of their ways also brings the gracious invitation of God to live in his holy presence. It brings people to faith in Christ and makes known to them God's grace.[34] And that faith is

---

32   It is to baptism by immersion that the verb *baptizō* most naturally refers.

33   Gunton, *The Actuality of Atonement*, p. 184.

34   As Barth puts it, 'We may say very generally that the goal of baptism [with

expressed in baptism. The Christian community baptizes someone with water with a view to what God has already done in reconciling the world to himself, the act of judgement and salvation in Christ Jesus. And those who are baptized, or those who bring infants for baptism, should do so to express their obedience to the divine command and submission to the divine judgement for themselves and for their children. Baptism with water is thus strongly bound up with baptism in the Holy Spirit, bringing people both outwardly and inwardly under the judgement and salvation of God.[35] As such, baptism both offers and demands a new beginning, a fresh start which should evoke profound gratitude.

The basis of this confidence in baptism does not lie in any cleansing properties of the water itself but in him in whose name they enter it. Baptism takes place in or into the name of Jesus.[36] C.K. Barrett interprets this phrase as, 'so as to become the property of Christ Jesus.'[37] So we may say that just as the property of those who sin against the Lord is judged in the judgement that God brings against them, as we see in the case of Achan,[38] so the property of Jesus Christ is judged in the judgement that came upon him. The judgement of all who become the property of Jesus Christ in baptism therefore lies in the past, just as much as his judgement now lies in the past. As Barth expresses it in his *Credo*, 'Burial *with* Christ would then mean, we were standing under His *Name* as actually those for whom that took place, who now may *live* as those for whom it did take place.'[39]

---

water] is God's act of reconciliation in Jesus Christ through the Holy Spirit, God's act of judgement and grace, of salvation and revelation' (IV/4, p. 72).

35 Barth tends to allow these two baptisms to become too distinct, as T.F. Torrance, John Webster and others point out. T.F. Torrance, *Theology in Reconciliation* (London: Geoffrey Chapman, 1975), p. 99, and John Webster in *Outstanding Christian Thinkers: Barth* (London: Continuum, 2000), p. 157.

36 Acts 2:38; 8:16; 10:48 and 19:5.

37 C.K. Barrett, *The Epistle to the Romans*, p. 114. This view is supported by Dunn and Marshall. J.D.G. Dunn *Romans 1-8*, p. 311 and I. H. Marshall, *Acts* (Leicester: Inter-Varsity Press, 1980), p. 81. In this regard, the question raised in Acts 8:16 of whether baptism into the name of Jesus is sufficient is not germane, since to become the property of Jesus Christ is to become the property of God, Father, Son and Holy Spirit.

38 Josh. 7:22-26.

39 K. Barth, *Credo* (translation by J. Strathearn McNab, London: Hodder and Stoughton, 1936), p. 94. Barth draws attention to the importance of this appeal to the name of Jesus when he says, 'This calling on the name of the Lord – in face of the ineluctable threat of judgement and consequently *e profundis* – is at issue in Christian baptism' (IV/4, p. 79).

The identification between those who are baptized and the name into which they are baptized is that close. Baptism into the name of Jesus means we now belong to him. There is a joining to Christ that takes place in baptism. So baptism is not only about passing through judgement, but also about coming through death to resurrection with Christ, and to all the riches that are in him. It is because this baptism with water is in the name of the Lord that it is not only about death and destruction but also about resurrection and new life. It can thus be not only an end, but also a new beginning, not only a uniting with the death of Christ, but also with his resurrection.[42]

Such baptism with water cannot be a solitary matter. As baptism 'in the name of the Lord', it not only involves a relationship with God, but also a relationship with those who have themselves been baptized in his name and been united with him. Barth draws this out when he says,

> Those who in baptism called very personally on His name, the name of the Head of the community, recognized and confessed herewith that they were *eo ipso* members of the body which is called in and with him, and as such, in this adherence to this community, they for their part became recognizable, and were recognized and pledged by those who baptized them, as members of the clearly manifested people of God of the fulfilled time, as brothers and sisters 'in the Lord.' (IV/4, p. 83)

So baptism has implications for those who have already been baptized and their relationship with the newly baptized. A community is formed of those who have passed through the waters of judgement. They have a common past, a common allegiance and a common future that unites them. Judgement is behind them, and joy is set before them. They have good news to proclaim to the world. All these things establish a commonality amongst people who might otherwise have little in common.[43] Baptism is not only about the

---

40 See also Rom. 1:6; Gal. 3:28 and 5:24.

41 '[W]hen you were buried with him in baptism, you were also raised with him through faith in the power of God, who raised him from the dead' (Col. 2:12).

42 This is also most clearly seen in baptism by immersion.

43 Gunton underlines the significance of this transformation when he says, 'This is something real: an ontic change, because to enter a new set of relationships – and particularly this one – is to be a new creation.' Gunton, *The Actuality of Atonement*, p. 188. He elaborates on this point in *Intellect and Action*, where, in his chapter on 'Election and Ecclesiology', he says, '[I]f the church is the body of Christ, those incorporate by baptism are more than merely called. There is an ontological change, because they have entered a new set of relationships, with God, with other people and with the created order.' C.E. Gunton, *Intel-*

formation of new people but also about the formation of a new community.

That baptism is about undergoing judgement is also brought out in the identification between baptism and death, since death is the sign of judgement. When Jesus asked the sons of Zebedee if they were able to be baptized with the baptism with which he would be baptized it was in the context of his death.[44] Paul puts it more explicitly, 'Do you not know that all of us who have been baptized into Christ have been baptized into his death?' and, 'you were buried with him in baptism.'[45] As Gunton says, the water of baptism not only cleanses, 'it is the stuff that drowns.'[46] So baptism with water marks a death to self, a burial of the old man or woman in the waters of judgement. It is not just a recognition of Christ's judgement but a submission to his judgement on me. It is not just to accept that I have died in the past death of Christ, but it is a death to sin now, in the present.[47] This is what distinguishes the baptized person from the non-baptized: they have died already. They have already faced

---

lect and Action (Edinburgh: T. & T. Clark, 2000), p. 152.
44 Mark 10:38ff. Both Cranfield and Lane provide arguments for interpreting baptism as death here. C.E.B. Cranfield, *The Gospel according to Mark* (Cambridge: Cambridge University Press, 1977), p. 338, and W.L. Lane, *The Gospel of Mark* (Grand Rapids: Eerdmans, 1974), p. 381.
45 Rom. 6:3 and Col. 2:12.
46 Gunton, *The Actuality of Atonement*, p. 184. Barth also speaks of baptism in terms of both the death and burial that drowning involves, 'This death is theirs, the death of their old being, as they have themselves been baptized; the community confirms this by baptizing them (Rom. 6:3; Col. 2:12): baptism is not a death but a solemn burial as befits the dead.' K. Barth *The Christian Life* (translation by G.W. Bromiley, Edinburgh: T. & T. Clark, 1975/1981), p. 145.
47 Professor Pannenberg develops this point in an illuminating way. He says, 'Representation and expiation do not mean that those who are represented do not have to die themselves. It means, rather, that those whom Jesus represents have the possibility in their death, by reason of its linking to the death of Jesus, of attaining to the hope of participating in the new resurrection life that has already become manifest in Jesus (Rom. 6:5). At issue, then, are the representation and expiation before the eschatological judgement of God. Recipients of the expiatory working of the death of Jesus may have confidence that their own death will not mean definitive exclusion from God and his life. This confidence expresses itself already in this life in works of righteousness (Rom. 6:13). With the hope of the new resurrection life, the covenant righteousness of God takes effect in sinners (2 Cor. 5:21), for God wills the life of his creatures.' W. Pannenberg, *Systematic Theology*, vol. 2 (translation by G.W. Bromiley, Grand Rapids: Eerdmans, 1994), p. 427.
48 Gal. 3:27.

God's judgement on their sin. They are already clothed with Christ.[48] As C.F.D. Moule puts it, 'In this sense, a baptized person has undergone the final judgement, and risen into new life; for such the "second death" of Rev. 20:6,14 has no power.'[49]

As such, baptism with water will also demand a radical change of lifestyle. Once someone has been baptized, there must be an ongoing rejection of sin and acceptance of Christ. A genuine participation in judgement will yield a new attitude to those thoughts, words and deeds that have been judged, and a new delight in doing the will of him who has borne that judgement for them and brought them into new life. So Paul goes on from describing baptism as baptism into the death of Christ by saying, 'Therefore we have been buried with him by baptism into death, so that, just as Christ was raised from the dead by the glory of the Father, we too might walk in newness of life.'[50] Forsyth characteristically emphasises the ethical implications of baptism when he says of how the Church has always baptized: 'It was *holy* Baptism, i.e. a Baptism affecting the soul and conscience of a moral being, by God's moral action in Christ, and applied by a society made entirely by that mystical bond.'[51] Barth also makes this point:

> Having called on His name, we have been set aside as those who could once sin, and wished to do so... In having themselves baptized they acknowledged that to wish to sin and to commit sin is a possibility which is closed to them.' (IV/4, 79)[52]

Barth's language here refers uniquely to the case of believers' baptism, which he advocates.[53] If we are to extend it to infant baptism, it is by making clear that this moral obligation falls initially, princi-

---

49   C.F.D. Moule, 'The Judgement theme in the Sacraments' in W. Daube and
     W.D. Davies, *The Background of the New Testament and its Eschatology* (Cambridge: Cambridge University Press, 1954), p. 467. As such, baptism with
     water demands to be understood as a sacrament, as an outward sign of
     an inward reality. This is contrary to Barth's position on the matter ('They
     [baptism and the Lord's Supper] are not what they have been called since
     the second century, namely mysteries or sacraments') because we maintain
     that baptism is not just an orientation towards judgement, but judgement
     itself. K. Barth, *The Christian Life*, p. 46.

50   Rom. 6:4.

51   P.T. Forsyth, *Lectures on the Church and the Sacraments*, (London: Longmans,
     Green and Co., 1917), p. 190.

52   Both John Webster and William Stacy Johnson draw attention to Barth's
     ethically-focussed view of baptism. Webster, *Barth's Ethics of Reconciliation*,
     p. 131 and W.S. Johnson, *The Mystery of God* (Kentucky: Westminster John
     Knox Press, 1997), p. 170.

53   Since water baptism is, for Barth, a response to God's grace, he is highly

pally, on those who bring up the child. They are undertaking to raise him or her in the covenant community which, through their baptismal identification with Christ, has accepted his judgement on sin, and submitted to his commands by the enabling of the Holy Spirit.

Many of these aspects of baptism we have already seen in relation to repentance. Both demand an act of faith in the word of God that results in a turning from sin to Christ by the power of the Spirit. The baptism of Jesus at the hands of John was an act of repentance, and the baptism of the disciples of Jesus is no less an act of repentance. The first responses demanded by the good news of God's gracious judgement, 'Repent and be baptized,'[54] belong together, because baptism is inseparable from repentance. Barth puts it remarkably simply: 'the meaning of baptism is man's conversion – the conversion of all who have a part in it' (IV/4, p. 138). R.S. Paul expands on this relationship between baptism and repentance:

> The Church's Baptism took over the 'general baptism' of our Lord's atoning work but with certain special emphases that were due to the fact that those who entered into the Baptism were sinners in need of cleansing before they could become the sons of God by adoption. For this reason it was bound to retain the element of repentance that had been in John's baptizing…'[55]

So the similarities in the description of repentance and baptism are no coincidence. Baptism cannot be understood apart from repentance, and repentance cannot be fully expressed without baptism. Both of them together are the primary responses of faith to the judgement of Jesus Christ.

---

critical of the practice of infant baptism (IV/4, pp. 165ff). But, as Johnson points out, this is on the basis of a highly individualistic interpretation of baptism, something for which Webster also criticizes him, that takes little note of the case of a child growing up in a Christian home where repentance and faith are expressed, however falteringly, as a daily reality. Johnson, *The Mystery of God*, p. 167, and Webster, *Barth's Ethics of Reconciliation*, p. 169. James Buckley responds to Barth's position on infant baptism by raising the important question of whether infant baptism and believers' baptism might be regarded as equivalent alternatives if baptism is viewed less as an event than as part of a continuum of catechumenal practices. J.J. Buckley, 'Community, baptism and Lord's Supper', in John Webster, ed., *The Cambridge Companion to Karl Barth*, (Cambridge: Cambridge University Press, 2000), p. 207.

54   Acts 2:38.
55   R.S. Paul, *The Atonement and the Sacraments*, p. 335.

C. Eucharist as the eschatological feast for those who have passed through judgement

We now turn our attention to the outworking of the life lived in repentance and baptismal faith and consider another of the central responses to Christ's saving work: participation in the Lord's Supper. How is this related to judgement?

Of special importance in addressing this question is the Pauline institution narrative and in particular the phrase, 'discerning the body' without which communicants 'eat and drink judgement against themselves' (1 Cor. 11:29). G.B. Caird acknowledges that this is not an easy text to interpret because there are lexical difficulties in taking *diakrinō* to mean 'to discern', since it does not have that meaning anywhere else in Greek literature, and it would hardly fit in v. 31 ('we would not be *judged*'). But he is still inclined to retain this traditional translation and follows C.F.D. Moule in interpreting the verse around the theme of discernment and the closely related term, to distinguish:[56]

> Because the eating and the drinking are a commemoration of the Lord's *death*, worthy participants take their stand with all who are united with the crucified body of their Lord, under the judgement which he bore for them. Unworthy participants evade the saving judgement only to share God's judgement on the world (i.e., on those who were responsible for the crucifixion). The attitude which 'fails to distinguish the body' (i.e. that which fails to see under the tokens of broken bread and shared cup the crucified body in which all Christians are made one with their Lord and therefore with one another), is the same as the attitude which fails to 'distinguish ourselves' (i.e. to see ourselves as sinners whose judgement Christ has borne).[57]

---

56 C.K. Barrett helpfully points out how many different ways Paul uses the word *diakrinō*, which in itself lends support to Caird's approach, and decides to render it 'to distinguish'. C.K. Barrett, *The First Epistle to the Corinthians* (London: A. & C. Black, 1971), p. 224. C.F.D. Moule and Gordon Fee also translate it 'to discern.' C.F.D. Moule, (1954) 'The Judgement theme in the Sacraments' in W. Daube and W.D. Davies, *The Background of the New Testament and its Eschatology* (Cambridge: Cambridge University Press, 1954), p. 472, and G.D. Fee, *The First Epistle to the Corinthians*, The New International Commentary of the New Testament (Grand Rapids: Eerdmans, 1987), p. 564.

57 G.B. Caird and L.D. Hurst, *New Testament Theology* (Oxford: Clarendon, 1994), p. 228. R.S. Paul also understands the text this way and makes the more general observation, 'In the thought of Paul judgement is but the obverse side of grace, and the greater the gift of sacramental grace, the greater is the judgement of the Sacraments upon those who ignore or abuse them.' Paul, *The Atonement and the Sacraments*, p. 366.

If Caird is right, this verse is about the need to recognize that those who eat and drink at this table are the body of Christ. They are united to him,[58] and now live in him. It is therefore a visible testimony to the reconciliation that has been secured by the broken body and out-poured blood of Christ. Where grudges are nursed and divisions perpetuated even at this table, as they were in Corinth, it is therefore judgement and not salvation that is proclaimed. As Gunton says of 1 Cor. 11:29,

> [T]o share the cup is to undergo judgement (meaning godly disci-pline) and so avoid judgement (meaning eschatological rejection), the latter of which is the unintended outcome revealed in some of the symptoms of the church's disordered life.[59]

So the Lord's Supper can never be a private matter; it is always corporate. It is not only a communing with the Lord but also with the Lord's people who are united by a common experience of the gracious judgement of God. As Barth says,

> In baptism and the Lord's Supper we are concerned in a uniquely dramatic way with the action of the community, and indeed with the action by which it establishes fellowship... [I]n the Lord's sup-per we have the repeated and conscious unification of this peo-ple, manifested in the sign of common eating and drinking, in new seeking and reception of the free grace which it constantly needs and is constantly given in its work of witness. (IV/ 3.2, p. 901)[60]

Those who receive the bread and wine discerning the body and

---

58 Barth does not hesitate to speak of Communion uniting us with the Lord and participating in him (IV/3, pp. 551, 737; IV/3, p. 761), or to say that it is this Jesus Christ who nourishes those who come to this table (IV/2, pp. 703ff, 706ff; IV/4, p. 40). T.F. Torrance, who also affirms the uniting char-acter of Communion, draws out the Trinitarian implications, saying, 'the eucharistic sacrifice means that we *through the Spirit* are so intimately united to Christ, by communion in his body and blood, that we participate in his self-consecration and self-offering to the Father and thus appear with him and in him and through him before the Majesty of God in worship, praise and adoration with no other sacrifice than the sacrifice of Jesus Christ our Mediator and High Priest.' T.F. Torrance, *Theology in Reconciliation*, p. 134.

59 C.E. Gunton, 'Towards an Eschatology of Church Membership', *Internation-al Journal of Systematic Theology* vol. 3, no. 1, (2001), p. 195.

60 The divisions which exclude Christians of other denominations from the communion table are fiercely criticized by Barth. He says, 'It is an impos-sible situation that either tacitly or expressly, with an open severity or a gentler friendliness, the one should say to the other, or, in fact, give it to be understood, or at any rate think of the other: You have another Spirit; You are not within but without; You are not what you presumptuously call yourselves, the community of Jesus Christ' (IV/1, p. 676).

blood of Christ are united in their need and in their recognition that it is Christ who can and does meet it. When they take, eat and drink, they admit their sin that separates them from God and from each other and acknowledge their collective indebtedness to Jesus Christ for reconciling them to God and to one another. So it is not only their relationship with God that is judged in this encounter, but also those with these neighbours. They are called together as those who have been reconciled to God and to one another in Christ Jesus. Those who have given offence and those who have been offended are alike invited to this table. They, together, must examine themselves and these relationships before they partake of this supper and their communion should bear witness to reconciliation, not continuing division.[61] Such a eucharist is then a powerful sign of the gospel of reconciliation and bears a vital testimony to a fragmented and litigious world.

This ecclesiological understanding of the eucharist gives it an inescapably eschatological orientation. To participate in Holy Communion is to participate in the reality of reconciliation with God and neighbour which will only be fully unveiled in the future. It is therefore a foretaste of the heavenly banquet, an 'anticipation of the marriage feast of the Lamb.'[62] This eschatological dimension was itself

---

61   The Lima document, which reflects theological convergence amongst virtually all the major church traditions, expresses this well. 'The eucharist shows us that our behaviour is inconsistent in the face of the reconciling presence of God in human history: we are placed under continual judgement by the persistence of unjust relationships of all kinds in society, the manifold divisions on account of human pride, material interest and power politics and, above all, the obstinacy of unjustifiable confessional oppositions within the body of Christ.' World Council of Churches, *Baptism, Eucharist and Ministry*, Faith and Order paper no. 111, (Geneva: World Council of Churches, 1982), p. 14. The introductory rubric to the Communion of the *Book of Common Prayer* (1662) of the Church of England is therefore wise to stipulate that, '[I]f any of those [intending to take Communion] be an open and notorious evil liver, or have done any wrong to his neighbour by word or deed, so that the Congregation be thereby offended; the Curate, having knowledge thereof, shall call him and advertise him, that in any wise he presume not to come to the Lord's Table, until he have openly declared himself to have truly repented and amended his former naughty life, that the Congregation may thereby be satisfied, which before they were offended; and that he have recompensed the parties, to whom he hath done wrong; or at least declare himself to be in full purpose so to do, as soon as he conveniently may. The same order shall the Curate use with those betwixt whom he perceiveth malice and hatred to reign; not suffering them to be partakers of the Lord's Table, until he know them to be reconciled' (p. 236).
62   Barth, *Dogmatics in Outline*, p. 155.

prefigured in the passover meal that Jesus shared with his disciples at the Last Supper. When passover was first celebrated it was on the eve of the judgement wrought in the land of Egypt by the angel of death and some time before the waters of the Red Sea engulfed the mighty Egyptian army. It was therefore a festival that anticipated something to celebrate. But the people of Israel could eat and drink in peace and with thanksgiving, confident that the Lord would indeed protect and preserve them in that divine judgement if they had the blood of the passover lamb on their door-posts and lintels.

But there is more to 'discernment of the body' than recognizing the social significance of the eucharist. There is also the question of the relationship with Christ whose body it is. Here again Barth is helpful. In his discussion of the sovereignty of the divine command he says, 'To examine ourselves means, therefore, to prepare ourselves for the encounter with our Judge.' Barth then clarifies what he has in mind by saying,

> To be prepared for our Judge is to be those who worthily partake in the communion of the body and blood of Christ, who expect their spiritual nourishment from this communion and find in it their life, who can say of Jesus Christ: 'I am His, and He is mine.' (II/2, pp. 640f)

The Lord's Supper is thus something much more than an act of remembrance, if that is understood to mean merely recalling to mind what has happened in the past. It is that, 'the One whom we remember is Himself in action now, today and here' (IV/2, p. 112), as the term *anamnēsis* suggests. The eucharist is about a present encounter with the living God through the activity of his Holy Spirit. Barth even goes so far as to say,

> We only show our failure to understand what it means that the earthly reality acquires this new *nota* by the Word of God if we regard this view of the new becoming as less realistic than that expressed in the Roman Catholic doctrine of transubstantiation or the Lutheran doctrine of consubstantiation (I/1, p. 89).

To prepare oneself for Communion is not merely to set right relationships that have gone wrong or to ensure against disorderly administration; it is to be ready to commune with the judge of all the earth.

This means that the self-examination required at the Communion table is not so much about introspection as about a consideration of the state of our relationship with Christ the judge. It is only in him that our sin may be seen as sin and it is only in him that our sin may be seen as forgiven. Barth draws this out in his discussion of discernment:

> And all examination of ourselves and our works, of the divine will

and the *diapheronta* and the time and its signs, can only be a repetition and modification of the self-examination in which we ask
ourselves how it stands between Jesus Christ and us, whether
we are such as may live in the strength of His life, death and
resurrection, of His Word and the power of His Spirit, whether
we are "in the faith," as Paul puts it very simply in 2 Cor. 13:5.
(II/2, p. 641)

Self-examination is thus an examination of self-in-Christ. It is not
about seeing if I am good enough to come to this table and fellowship with the holy God who is my judge, for that could only yield
the answer, No. Instead, it calls attention to Christ and what he has
done for me and for us. It brings me back to my position before this
God as one for whom Christ died.[63] My sin has already been judged
in him and I can come to this table at his invitation because he has
forgiven my sin. As such, Barth can confidently say, 'If we "are in the
faith," God will find our heart and works pure, and we shall not fail
to hear the *dokimē* of our walking which He will pronounce upon us'
(II/2, p. 641).[64] The judge who calls us to his table has made us worthy to take our place at it because he has been judged in our place.
The eucharist is therefore an event in which the gospel is repeatedly
encountered afresh. As such, this self-examination is a call to look at
Christ and ourselves in him as those who have died to sin and risen
to eternal life, because Christ has done these things for us.

Understood as such, the eucharist is brought into close connection
with baptism. Both entail an encounter with the divine judge, and
both celebrate the judgement which the judge has borne in our place.
C.F.D. Moule brings this out well when he says,

> The preaching of the Christian Gospel of man's sin and God's grace
> is a focal point for repentance and renewal; and all sorts of circum-
> stances provide similar grasping-points of a Christian's ascent; but
> sacramentally speaking, *the* renewal-point [of baptismal prom-
> ises] *par excellence* is the Eucharist, with its antecedent preparation
> of self-judgement and fresh acceptance of God's verdict on sin,
> whether such preparation takes the form of confession and absolu-
> tion or of a more simple (though not necessarily any less profound)
> private self-searching and acceptance of forgiveness.[65]

Colin Gunton reaches the same conclusion through a discussion

---

63   There is a parallel here with the first passover meal, when the Hebrews ate
     and drank under the protection of the blood of the lamb on the lintel and
     door-posts (Exod. 12:7).
64   Cp. '[W]hen we are judged by the Lord, we are disciplined so that we may
     not be condemned along with the world' (1 Cor. 11:31).
65   Moule, 'The Judgement theme in the Sacraments', p. 469.

of the metaphor of sacrifice by appealing to the judgement to which both baptism and Communion refer. He says, 'Paul links sacrifice with judgement and so, we might say, the eucharist with a renewal of baptism.'[66] Those who have not yet been baptized should not therefore take this Communion. There must be an (unrepeatable) baptism which the eucharist can (repeatedly) renew; a recognition that the judgement of God has been revealed in Christ Jesus and come upon us in baptism, and an ongoing living in the light of that judgement and facing its scrutiny in the eucharist. There can be no short-cut to this table that evades the challenge of the gospel message and the passing through the waters of judgement in the name of the Lord that it demands. To do so would be to risk eating and drinking judgement on oneself. For that is to come to the table of the judge trusting in our own righteousness, which is as filthy rags to him. For those who have not yet turned from their sin and thus still live under the Lord's condemnation, to participate in the Lord's Supper is to celebrate something which is for them a matter for serious alarm, not great rejoicing. Those who give the invitation to Communion need somehow to make this clear. The call is to those who are disciples of Jesus, not to those who are inquirers. They may come forward for prayer for the gift of the Holy Spirit to lead them into all truth, but they should refrain from taking the bread and cup until they have themselves come to repent and be baptized.

Realizing that the host of the eucharist is the judge also means that those who have repented and been baptized must not come to this table casually. A proper recognition that he with whom we have to do is the host will demand that we take the bread and the cup as those who come before the One who knows the secrets of the heart. This is, of course, not uniquely true of the eucharist. Our whole life is lived under this same gaze. But if this particular encounter does not make us stop and think, nothing will. As Barth says, 'If we examine ourselves at this point, we examine ourselves always and everywhere. If we fail to examine ourselves at this point, we do not examine ourselves at all' (II/2, p. 641). It is by taking this moment with great seriousness that we are set free to take all moments with proper seriousness.

In practice, this will mean that each participation in the Lord's Supper will demand a fresh repentance. The call to an ongoing repentance that we have already considered will therefore come particularly sharply at Communion and involve a turning away from sin as well as a turning to Christ. The self-examination required at the Lord's table will bring to light thoughts, words and deeds for which

---

66   Gunton, *The Actuality of Atonement*, p. 197.

Christ died and which would in themselves bring us under such a death had Christ not suffered that death for us. It should include a true acknowledgement of guilt before the Lord.[67] Action may then be required in order to prepare for Communion. Forgiveness must be sought from those we have offended and given to those who have offended us. If we have taken anything which is not ours it should be returned. Thoughts which we have not taken captive to Christ should be subdued. There must be a frank admission of fault, a willingness to address the implications, and a humble acceptance of forgiveness if the eucharist is indeed to be a joyful thanksgiving.[68]

Due recognition of the judicial element of the eucharist should ensure that it is not allowed to become a merely routine rite. As P.T. Forsyth aptly says,

> It is not an hour of instruction but of communion. It is an act, not a lesson; and it is not a spectacle or a ceremony. It does something. It is *opus operatum*. More, it is an act of the Church more than of the individual. Further still, it is an act created by the eternal Act of Christ which made and makes the Church. At the last it is the Act of Christ present in the Church, which does not so much live as Christ lives in it. It is Christ's act offering Himself to men rather than the act of the Church offering Christ to God.[69]

This is a highly dynamic understanding of the eucharist which centres its transforming power in Jesus Christ. He it is who, as the merciful judge, meets with us at the table by his Spirit and applies his saving work to all who come to his table in humble obedience.

D. Holiness as the formation of Christlike character under the purifying judgement of God

Having considered repentance, baptism and eucharist in their relation to judgement, we now turn finally to the subject of holiness, to

---

67   As Paul Molnar says, 'In understanding the Lord's Supper from the human side, we cannot think away the fact that God's judgement was right. Practically speaking this means admitting the need for forgiveness of sin.' P.D. Molnar, *Karl Barth and the Theology of the Lord's Supper*, (New York: Lang, 1996), p. 171.

68   Any temptation to avoid the eucharist rather than face up to this need to repent must itself be resisted. Not to come to the table in response to the Lord's invitation is as much a sin as any other defiance of the word of the Lord. This too brings us under God's judgement. Thus Communion becomes a repeated demand to obedience to the gospel of Christ, each time bringing a fresh call to repentance and living in right relationship with God, our neighbour and ourselves.

69   Forsyth, *Lectures on the Church and the Sacraments*, p. 216.

which repentance, baptism and eucharist are directed. How is holiness related to the saving judgement of God?

An important biblical text in this connection is Eph. 5:26. Here Paul commands husbands to love their wives as Christ loved the Church, 'in order to make her holy by cleansing her with the washing of water by the word.' After noting the baptismal reference here, Barth comments on this verse,

> [The community's] sanctification, effected in Jesus Christ on the cross of Golgotha, can be its true cleansing, and in fact it is. For it is not a remote or silent act. As the work of Jesus Christ, it is also a living and present word, and *en rhemati* it is thus at work among us and in them as the divine work which has spoken and which speaks to Christians. On this view we have a parallel here to John 15:3: 'Now we are clean through the word which I have spoken to you.' (IV/4, p. 114)

Holiness in sinful people issues from cleansing, from washing sin away, and that is achieved by the word of Jesus. His word declares what is right and what is wrong and exposes where we fall short of his holiness and what must be done about it. So we may say that his word cleanses through judgement. His is the word that sets the standards, declares where we stand in relation to them, and pronounces what is to become of us as a result. And his is the word that offers forgiveness of our sins and promises the gift of the Holy Spirit to make us holy. It is by his word that those things which mar his image in us are relentlessly exposed and cut off in order that his glory may be revealed. Such sanctification through the purifying word of God is sanctification by his word of judgement.[70]

The formation of holiness through judgement is something to which Barth draws attention. He observes:

> It is by His acts of judgement and grace among and to this people that He sanctifies it as its Lord (Ezek. 37:28) 'before the heathen' (Ezek. 20:41), 'before their eyes' (Ezek. 36:23) – and in so doing sanctifies Himself in the world, i.e., activates and reveals Himself in His majesty in the forms and circumstances of human history. (IV/2, p. 501)

He even speaks of 'sanctification in God's judgement' (II/2, p. 768). Barth makes this connection because he sees sanctification as inseparable from justification, and, as we have seen, he understands justification primarily in terms of judgement. Barth regards sanctifi-

---

70 As such, the cleansing word may be described as the word of the gospel of Jesus Christ, or, as Barrett puts it, 'the message of salvation which he brings, and in himself is.' C.K. Barrett, *The Gospel According to St John*, (London: SPCK, 1978), p. 474.

cation as a direct and inevitable consequence of justification. It cannot be separated from it as some second stage in a process;[71] it is
what justification brings about.[72]

> The divine act of atonement accomplished and revealed in Jesus
> Christ does not consist only in the humiliation of God but in and
> with this in the exaltation of man... It does not consist, therefore,
> only in the justification of man. It consists also in the sanctification
> which is indissolubly bound up with his justification, i.e., in the
> fact that as He turns to man in defiance of his sin He also, in defi-
> ance of his sin, turns man to Himself. (IV/2, p. 499)[73]

Since this sanctification is wrought through judgement and that
judgement comes through the word of God, we are reminded that
response to the gracious judgement of God will require attentive-
ness and obedience to God's word. It is this word that sets out what
is good and required, and what is wrong and forbidden, and which
as such guides and directs holy living. The process of sanctification
thus requires ears that are open to this word and a willingness to
be unsettled, discomforted and changed. Barth takes up this theme
by combining imagery from Heb. 4:12 and Rom. 5. He describes a
two-edged sword cutting through the old Adam and wounding him,
causing the man of sin,

---

71 'The one is done wholly and immediately with the other' (IV/2, p. 502).
    Barth here rejects the two stage dogmatics of the older Protestants in favour
    of a simultaneous act. He argues that to maintain a division between the
    two is to separate the forgiveness of sins from the liberation from sin, or
    of faith from obedience. It also creates problems for Christology, because
    it involves, 'an isolation of the self-humiliating Son of God on one side,
    and of the exalted Son of Man on the other' (IV/2, p. 505). This joining
    together of justification and sanctification is one of the conclusions reached
    by ARCIC II on *Salvation and the Church*, where we have, 'Justification and
    sanctification are two aspects of the same divine act (1 Cor. 6:11).' Anglican
    Roman Catholic International Commission II, *Salvation and the Church* (Lon-
    don: Catholic Truth Society and Church House Publishing, 1989), section III
    paragraph 15.
72 Since, for Barth, justification is not simply an imputation of righteousness
    but an actual making righteous, sanctification cannot be separated from it as
    a subsequent event. As we have seen, Barth says of justification, 'Negative-
    ly, the justification of sinful man means a basic turning away from wrong
    and from himself as the doer of it. Positively, it means his basic turning
    to God' (IV/1, p. 556). It is this positive element of justification that Barth
    now identifies as sanctification. As he explains, '"I will be your God" is the
    justification of man. "Ye shall be my people" is his sanctification' (IV/2, p.
    499).
73 And, 'God who in His humiliation justifies us is also the man who in His
    exaltation sanctifies us' (IV/2, p. 503).

[A] pain from which he can never again be free, which from the heart, the affected centre of his existence, will continually accompany and penetrate all his thoughts and words and works, which will constantly thwart and disturb him in his pride, which will not allow him to give himself up to his evil cause and to himself and the world. (IV/1, p. 772)

Once the word of God has entered into someone, they can never be the same. The effect it brings to bear is as indelible as that of the surgeon's knife. Each time it comes, it cuts in order to heal, and a scar remains. But as these words are received, trusted and obeyed, they are found to be the very words of life that liberate us from sin and form in us the character of Christ.

The word of God not only brings pain, it also brings joy, because it not only condemns what is wrong but also vindicates what is right. This too forges holiness in the people of God. So we see that it is the word of God that says we are cleansed by the words of Jesus. It is the word of God that says, 'you were washed, you were sanctified, you were justified in the name of the Lord Jesus Christ and in the Spirit of our God' (1 Cor. 6:11). Those who put their faith in Christ are promised sanctification in the name of him who was sanctified for them. As Jesus prayed, 'And for their sakes I sanctify myself, so that they also may be sanctified in truth' (John 17:19). So Barth can write,

We are saints and sanctified because we are already sanctified, already saints, in this One… Our sanctification consists in our participation in His sanctification as grounded in the efficacy and revelation of the grace of Jesus Christ. (IV/2, pp. 516f)

It is because Christ was not only justified but also sanctified that we are not only justified but also sanctified. Those who, by faith, take this to be true for themselves will live as those who know that they have died with him and have been raised with him. In that regard, they live as those who have been sanctified. This should bring relief from the stifling effects of morbid introspection and the anxious thoughts that condemn. It is in the light of the great declaration that, 'There is therefore now no condemnation for those who are in Christ Jesus' (Rom. 8:1) that the Christian life must be lived. So the word of God comes not only to rebuke and correct but also to console and encourage.

This work of the word of God does not stand in isolation from that of the Spirit of God. Both Jews and Gentiles are, 'sanctified by the Holy Spirit' (Rom. 15:16).[74] So it is the Spirit's task too to sanctify. This sanctification also comes through judgement in twofold manner, in both condemning what is wrong and vindicating what

---

74 Cf. 2 Thess. 2:13 and 1 Pet. 1:2.

is right. With respect to the condemnatory aspect, Jesus taught that
it is the work of the Spirit to 'convict the world of sin and righteousness and judgement' (John 16:8).[75] The work of Jesus was thus to be
continued after his ascension by the work of Spirit, who would go on
exposing the sin of unbelief in Jesus, the outward righteousness of
the Pharisees, and the false judgements of the world.[76] This is again a
purifying work because its purpose is to disturb and unsettle all that
is unrighteous in order to lead people to repentance and bring them
to new birth.[77] The Holy Spirit thus convicts in order to cleanse, so
that sinful people may be made holy.[78]

But the work of the Spirit is not only to convict; it is also to
comfort.

> When we cry "Abba! Father!" it is that very Spirit bearing wit-
> ness with our spirit that we are children of God, and if children
> then heirs, heirs of God and joint heirs with Christ – if in fact, we
> suffer with him so that we may also be glorified with him. (Rom.
> 8:15b-17)

This joyful acclamation also reflects the gracious judgement of
God. It is the Spirit who raised Jesus from the dead that is at work in
us,[79] promising that the Father who vindicated the Son in his resurrection from the dead will vindicate all his children. And there will be
evidence of that work of glorification in the fruit that the Spirit yields
in the sons and daughters of God as they show forth increasingly the
love, joy, peace, patience, kindness, generosity, faithfulness, gentle-
ness and self-control that reflect the Father's likeness.[80] It is also the
Holy Spirit who empowers believers to take hold of the promise of

---

75   Here we take the alternative form from the footnote in the NRSV rather
      than, 'to prove the world wrong about...' D. A. Carson provides a discus-
      sion of several alternative interpretations of this text and advocates the
      view taken here. D. A. Carson, *The Gospel According to John* (Leicester: Inter-
      Varsity Press, 1991), pp. 534-539.
76   Here we are following Carson's interpretation. Carson, *The Gospel of John*,
      pp. 537ff.
77   John 3:5f. and Tit. 3:5.
78   D. Lyle Dabney, I think rightly, sees evidence of this work of the Spirit in the
      people of God, 'through confronting the demonic powers that would en-
      slave creation, through the forgiveness of sin, through feeding the hungry
      and healing the sick, declaring the last to be first and attending to the least
      among us, giving rest to the weary and calling the proud and the powerful
      to repentance, through summoning us one and all to follow him in the way
      of the cross to resurrection. D. Lyle Dabney, 'Justified by the Spirit', *Interna-
      tional Journal of Systematic Theology* vol. 3, no. 1, (2001), p. 66.
79   Rom. 8:11.
80   Gal. 5:22f.

new life and offers the strength to resist what is evil and to embrace what is good. It that way, believers are enabled to follow in the way of Christ and to increasingly show his qualities of character in their lives. So the Spirit not only humbles, but also exalts, and this too is part of the purifying judgement of God.[81]

The Spirit also creates a constant thirst for more of that cleansing work. The process of purification is thus itself something that will increase as the child of God continues to grow. As Barth comments,

> To put it another way, the receiving of the Holy Spirit which makes the community a Christian community and a man a Christian will work itself out and show itself in the fact that only now will they really expect Him, only now will they want to receive Him; and where He is really expected, where there is a desire to receive Him, that is the work which He has already begun, the infallible sign of His presence. (IV/1, p. 647)

Where the Holy Spirit is at work there will be a desire for more of that work. The will to be holy is thus a sign that the Spirit has provoked a godly dissatisfaction with sinful life and a yearning for greater purity. This too is evidence that the Spirit is the bearer of God's vindicating judgement, through which he creates holiness.

These actions of the Word and of the Spirit are themselves insepa-rable. It is the Spirit who is the bearer of God's word of cleansing judgement, and brings it as a word of grace.[82] And it is the Spirit who makes real to human beings that this is the judgement of God, because he not only brings the word of God to human hearing but also sets people free to receive that word as God's word. It is the work of the Holy Spirit to awaken human beings to the word which addresses their sinful condition in order that their sin may be put away. He enables people to humble themselves and repent, and to put their faith in Christ. So the Word and Spirit of God together con-vey God's judgement as his judgement and as the judgement that

---

81 This purification by the Spirit is itself only possible because the judgement of God had fallen on Christ. It was only when Christ was glorified as the suffering servant-king that the Spirit could come (John 7:39), for only in view of that cleansing from the sin of the world could God dwell with his people again. Pentecost could only follow Holy Week, not precede it.

82 So Barth can say, 'That power [of the Holy Spirit] and that power alone is his possibility. It is the possibility of that saving poverty, that saving humil-ity, or that saving death, which carries with it existence in Christ, and the wealth and exaltation and life of that existence' (I/2, p. 260).

has been borne for us by Jesus Christ.[83]

This sanctification that the Word and Spirit bring about is not to be conceived as something narrowly solitary or individualistic. Sanctification takes place principally in the context of community and in the formation and constant reformation of that community. No individual is called a saint in the New Testament, there are only 'saints'. The sense of collective identity is part of the vindicating work of the Spirit, and the desire to come together as the people of God to hear his word are signs of the vindicating work of the Spirit, who is bringing all things into union in Christ.[84] Those who have repented and been baptized are given a desire (albeit one that evidently may be resisted or overcome by other desires) to join with others to hear the word of the Lord, to celebrate the goodness and grace of God, to participate in the Lord's Supper, and to be renewed by the Holy Spirit in order to live out holy lives. This will not merely be a formal duty and obligation but also an expression of their new identity as the adopted children of God. They have become members of the family of God who are being cleansed by God's Word and Spirit, and liberated for ever greater acts of service. As such they will be witnesses to the majesty of God, and, if they remain faithful to the Lord, ready for the judgement of the Last Day, when all that is unholy will be consumed and all that is righteous and good will be revealed in all its glory.

Conclusion

So there is considerable evidence to suggest that the response elicited by the gospel of God's gracious judgement can itself be understood in terms of judgement as a response to that judgement and a living under that judgement as a judgement that has taken place in Jesus Christ. Repentance, baptism, eucharist and holiness, to which reconciliation with God is directed, can be and should be described in terms of judgement. These expressions of faith in the grace of God are expressions of belief that God's judgement is both just and merci-

---

83   John Webster's summary of the work of the Holy Spirit is apposite here. He says it is, 'that personal activity of God whereby the risen Lord Jesus imparts himself to a particular person and makes them new.' Webster, *Barth's Ethics of Reconciliation*, p. 145.

84   This is not limited to human beings alone, but extends to delivering the whole earth from its current bondage to decay. 'We know that the whole creation has been groaning in labour pains until now; and not only creation but we ourselves, who have the first fruits of the Spirit, groan inwardly while we wait for adoption, the redemption of our bodies' (Rom. 8:22-24).

ful, that this judgement has come to pass in the judgement of Jesus Christ, and that this judgement is our judgement which we acknowledge in repentance, endure in baptism, celebrate in eucharist and reveal in holiness.

CHAPTER 8

Conclusion: Proposals for Proclaiming the Atonement

Introduction

Our concern in this study has been to identify problems with the contemporary preaching of the gospel and to put forward a proposal designed to overcome them. With this aim in view, we have examined twentieth century British atonement theology by considering six of the most influential authors on the subject, looking both at their general arguments and then at how they utilize the Bible in support of their position. After that we investigated the claims of P.T. Forsyth to have unified the fragmented doctrine of atonement around the perfect obedience of Christ, a claim we found to be unsubstantiated. We then advanced the proposal that the doctrine of reconciliation could be properly systematized by treating the judgement of Jesus Christ as the paradigmatic metaphor of atonement. This assertion was based on the exposition of the doctrine of reconciliation by Karl Barth in his *Church Dogmatics*, where he gives judgement such a central place that victory, redemption and sacrifice may be seen as subordinate metaphors of atonement to that of judgement. Finally, we considered the response to the gospel message and found that repentance, baptism, eucharist and holiness each have important connections with judgement. In this final chapter, we evaluate the results of this work in order to draw our conclusions.

A. Results of the Study

Several important results have emerged in the course of this investigation. The first is that we found serious problems in contemporary gospel preaching.[1] There is a timidity about it that fails to do justice to the importance and urgency of the message. It is hardly likely to bring home to its hearers the seriousness of sin and the enormity of God's grace. In the *Times Books of Best Sermons* published annually since 1995, sermons that discuss the gospel message tend to either take a single image of atonement in isolation from the others or to try

---

1   See Chapter 1.

to bring several of them together. The former approach tends to give little more than a partial glimpse of what Christ has achieved, and the latter to obscure the subject by combining apparently unrelated images. In both cases it is also assumed that congregations understand what it means to say that the blood of Christ purifies us from sin, that Jesus won a victory on the cross, that his death was God's judgement on sin, that it brought reconciliation with God, and that his suffering was redemptive. These assertions are rarely explained and, when they are, heavy reliance is made on illustrations which raise serious questions about the justice of God and his freedom to act in his creation. We also found that where preachers try to combine several atonement images, the question of how they stand in mutual relation is only occasionally addressed. When it is, they are generally regarded pluralistically, whether as complementary facets of a diamond or as the partial views afforded by different windows or pictures. With such ideas prevailing, we can hardly expect gospel preaching to be anything other than hesitant and provisional, and we should not be surprised that the subject of atonement arises remarkably infrequently in these sermons.

The second result is the observation that six of the standard British texts on atonement of the twentieth century tend to promote such fragmentary views of the doctrine.[2] Analysis of the overall arguments of these works reveals how Rashdall, Aulén and Young take one aspect of atonement (moral response, victory and sacrifice respectively) and Dillistone, Fiddes and Gunton collect several images and seek to hold them together. The former approach promises greater clarity about the work of Christ but fails to reflect the breadth of his achievement (e.g. Rashdall), or else finds the chosen image or idea itself unravels into a multiplicity of images or ideas (e.g. Aulén and Young). In this case they give rise to the problems of the latter approach, namely that whilst the scope of the work of Christ is more fully articulated, exactly what that work is remains obscure. Analysis of these atonement texts and the use of Scripture on which they rely provides support for Colin Gunton's proposal that victory, judgement, and sacrifice should be seen as metaphors of atonement. But it also highlights the need for further work to be done on how these metaphors are related to one another.

The third result was finding that the attempt by P.T. Forsyth to harmonize these atonement metaphors around the perfect obedience of Christ fails.[3] Forsyth essayed to bring together redemption, justification and sanctification by showing that each was a dimension of the

---

2   See Chapters 2 and 3.
3   See Chapter 4, especially section D.

perfect obedience of Christ. But, whilst he succeeded in showing that Christ's sacrifice was acceptable to God because it exhibited perfect obedience to him, Forsyth did not establish how perfect obedience is central to redemption, judgement (the second aspect of justification to complement sacrifice) or sanctification. Redemption is expounded as the decisive action in the cross of Christ when the kingdom of God broke into history in order to restore the world into relationship with God. Judgement is treated as the means of establishing the just rule of God in a rebellious world. And sanctification is interpreted as the formation of holiness in the human race by the solidary act of Christ crucified. They all require the obedience of Christ, but they are not fundamentally about that obedience. As such, we could not accept his claim that the perfect obedience of Christ unifies the various aspects of his atoning work. We also found in the writings of Forsyth on the atonement other competing claims to such a unifying role being made by redemption and judgement, which further undermined his argument.

Our fourth result was the crucial finding for our purposes that the exposition of the doctrine of reconciliation by Karl Barth in terms of the judgement of Jesus Christ provides a means to co-ordinate judgement with other metaphors of atonement, such as victory, redemption and sacrifice.[4] Barth sees judgement in the twofold sense of the action of God in Christ to restore justice under the covenant of grace, and the verdict of condemnation on those who breach that covenant, a condemnation mercifully borne by Christ on the cross. This judgement may then be related to the victory, redemption and sacrifice of Christ by saying that victory is an act of God's judgement against his enemies and for his obedient people, redemption is the liberation of his covenant people brought about through that judgement, and sacrifice is the judgement on sin revealed in death. From this we conclude that judgement should be seen as the paradigmatic metaphor of atonement. That is to say judgement so fully expresses the atonement that it provides the pattern to which other metaphors of atonement may be compared and to which they may be related subordinately. It may not contain all that is said by these other metaphors, nor can it articulate the whole work of reconciliation, but judgement should be treated as the primary metaphor to which the other atonement metaphors may be related. Judgement should therefore be given greater prominence as the co-ordinating principle of atonement, and victory, redemption and sacrifice treated as aspects of this gracious judgement, thus overcoming the current problems of incoherence in the proclamation of the gospel.

The fifth and final result lies in the response to the message of God's justifying judgement. This is that four of the central responses of faith to the gospel proclamation: repentance, baptism, eucharist and holiness, may themselves be seen in relation to judgement.[5] Repentance demands accepting God's condemnation of sin and vindication of Christ, baptism involves passing through the waters of judgement in the name of the Lord, the eucharist is the eschatological feast for those who have passed through judgement, and holiness comes about through the formation of Christlike character under the purifying judgement of God. Thus these responses to the message of God's saving judgement may themselves be understood in relation to that judgement.

At this point we must pause to evaluate these results, and especially the fourth result about the ability of judgement to co-ordinate the metaphors of atonement, which is so central to our thesis. What problems might there be with this? There are two main possibilities. The first lies in an over-schematizing of the doctrine of atonement. Have we merely imposed a structure which is not present in the New Testament material? In response to such concern we should acknowledge that there is no particular biblical text that provides the spur to this proposal. We have, however, endeavoured to show scriptural evidence for the claims that victory is judgement against God's enemies and for his obedient people, redemption is the liberation of God's covenant people brought about through that judgement, and sacrifice is the judgement on sin revealed in death. It is from these observations that the proposal is made that judgement is the paradigmatic metaphor of atonement. In other words, the argument rests on these understandings of the nature of victory, redemption, sacrifice and their relationship to judgement. Further support for this proposal is then to be found in the analysis of biblical texts where more than one atonement metaphor arises.[6] There we find evidence of a prioritizing of these metaphors, with redemption and victory being described in terms of sacrifice, giving sacrifice a more important place than victory or redemption. When we later showed that sacrifice itself needed to be understood within the framework of covenantal law in order to expound the significance of the death of a sin offering, we saw that sacrifice in turn needs to be understood in terms of judgement,[7] supporting our contention that judgement is the primary atonement metaphor. It is also from the biblical testimony that we see the extent to which these metaphors illuminate the atonement and discover where their limits lie. The ability of judge-

---

4   See Chapters 5 and 6.
5   See Chapter 7.
6   See Chapter 3, section F.
7   See Chapter 6, section C.

ment to comprehend so much of the saving work of Christ, more than can victory, redemption or even sacrifice, is further evidence that it is to be regarded as the paradigmatic metaphor. It is for these reasons that this claim should be seen as arising from within the biblical material rather than being imposed upon it.[8]

The second problem lies in claiming such prominence for judgement, since it is such an unpopular topic in the Church and in society at large. This, indeed, might well be a reason why this thesis has not been proposed before.[9] We may give three responses to this criticism. The first is that issues of popularity should not be allowed to shape Christian theology. Our concern is to articulate faithfully the Christian message even if it might be unpalatable, as, of course, many found the teaching of Jesus in the first century.[10] The second is that the human resistance to the message of judgement is part of the evidence of our inclination towards sin and of an understandable reluctance to be exposed to our true condition.[11] And, thirdly, we must be clear that by judgement we do not just mean condemnation, as is commonly assumed, but the whole task of seeing, weighing, separating, rewarding and punishing. Once it is explained that we are considering judgement in this broader sense as the means of secur-

---

8   There are, of course, many other metaphors used to describe the atonement to which we have made sparse reference, such as those from medicine (healing and saving), and new images are still being added to this list, like 'facing' in David Ford's recent study on *Self and Salvation*. D.F. Ford, *Self and Salvation* (Cambridge: Cambridge University Press, 1999). It might be suggested that our thesis only succeeds, in as far as it does, by its selecting only the four images of judgement, victory, redemption and sacrifice. But here too we notice that images like medicine and facing, where they have a direct connection to atonement, contain elements of judgement: e.g. radical surgery and the facing down of enemies in the trials of Jesus. So we may say, in so far as these are being used as metaphors of atonement, it is by virtue of their judicial associations.

9   It is also the case that this thesis relies heavily on the work of Karl Barth on the centrality of judgement to the doctrine of reconciliation and that of Colin Gunton on the metaphorical nature of the New Testament imagery of atonement. Prior to those, no judicial account of atonement had been given which so effectively drew together so much of this central doctrine, and the question of the status of the New Testament images of atonement remained highly problematic.

10 For instance, after teaching about himself as the bread of life and giving his flesh to eat 'many of his disciples turned back and no longer went about with him' (John 6:66).

11 As Derek Kidner points out in his commentary on Genesis, 'the first doctrine to be denied is judgement' when the serpent contradicts God's word to Adam. Derek Kidner, *Genesis*, (Leicester: Inter-Varsity Press, 1967), p. 68.

ing justice, it may not be received with such dismay. Understood as such, we may also see that judgement occurs frequently in daily life, making it a highly suitable vehicle for the public proclamation of the gospel of Jesus Christ.

B. Implications of the Study

As we indicated in the introduction, the concern that lies behind this thesis is with the content of the preaching of the gospel. Our chief interest in the implications of this study will therefore be with regard to how the current weakness of evangelistic preaching may be addressed.

The most important implication of this study is the demand it makes that greater prominence be given to judgement in the proclamation of the gospel. It currently occupies only a relatively minor place in the theology of many preachers. For instance, the subject only occurs very infrequently in the *Times Books of Best Sermons*. Zena Helliwell spoke at Redland Parish Church of how John the Baptist called people to 'Flee from the coming judgement!',[12] although she went on to expound the passage in terms of John being an example of standing out and standing firm rather than as a call to her hearers to prepare for judgement. Harry Potter, barrister and honorary Curate of St Giles, Camberwell, told King's School, Canterbury, that the nations will be judged, and that by the quality of their compassion. He then considered some recent trials in which he had been involved and reminded the congregation that the courts punish crime, not sin.[13] Dr Arnold Kellett spoke of the Day of Judgement, warning against expecting it in the year 2000 but encouraging people to regard judgement as being 'just round the corner.'[14] Andrew Sails commented to the congregation at Central Hall Methodist Church, Walsall, that after death we face judgement when our lives will be tested by fire.[15] In each of these cases, judgement is only briefly mentioned and does not receive a sustained treatment.

Only two of the one-hundred-and-forty Christian sermons in first five *Times Books of Best Sermons* develop the theme of judgement

---

12 Z. Helliwell, 'Who was John?' in Gledhill, ed., *The Times Best Sermons for 1998*, p. 77.
13 H. Potter, A Sermon Preached on Advent Sunday' in Gledhill ed., *The Times Best Sermons for 1998*, p.104.
14 A. Kellett, 'A Thief in the Night' in Gledhill, ed., *The Fourth Times Book of Best Sermons*, p. 9.
15 A Sails, 'Blessed are the Meek' in Gledhill, ed., *The Fifth Times Book of Best Sermons*, p. 172.

in any detail. The first of these is by Jim Rea, whose illustration of atonement in terms of the judge forgiving his friend in the dock we considered in the Introduction.[16] The second is John Thompson, who boldly declared to a congregation at Totley Rise Methodist Church, Sheffield, 'the whole world is under God's judgement'[17] and went on to stress the seriousness of disobeying the commands of God. But these are rare exceptions in this collection.

The recent report of the Doctrine Commission of the Church of England on the atonement, *The Mystery of Salvation*, is further evidence of the avoidance of this theme. It accords judgement only a minor place and recommends it be used with great caution. The Commission writes,

> [T]here is little doubt that the traditional patriarchal images of God as king, lord, judge, warrior, etc. that belong to the traditional vocabulary of atonement with its central themes of law, wrath, guilt, punishment and acquittal, leave many Christians cold and signally fail to move people, young and old, who wish to take steps towards faith. These images do not correspond to the spiritual search of many people today and therefore hamper the Church's mission.[18]

They also say judicial accounts, 'appear to eclipse moral considerations by legal ones.'[19] These are strong criticisms, but hardly a basis for sidelining such a major strand of the New Testament teaching on the atonement. And whilst they may apply to some formulations of penal substitution theories, they can hardly be said of the account of the doctrine of reconciliation given by Karl Barth. His emphasis on the covenantal relationship between the judge and the people he comes to judge ensures it is not 'cold', and by taking judgement to refer to the whole process of bringing about justice it cannot be said to be legalistic.[20] So judicial accounts of atonement should not be marginalised for these reasons.

The new three year *Revised Common Lectionary*, now used in the Roman Catholic Church, the Anglican Communion and many Free

---

16 See Chapter 1, section B.
17 J. Thompson, 'Everyone Did as They Pleased' in Gledhill, ed., *The Times Best Sermons of 1996*, p. 57.
18 The Doctrine Commission of the Church of England, *The Mystery of Salvation*, (London: Church House Publishing, 1995), p.113.
19 Doctrine Commission of the Church of England, *The Mystery of Salvation*, p. 212.
20 Karl Barth is acknowledged as giving, 'a generally acceptable sense to penal imagery' (Doctrine Commission of the Church of England, *The Mystery of Salvation*, p. 123), but the report retains its criticisms in view of the less adequate versions of judicial accounts of atonement.

Churches, also reflects and exacerbates this tendency to avoid the subject of divine judgement. In a sequence of readings in a given biblical book, passages about the judgement of God are frequently omitted, especially on Sundays when they are most likely to be a sermon text. Perhaps the most notorious case in point is the reading for the Principal Service on the Seventh Sunday of Easter in Year C, when the verses to be read from Revelation 22 are specified as 12-14, 16-17, 20-21. The verses omitted are: 'Outside [the gates of the new Jerusalem] are the dogs and sorcerers and fornicators and murderers and idolaters, and everyone who loves and practices falsehood' (v. 15), and, amazingly,

> I warn everyone who hears the words of the prophecy of this book: if anyone adds to them, God will add to that person the plagues described in this book; if anyone takes away from the words of this prophecy God will take away that person's share in the tree of life and in the holy City, which are described in this book (vv. 18-19).[21]

Preachers face temptation enough to say nothing about verses that refer to God's judgement when they arise in a sermon text, but if they do not even arise there is an even graver danger that this aspect of the counsel of God will not be declared.

Our survey of *Times Books of Best Sermons* combined with the evidence of the Doctrine Commission of the Church of England and of the notable omissions in the lectionary suggest that judgement is not receiving the attention that may be warranted by the more satisfactory account that we have offered. If we are to see judgement given much greater prominence in gospel proclamation, and reverse the trend to minimize it set in place by Schleiermacher and Ritschl, considerable work will be required. At the heart of this project will stand a re-formulation of what exactly we mean by judgement. It needs to be seen as the whole process of bringing about God's justice in an unjust world. So, as both Forsyth and Barth say, judgement must be understood as a means of bringing about salvation and therefore as an act of grace, as an expression of God's love and not the withdrawal of it. This judgement is brought to bear in order to remove the corruption of a sinful world so that the kingdom of God may be established here, and all his gracious blessings enjoyed. As such, judgement is to be compared with the incision of a skilled surgeon, or the painful discipline of a loving father, or, better still,

---

21 It should be noted, however, that on the Fourth Sunday of Advent of Year A, the epistle for the Second Service is Rev. 22:6-21. There are numerous other examples of passages on judgement being avoided. Two such cases are the Principal Services on Trinity 4, Year C, when Luke 10:12-15 is omitted and on Trinity 10, Year C when Luke 12:57-59 is omitted.

with the return of a just and powerful king to a land overrun by his enemies.[22] The judge who brings forth this judgement is not so much to be imagined in a contemporary western courtroom as in a royal palace in the Ancient Near East. It is the kingly judge who brings this judgement, who not only interprets and applies the law but also formulates and publishes it. Such judgement will involve punishment, but it will also embrace the whole task of evaluating what must be done and vindicating what is good as well as condemning all that is evil. Only by such a judgement can a just and lasting peace be established and God's good purposes for his creation fulfilled.

We must also be clear that the condemnatory aspect of this judgement is not simply inflicted on sinful people as they deserve but instead borne by the sinless Jesus Christ in their place.[23] He suffered death on the cross as the judgement of God on the sin of the world. He hung there as representative of the sinful human race, revealing the judgement that our sins deserve and bearing that judgement for us as our substitute so that we might be forgiven. By his total obedience to the Father's will, even to the point of laying down his life, Christ freely overcame the disobedience of the human race in order to bring it to an end in his death. Then, in raising him from the dead, God delivered his own verdict: that Jesus is his beloved Son, his anointed, his holy one, whom he would not allow to see corruption. Christ's righteousness was thus vindicated, and a new age of abundant and eternal life begun. That is why this judgement should be seen as yielding mercy, and not withholding it. As Forsyth remarks, 'His mercy is by judgement unto holy victory and endless peace.'[24] So it is profoundly good news that Jesus Christ comes bringing judgement on the earth, not only because that is the assurance

---

22 It might also be compared with educational examinations, job interviews, work appraisals, inspections (such as those by OFSTED, the Health and Safety Executive, auditors *etc.*), Annual General Meetings, court appearances *etc.* Each of these involves an assessment taking place on the basis of which important decisions rest. They are undertaken by those deemed qualified to make such a judgement and who have the power to enforce the results of their evaluation. They may also be the originator of the standard against which they test, such as the academic examiner who sets the paper and decides the pass mark. All of these have limitations as sermon illustrations, but they do include both discernment and decision and as such are able to express something of what we mean by judgement.

23 This aspect of God's merciful judgement might be illustrated by the story of the Memphis express, or of the judge who paid the fine for his friend in the dock, or of the prisoner of war clubbed to death for stealing a shovel, which were discussed in Chapter 1.

24 Forsyth, *The Justification of God*, p. 58.

that justice will be done, but also because it secures the hope for the elect that mercy will be received on the day of judgement. We may therefore say that this judgement is not so much a destroying judgement as a saving judgement, a justifying judgement, and as such, for all who will respond to it, a cause for great thanksgiving and joy.

Such an emphasis on judgement promises to restore iron to the anaemic blood of much contemporary gospel preaching. An account of atonement centering on the justifying judgement of God is able to face with due seriousness the world as it is, with all its potential for good and all its propensity towards evil. And it can provide the vocabulary to describe how the ever urgent need to root out corruption and establish righteousness, to bring down the proud and raise up the humble, is met in Jesus Christ. He alone has the wisdom, power and authority as the divine-royal judge to disclose the true state of the world, to separate the righteous from the wicked, and to distribute his blessing and curse accordingly. And he alone has the loving compassion to stand in the place of sinners and bear the curse of condemnatory judgement due to them in order to set them free from the sentence justly dispensed against them. This is a strong and gracious gospel and not mere sentiment or theodicy.

Such a view of judgement also opens up the way for preachers to express the urgency of the call to come to Jesus Christ. His crucifixion reveals the place of the sinner, and his death upon the cross discloses the end to the life of sin. A godforsaking life will lead to a godforsaken death. Any hope that disobedience to God will have no adverse consequences must be laid to rest. By suffering and dying in the place of sinful humanity Christ represented the human race and bore the sin of the world, but that is not to say that every sinner stands forgiven. There needs to be a repentance of sin and a turning to Christ to receive his forgiveness and the gift of the Holy Spirit. And there is the call to baptism with water which signifies and seals the death to sin and the rising with Christ to new life in the Spirit. To continue in sin knowing that Christ has died for the sins of the world is only to compound the judgement that is due. But to turn from sin to Christ and be baptized is to die to sin and be born again of water and the Spirit. From then on, the person is to inhabit the eucharistic community, orientated towards praise and thanksgiving for the one who has borne judgement for them, witnessing to his justice and glory in the world, and calling people everywhere to turn to him. Such a life will be lived with the people of God under the purifying judgement of God directed towards holiness, brought about through the cleansing and renewal of the Word and Spirit of God. So judgement remains a continuing reality for the Christian, but as sanctification, not condemnation, for all condemnation has been borne already by Jesus Christ the Lord.

Another consequence of increased emphasis on judgement in preaching should be a greater prominence for the judgement of the last day, with all its power to effect a proper seriousness about the ethical decisions of daily life. To know that we shall be called to account for all we do should play an important part in encouraging righteous living. Recognizing that we live under the eyes of the judge of all the earth, 'from whom no secrets are hidden'[25] offers an important perspective on the significance of our every action and inaction, which has been largely eroded from public consciousness in Britain. It also confers a sense of dignity on human persons, as Wolf Krötke has recently argued,[26] since our actions are being treated with such seriousness by God. This increased prominence for judgement therefore has important implications not only for presenting the Christian message to the world, but also for Christian behaviour and for the life of the Christian Church.

Conclusion

In this study we have observed problems with contemporary proclamation of the Christian gospel and sought to expose the roots of these problems in the treatment of the biblical metaphors of atonement as if they are essentially independent. The selection of one aspect to the exclusion of others and the pluralistic combination of these metaphors that arise from this understanding diminish the gospel message by restricting its range or confusing its content. P.T. Forsyth was unable to resolve the problem because he could not make the perfect obedience of Christ co-ordinate these various aspects of atonement. Karl Barth does, however, provide such a possibility in his exposition of the doctrine of reconciliation chiefly in terms of judgement. The victory of Christ can then be seen as God's judgement against his enemies and for his obedient people, redemption as the resultant liberation of God's covenant friends, and sacrifice the judgement of sin revealed in death. As such we have argued that judgement is the paradigmatic metaphor of atonement and should be privileged over the others by those who proclaim the gospel message, as well as in the call to respond in repentance, baptism, eucharist and holiness. As such, other biblical metaphors of atonement may be given their full place, not as alternative accounts of atonement, but as metaphors of judgement.

---

25 From the 'Collect for Purity' attributed to St Gregory, Abbot of Canterbury *c.* 780. Cf. 1 Sam. 16:7.

26 W. Krötke, 'Hope in the Last Judgement and Human Dignity,' *International Journal of Systematic Theology*, vol. 2, no. 3 (2000), pp. 270-282.

Bibliography

Biblical quotations are taken from the New Revised Standard Version (1989), Oxford: Oxford University Press

Anderson, M.W., ed., (1971) *The Gospel and Authority: A P.T. Forsyth Reader: Eight Essays Previously Published in Journals* Minneapolis: Augsburg

Anglican Roman Catholic International Commission II (1989) *Salvation and the Church* London: Catholic Truth Society and Church House Publishing

Anselm, (1098/1909) *Cur Deus Homo?* E. T. by Rose Corbet, London: Griffith, Farran, Okedan and Welsh

Aulén, G., (1930/1931) *Christus Victor* E. T. by A.G. Herbert, London: SPCK

Baillie, D.M., (1947) *God was in Christ* London: Faber and Faber

Balthasar, H.U. von, (1971) *The Theology of Karl Barth* E. T. by J. Drury, New York, Chicago, San Francisco: Holt, Rinehart and Winston

Barrett, C.K., (1978) 2nd edn. *The Gospel According to St John* London: SPCK

Barrett, C.K., (1991) 2nd edn. *The Epistle to the Romans* London: A. & C. Black

Barrett, C.K., (1971) 2nd edn. *The First Epistle to the Corinthians* London: A. & C. Black

Barth, K., (1928/1981) *Ethics* E. T. by G.W. Bromiley, edited by D. Braun, New York: Seabury Press

Barth, K., (1932/1975) *Church Dogmatics vol. I, part 1* E. T. by G.W. Bromiley, edited by G.W. Bromiley and T.F. Torrance, Edinburgh: T. & T. Clark – (I/1)

Barth, K., (1935/1936) *Credo* E. T. by J. Strathearn McNab, London: Hodder and Stoughton

Barth, K., (1938/1956) *Church Dogmatics vol. I, part 2* E. T. by G.W. Bromiley, edited by G.W. Bromiley and T.F. Torrance, Edinburgh: T. & T. Clark – (I/2)

Barth, K., (1940/1957) *Church Dogmatics vol. II, part 1* E.T. by T.H.L. Parker, W.B. Johnston, H. Knight and J.L.M. Haire, edited by G.W. Bromiley and T.F. Torrance, Edinburgh: T. & T. Clark – (II/1) Barth, K., (1942/1957) *Church Dogmatics vol. II, part 2* E. T. by G.W. Bromiley, J.C. Campbell, I. Wilson, J. Strathearn, H. Knight and R.A. Stewart, edited by G.W. Bromiley and T.F. Torrance, Edinburgh: T. & T. Clark – (II/2)

Barth, K., (1947/1959) *Dogmatics in Outline* E. T. by G.T. Thompson, New York: Harper and Brothers

Barth, K., (1947-1949, 1961/1964) *Prayer and Preaching* E. T. by B.E. Hooke, London: SCM Press

Barth, K., (1948/1960) *Church Dogmatics vol. III, part 2* E. T. by G.W. Bromiley, edited by G.W. Bromiley and T.F. Torrance, Edinburgh: T. & T. Clark – (III/2)

Barth, K., (1950/1960) *Church Dogmatics vol. III, part 3* E. T. by G.W. Bromiley, edited by G.W. Bromiley and T.F. Torrance, Edinburgh: T. & T. Clark – (III/3)

Barth, K., (1953/1956) *Church Dogmatics vol. IV, part 1* E. T. by G.W. Bromiley, edited by G.W. Bromiley and T.F. Torrance, Edinburgh: T. & T. Clark – (IV/1)

Barth, K., (1955/1958) *Church Dogmatics vol. IV, part 2* E. T. by G.W. Bromiley, edited by G.W. Bromiley and T.F. Torrance, Edinburgh: T. & T. Clark – (IV/2)

Barth, K., (1959/1961) *Church Dogmatics vol. IV, part 3.1* E. T. by G.W. Bromiley, edited by G.W. Bromiley and T.F. Torrance, Edinburgh: T. & T. Clark – (IV/3.1)

Barth, K., (1959/1962) *Church Dogmatics vol. IV, part 3.2* E. T. by G.W. Bromiley, edited by G.W. Bromiley and T.F. Torrance, Edinburgh: T. & T. Clark – (IV/3.2)

Barth, K., (1967/1969) *Church Dogmatics vol. IV, part 4, fragment* E. T. by G.W. Bromiley, edited by G.W. Bromiley and T.F. Torrance, Edinburgh: T. & T. Clark – (IV/4)

Barth, K., (1975/1981) *The Christian Life* E. T. by G.W. Bromiley, Edinburgh: T. & T. Clark

Bennett, M.L.B., (1985) *Christianity Explained* London: Narrowgate Press

Berkouwer, G.C., (1956) *The Triumph of Grace in the Theology of Karl Barth* E.T. by H.R.Boer, London: Paternoster Press

Bonhoeffer, D., (1927/1963) 3rd edn. *Sanctorum Communio* E. T. by R. Gregor Smith, London: Collins

Bradley, I., (1995) *The Power of Sacrifice* London: Darton, Longman and Todd

Bromiley, G.W., (1979) *Introduction to the Theology of Karl Barth* Edinburgh: T. & T. Clark

Bruce, F.F., (1964) *The Epistle to the Hebrews* The New London Commentary on the New Testament, London: Marshall, Morgan and Scott

Brunner, E., (1934/1927) *The Mediator* E. T. by O. Wyon, London: Lutterworth Press

Brunner, E., (1949) *The Christian Doctrine of God* E. T. by O. Wyon, London: Lutterworth Press

Buckley, J.J., (2000) 'Community, baptism and Lord's Supper', in John Webster, ed., *The Cambridge Companion to Karl Barth* Cambridge: Cambridge University Press

Bushnell, H., (1866) *The Vicarious Sacrifice* London: Alexander Strahan

Caird, G.B., (1956) *Principalities and Powers* Oxford: Clarendon Press

Caird, G.B., and Hurst, L.D. (1994) *New Testament Theology* Oxford: Clarendon Press

Calvin, J., (1536/1989) *The Institutes of the Christian Religion* E. T. by Henry Beveridge, Grand Rapis: Eerdmans

Campbell, J. McLeod, (1886) 5th edn. *The Nature of the Atonement* London: Macmillan

Carr, A.W., (1981) *Angels and Principalities* Cambridge: Cambridge University Press

Carson, D.A., (1991) *The Gospel According to John* Leicester: Inter-Varsity Press

Cave, S., (1937) *The Doctrine of the Work of Christ* London: University of London Press and Hodder and Stoughton

Cleverley Ford, D.W., (1993) *Preaching on the Crucifixion* London: Mowbray

Cole, R.A., (1973) *Exodus* Tyndale Old Testament Commentaries, Leicester: Inter-Varsity Press

Cottrell, S., Croft, S., Finney, J., Lawson F., and Warren, R., (1996) *Emmaus: The Way of Faith* Stage 2, Nurture, London: National Society/Church House Publishing, and Swindon: The Bible Society

Cranfield, C.E.B., (1977) *The Gospel according to Mark* The Cambridge Greek Testament Commentary, Cambridge: Cambridge University Press

Cunningham, R.M., (1994) *The DC Course* Leicester: Universities and Colleges Christian fellowship

Dabney, D.L., (2001) 'Justified by the Spirit', *International Journal of Systematic Theology* vol. 3, no. 1

Dale, R.W., (1888) 11th edn. *The Atonement* London: Congregational Union of England and Wales

Daly, R.J., (1978) *The Origins of the Christian Doctrine of Sacrifice* London: Darton, Longman and Todd

Denney, J., (1903) *The Atonement and the Modern Mind* London: Hodder and Stoughton

Denney, J., (1918/1959) *The Christian Doctrine of Reconciliation* Carlisle: Paternoster

Dillistone, F.W., (1983) 'Atonement', in Alan Richardson and John Bowden, ed., *A New Dictionary of Christian Theology* London: SCM Press

Dillistone, F.W., (1984) 2nd edn. *The Christian Understanding of Atonement* London: SCM Press

Dix, G., (1945) *The Shape of the Liturgy* London: A. & C. Black

Doctrine Commission of the Church of England (1995) *The Mystery of Salvation* London: Church House Publishing

Dunn, J.D.G., (1988) *Romans 1-8* Word Biblical Commentary, vol 38A, Dallas, Texas: Word Books

Farrow, D., (1999) 'Robert Jenson's Systematic Theology, Three Responses', *International Journal of Systematic Theology* vol. 1, no. 1, p. 92

Fee, G.D., (1987) *The First Epistle to the Corinthians* The New International Commentary of the New Testament, Grand Rapids: Eerdmans

Feenstra, R.J. and Plantinga Jr, C. eds., *Trinity, Incarnation and Atonement* Indiana, USA: University of Notre Dame Press

Fiddes, P.S., (1989) *Past Event and Present Salvation: The Christian Idea of Atonement* London: Darton, Longman and Todd

Ford, D.F., (1985) *Barth and God's Story* Frankfurt: Verlag Peter Lang

Ford, D.F., (1999) *Self and Salvation* Cambridge: Cambridge University Press

Forsyth, P.T., (1902) *The Atonement in Modern Religious Thought* London: James

Clarke

Forsyth, P.T., (1907) *Positive Preaching and the Modern Mind* London: Independent Press

Forsyth, P.T., (1909) *The Person and Place of Jesus Christ* London: Independent Press

Forsyth, P.T., (1909/1997) *The Cruciality of the Cross* Carlisle: Paternoster Press

Forsyth, P.T., (1910/1938 with memoir) *The Work of Christ* London: Independent Press

Forsyth, P.T., (1912/1952) 2nd edn. *The Principle of Authority in Relation to Certainty Sanctity and Society* London: Independent Press

Forsyth, P.T., (1912/1955) 2nd edn. *Faith, Freedom and the Future* London: Independent Press

Forsyth, P.T., (1915/1987) *The Preaching of Jesus and the Gospel of Christ* Blackwood, South Australia: New Creation Publications

Forsyth, P.T., (1916/1949) *The Soul of Prayer* London: Independent Press

Forsyth, P.T., (1917/1948) *The Justification of God* London: Latimer House

Forsyth, P.T., (1917) *Lectures on the Church and the Sacraments* London: Longmans, Green and Co.

Franks, R.S., (1918/1962) *The Work of Christ* (the 1918 edition was entitled, *A History of the Doctrine of the Work of Christ*) Edinburgh: Thomas Nelson

Garvie, A.E., (1944) 'A Cross-Centered Theology', *Congregational Quarterly* 22

Gledhill, R., ed. (1995) *The Times Book of Best Sermons* London: Cassell

Gledhill, R., ed. (1996) *The Times Best Sermons of 1996* London: Cassell

Gledhill, R., ed. (1997) *The Times Best Sermons of 1998* London: Cassell

Gledhill, R., ed. (1999) *The Fourth Times Book of Best Sermons* London: Cassell

Gledhill, R., ed. (1999) *The Fifth Times Book of Best Sermons* London: Cassell

Goldingay, J., ed. (1995) *Atonement Today* London: SPCK

Gordon, E., (1967) *Miracle on the River Kwai* London: Collins

Grant, C., (1986) 'The Abandonment of Atonement', *Kings Theological Review*, 9

Green, M., (1979) *Why bother with Jesus?* London: Hodder and Stoughton

Grey, M., (1989) *Redeeming the Dream: Feminism, Redemption and Christian Tradition* London: SPCK

Gumbel, N., (1993) *Questions of Life* Eastbourne: Kingsway

Gunton, C.E., (1988) *The Actuality of Atonement* Edinburgh: T. & T. Clark

Gunton, C.E., (1997) 2nd edn. *Yesterday and Today* London: SPCK

Gunton, C.E., (2000) *Intellect and Action* Edinburgh: T. & T. Clark

Gunton, C.E., (2001) 'Towards an Eschatology of Church membership', *International Journal of Systematic Theology* vol. 3, no. 1, p. 195

Gunton, C.E., (2002) *The Christian Faith* Oxford: Blackwell

Harnack, A. von, (1893/1899) *History of Dogma* vol. VI, E. T. by W. McGilchrist, London, Edinburgh and Oxford: William and Norgate

Hart, T., ed. (1995) *Justice the True and Only Mercy* Edinburgh: T. & T. Clark

Hays, R.B., (1996) *The Moral Vision of the New Testament* Edinburgh: T. & T. Clark

Heim, D.K., (1952/1959) 2nd edn. *Jesus the World's Perfector: The Atonement and the Renewal of the World* E.T. by D.H. van Daalen, Edinburgh and London: Oliver and Boyd

Hengel, M., (1980/1981) *The Atonement: The Origins of the Doctrine in the New Testament* E. T. by J. Bowden, London: SCM Press

Hodges, H.A., (1955) *The Pattern of Atonement* London: SCM Press

Holmes, S., (1999) 'Edwards on the Will', *International Journal of Systematic Theology* vol. 1, no. 3, p. 271

Hooker, M.D., (1994) *Not Ashamed of the Gospel* Carlisle: Paternoster Press

Hughes, T.H., (1940) 'Dr Forsyth's View of the Atonement' *Congregational Quarterly* 18

Hughes, T.H., (1949) *The Atonement: Modern Theories of the Doctrine* London: George Allen and Unwin

Hunsinger, G., (1991) *How to Read Karl Barth* Oxford: Oxford University Press

Hunsinger, G., (1998) 'The Politics of the Non-violent God', *Scottish Journal of Theology*, vol. 51, no. 1

Hunter, A.M., (1974) *P.T. Forsyth* London: SCM Press

Hurst, L.D. and Wright, N.T., eds. (1987) *The Glory of Christ in the New Testament* Oxford: Clarendon Press

Hyatt, J.P., (1980) rev. edn. *Exodus* The New Century Bible Commentary, London: Marshall, Morgan and Scott

Jenson, R.W., (1963) *Alpha and Omega: A Study in the Theology of Karl Barth* New York: Thomas Nelson

Jeremias, J., (1964/1966) *The Eucharistic Words of Jesus* New Testament Library, E. T. by N. Perrin, London, SCM Press

John, J., (2000) *Calling Out* Milton Keynes: Word

Johnson, W.S., (1997) *The Mystery of God* Kentucky: Westminster John Knox Press

Jüngel, E., (1986) *Karl Barth: A Theological Legacy* Philadelphia: Westminster Press

Jüngel, E., (1999) 'On the Doctrine of Justification', *International Journal of Systematic Theology* vol. 1, no.1, p. 26.

Kant, I., (1794/1960) *Religion Within the Limits of Reason Alone* E. T. by T.M. Greene and H.H. Hudson, New York: Harper and Row

Kapic, K., (2001) 'The Son's Assumption of a Human Nature: A Call for Clarity', *International Journal of Systematic Theology* vol. 3, no. 2, pp. 154ff

Kelsey, D.H., (1975 *The Uses of Scripture in Recent Theology* London: SCM Press

Kidner, D., (1967) *Genesis* Tyndale Old Testament Commentaries, Leicester: Inter-Varsity Press

Kittel, G., ed. (1949f, 1964f) *Theological Dictionary of the New Testament* vol. I,

Grand Rapids: Eerdmans

Krötke, W., (2000) 'Hope in the Last Judgement and Human Dignity,'   *International Journal of Systematic Theology*, vol. 2, no. 3, pp. 270ff.

Küng, H., (1957/1964) *Justification: The Doctrine of Karl Barth and a Catholic Reflection* E. T. by T. Collins, E.E. Tolk and D. Grandskou, London: Burns and Oates

Lane, W.L., (1974) *The Gospel of Mark* The New International Commentary of the New Testament, Grand Rapids: Eerdmans

Leivestad, R., (1955) *Christ the Conqueror* London: SPCK

Letham, R., (1993) *The Work of Christ* Leicester: Inter-Varsity Press

Luther, M., (1535/1953) *Commentary on the Epistle to the Galatians* E. T. by P.S. Watson, London: James Clarke and Co.

Lyonnet, S. and Sabourin, L., (1970) *Sin, Redemption and Sacrifice – A Biblical and Patristic Study* E. T. by L. Sabourin, Analecta Biblica 48, Rome: Biblical Institute Press

MacKinnon, D.M., (1966) 'Subjective and Objective Conceptions of Atonement' in *Prospects for Theology: Essays in Honour of H.H. Farmer* ed. F.G. Healey, Letchworth: Nisbet

Marshall, I.H., (1978) *The Gospel of Luke* The New International Greek Testament Commentary, Exeter: Paternoster Press

Marshall, I.H., (1980) *Acts* Leicester: Inter-Varsity Press

Maurice, F.D., (1893) 2nd edn. *The Christian Doctrine of Sacrifice* London: Macmillan

McCulloh, G.W., (1990) *Christ's Person and Life-Work in the Theology of Albrecht Ritschl with Special Attention to Minus Triplex* Maryland: University Press of America

McGrath, A.E., (1985) 'The Moral Theory of the Atonement: An historical and theological critique', *Scottish Journal of Theology* 38

McGrath, A.E., (1994) 2nd edn. *The Making of Modern German Christology* Leicester: Apollos

McIntyre, J., (1954) *St Anselm and his Critics: A Re-interpretation of the Cur Deus Homo* Edinburgh and London: Oliver and Boyd

McIntyre, J., (1992) *The Shape of Soteriology* Edinburgh: T. & T. Clark

McKenzie, J.L., (1968) *Second Isaiah* New York: Doubleday

Moberley, R.C., (1902) *Atonement and Personality* London: John Murray

Molnar, P.D., (1996) *Karl Barth and the Theology of the Lord's Supper* New York: Lang

Moltmann, J., (1972/1973) *The Crucified God* E. T. by R. A. Wilson and John Bowden, London: SCM Press

Morris, L., (1965) 2nd edn. *The Apostolic Preaching of the Cross* Grand Rapids, Michigan: Eerdmans

Morris, L., (1965) *The Cross in the New Testament* Grand Rapids, Michigan: Eerdmans

Moses, J., (1992) *The Sacrifice of God: A Holistic Theory of Atonement* Norwich: Canterbury Press

Moule, C.F.D., (1954) 'The Judgement theme in the Sacraments' in Daube, W. and Davies, W.D., *The Background of the New Testament and its eschatology* Cambridge: Cambridge University Press

Mozley, J.K., (1915) *The Doctrine of the Atonement* London: Duckworth

Mozley, J.K., (1925) *The Heart of the Gospel* London: SPCK

Nolland, J., (1993) *Luke 9:21-18:34* Word Biblical Commentary, vol. 35B, Dallas, Texas: Word

Pannenberg, W., (1991/1994) *Systematic Theology, vol. 2* E. T. by G.W. Bromiley, Grand Rapids: Eerdmans

Paul, R.S., (1961) *The Atonement and the Sacraments* London: Hodder and Stoughton

Peterson, R.A. Sr., (1999) 2nd edn., *Calvin on the Atonement* Ross-shire: Christian Focus Publications

Quick, O.C., (1938) *Doctrines of the Creed* London: Nisbet

Rashdall, H., (1919) *The Idea of Atonement in Christian Theology* London: Macmillan

Richardson, A. and Bowden, J., ed. (1983) *A New Dictionary of Christian Theology* London: SCM Press

Riddell, J.G., (1938) *Why did Jesus die?* London: Hodder and Stoughton Ritschl, A., (1872) *A Critical History of the Christian Doctrine of Justification and Reconciliation* E.T. by J.S. Black, Edinburgh: Edmonston and Douglas

Ritschl, A., (1876/1900) 3rd edn. *The Christian Doctrine of Justification and Reconciliation* vol. 3, E. T. by J.S. Black, Edinburgh: T. & T. Clark

Rivière, J., (1905) *Le Dogma de la Rédemption* Paris: Victoire Lecoffre

Rodgers, J.H., (1965) *The Theology of P.T. Forsyth* London: Independent Press

Rogers, C.F., (1932) *The Atonement* London: SPCK

Saiving Goldstein, V., (1960) 'The human situation: A feminine view', *Journal of Religion*, vol. 40

Schweizer, E., (1984) *The Good News According to Luke* E. T. by D.E. Green, London: SPCK

Selby, P., (1997) *Grace and Mortgage* London: Darton, Longman and Todd

Smith, H.M., (1925) *Atonement* London: Macmillan

Sölle, D., (1967) *Christ the Representative* London: SCM Press

Soskice, J M., (1985) *Metaphor and Religious Language* Oxford: Clarendon Press

Storr, V.F., (1924) 2nd edn. *The Problem of the Cross* London: SCM Press

Stott, J.R.W., (1986) *The Cross of Christ* Leicester: Inter-Varsity Press

Swinburne, R., (1989) *Responsibility and Atonement* Oxford: Clarendon Press

Sykes, S., ed. (1991) *Sacrifice and Redemption: Durham Essays in Theology* Cambridge: Cambridge University Press

Sykes, S., (1997) *The Story of Atonement* London: Darton, Longman and Todd

Talbert, C.H., (1990) *Reading Luke* A Commentary for Preachers, London: SPCK

Taylor, V., (1945) 2nd edn., *The Atonement in New Testament Teaching* London: Epworth Press

Thompson, K.C., (1962) *Once for All: A Study of the Christian Doctrine of Atonement and Salvation* London: Faith Press

Tidball, D., (2001) *The Message of the Cross* Leicester: Inter-Varsity Press

Torrance, T.F., (1975) *Theology in Reconciliation* London: Geoffrey Chapman

Torrance, T.F., (1990) *Karl Barth, Biblical and Evangelical Theologian* Edinburgh: T. & T. Clark

Turner, H.E.W., (1959) *The Meaning of the Cross* London: Mowbray

Vidler, A.R., ed. (1962) *Soundings: Essays Concerning Christian Understanding* Cambridge: Cambridge University Press

Von Rad, G., (1957/1975) *Old Testament Theology* vol. 1, E. T. by D.M.G. Stalker, London: SCM Press

Watson, D., (1976) *I Believe in Evangelism* London: Hodder and Stoughton

Watson, D., (1980), 3rd edn., *My God is Real* Eastbourne, Falcon

Watts, J.D.W., (1987) *Isaiah 34-44* Word Biblical Commentary vol 25, Texas: Word

Webster, J., (2000) *Outstanding Christian Thinkers: Barth* London: Continuum

Webster, J., (2000) *The Cambridge Companion to Karl Barth* Cambridge: Cambridge University Press

Webster, J., (1995) *Barth's Ethics of Reconciliation* Cambridge: Cambridge University Press

Westermann, C., (1969) *Isaiah 40-66: A commentary* Old Testament Library, London: SCM Press

Whale, J.S., (1960) *Victor and Victim* Cambridge: Cambridge University Press

White, V., (1991) *Atonement and Incarnation* Cambridge: Cambridge University Press

Wink, W., (1984) *Naming the Powers* Philadelphia: Fortress Press

Winter, M., (1995) *The Atonement* London: Geoffrey Chapman

World Council of Churches (1982) *Baptism, Eucharist and Ministry*, Faith and Order paper no. 111, Geneva: World Council of Churches

Wright, N.T., (1996) *Jesus and the Victory of God* London: SPCK

Young, F.M., (1975) *Sacrifice and the Death of Christ* London: SPCK

Young, F.M., (1979) *The Use of Sacrificial Ideas in Greek Christian Writers from the New Testament to John Chrysostom* Cambridge MA: The Philadelphia Patristic Foundation

Index

scripture; 42, 44-46, 49-51, 54-55, 58-
59, 61-62, 65, 68, 89-90, 140, 158,
204
Selby, Peter; 41
self-substitution; 12, 115
Sell, Alan; 84, 85, 105
service; 125
sin; 7, 11, 17, 19, 22-23, 32-33, 35-37,
43-44, 47, 55, 59, 61, 65, 68, 72, 77-
78, 84, 86-88, 91-92, 94-99, 101, 103,
108, 111-122, 124-125, 127, 129-131,
136, 141, 147, 150-152, 154-169, 171,
173--183, 185-187, 190-199, 203-208,
211-213
slavery; 28, 43
sloth; 175, 176
sola scriptura; 65
Soskice, Janet Martin; 66
Storr, V.F.; 22, 23
Stott, John; 12, 20, 34, 41
substitution; 13-14, 19-20, 51, 84-85,
114-115, 151, 162, 166, 211
punishment; 20
suffering; 7, 35, 52
Swinburne, Richard; 41
Sykes, Stephen; 41, 74, 169

T

Taylor, Vincent; 96
Tertullian; 155
theories of the atonement; 41
theory of atonement; 22, 167
Thompson, John; 209
Tidball, Derek; 41
Til, Cornelius van; 130
The Times Book of Best Sermons; 4
Torrance, T.F.; 113, 147, 183, 189
tradition; 51, 65, 68

U

universalism; 130-131, 133-134

V

victory; xiii, 2-3, 5-8, 15-17, 19, 24-25,
27-28, 30, 33-37, 39-40, 42, 44-45,
52, 53, 55-57, 62, 65-69, 71-72,
74-76, 78-79, 88, 108, 116, 139, 143,
145-154, 156, 158, 166-171, 203-207,
211, 213
of Christ; 36
of God; 62
vindication; viii, 73-74, 83, 86, 88-90,
122, 126, 155, 163-164, 168, 173,
177-179, 181, 206, 211
vocation; 112
Von Rad, G.; 166

W

Watson, David; 7
Watts, John D.W.; 119
Webster, John; 133, 183, 186-187, 200
Westcott, B.F.; 96
Westermann, Claus; 119
Whale, J.S.; 38
White, Vernon; 121
wickedness; 111, 117, 163
Williamson, Colin; 5
Winter, Michael; 41
wrath; 87-88, 96, 119-120, 135, 179, 209
of God; 1, 50, 59, 61, 182
Wrede, William; 54
Wright, N.T.; 40, 48

Y

Young, Frances; 32, 33, 36, 38, 42-43,
45, 59-62, 67-68, 92, 157-159, 165,
167, 169, 204

Paternoster Biblical Monographs

(All titles uniform with this volume)
Dates in bold are of projected publication

Joseph Abraham
Eve: Accused or Acquitted?
A Reconsideration of Feminist Readings of the Creation Narrative Texts in Genesis 1–3

Two contrary views dominate contemporary feminist biblical scholarship. One finds in the Bible an unequivocal equality between the sexes from the very creation of humanity, whilst the other sees the biblical text as irredeemably patriarchal and androcentric. Dr Abraham enters into dialogue with both camps as well as introducing his own method of approach. An invaluable tool for any one who is interested in this contemporary debate.

2002 / 0-85364-971-5 / xxiv + 272pp

Octavian D. Baban
Mimesis and Luke's on the Road Encounters in Luke-Acts
Luke's Theology of the Way and its Literary Representation

The book argues on theological and literary (mimetic) grounds that Luke's on-the-road encounters, especially those belonging to the post-Easter period, are part of his complex theology of the Way. Jesus' teaching and that of the apostles is presented by Luke as a challenging answer to the Hellenistic reader's thirst for adventure, good literature, and existential paradigms.

2005 */ 1-84227-253-5 / approx. 374pp*

Paul Barker
The Triumph of Grace in Deuteronomy

This book is a textual and theological analysis of the interaction between the sin and faithlessness of Israel and the grace of Yahweh in response, looking especially at Deuteronomy chapters 1–3, 8–10 and 29–30. The author argues that the grace of Yahweh is determinative for the ongoing relationship between Yahweh and Israel and that Deuteronomy anticipates and fully expects Israel to be faithless.

2004 / 1-84227-226-8 / xxii + 270pp

Jonathan F. Bayes
The Weakness of the Law
God's Law and the Christian in New Testament Perspective

A study of the four New Testament books which refer to the law as weak (Acts, Romans, Galatians, Hebrews) leads to a defence of the third use in the Reformed debate about the law in the life of the believer.

2000 / 0-85364-957-X / xii + 244pp

Mark Bonnington
The Antioch Episode of Galatians 2:11-14 in Historical and Cultural Context
The Galatians 2 'incident' in Antioch over table-fellowship suggests significant disagreement between the leading apostles. This book analyses the background to the disagreement by locating the incident within the dynamics of social interaction between Jews and Gentiles. It proposes a new way of understanding the relationship between the individuals and issues involved.
2005 / 1-84227-050-8 / approx. 350pp

David Bostock
A Portrayal of Trust
The Theme of Faith in the Hezekiah Narratives
This study provides detailed and sensitive readings of the Hezekiah narratives (2 Kings 18–20 and Isaiah 36–39) from a theological perspective. It concentrates on the theme of faith, using narrative criticism as its methodology. Attention is paid especially to setting, plot, point of view and characterization within the narratives. A largely positive portrayal of Hezekiah emerges that underlines the importance and relevance of scripture.
2005 / 1-84227-314-0 / approx. 300pp

Mark Bredin
Jesus, Revolutionary of Peace
A Non-violent Christology in the Book of Revelation
This book aims to demonstrate that the figure of Jesus in the Book of Revelation can best be understood as an active non-violent revolutionary.
2003 / 1-84227-153-9 / xviii + 262pp

Robinson Butarbutar
Paul and Conflict Resolution
An Exegetical Study of Paul's Apostolic Paradigm in 1 Corinthians 9
The author sees the apostolic paradigm in 1 Corinthians 9 as part of Paul's unified arguments in 1 Corinthians 8–10 in which he seeks to mediate in the dispute over the issue of food offered to idols. The book also sees its relevance for dispute-resolution today, taking the conflict within the author's church as an example.
2006 / 1-84227-315-9 / approx. 280pp

Daniel J-S Chae
Paul as Apostle to the Gentiles
*His Apostolic Self-awareness and its Influence on the Soteriological Argument
in Romans*
Opposing 'the post-Holocaust interpretation of Romans', Daniel Chae com-
petently demonstrates that Paul argues for the equality of Jew and Gentile in
Romans. Chae's fresh exegetical interpretation is academically outstanding and
spiritually encouraging.
1997 / 0-85364-829-8 / xiv + 378pp

Luke L. Cheung
The Genre, Composition and Hermeneutics of the Epistle of James
The present work examines the employment of the wisdom genre with a certain
compositional structure and the interpretation of the law through the Jesus
tradition of the double love command by the author of the Epistle of James to
serve his purpose in promoting perfection and warning against doubleness
among the eschatologically renewed people of God in the Diaspora.
2003 / 1-84227-062-1 / xvi + 372pp

Youngmo Cho
Spirit and Kingdom in the Writings of Luke and Paul
The relationship between Spirit and Kingdom is a relatively unexplored area in
Lukan and Pauline studies. This book offers a fresh perspective of two biblical
writers on the subject. It explores the difference between Luke's and Paul's
understanding of the Spirit by examining the specific question of the
relationship of the concept of the Spirit to the concept of the Kingdom of God in
each writer.
2005 */ 1-84227-316-7 / approx. 270pp*

Andrew C. Clark
Parallel Lives
The Relation of Paul to the Apostles in the Lucan Perspective
This study of the Peter-Paul parallels in Acts argues that their purpose was to
emphasize the themes of continuity in salvation history and the unity of the
Jewish and Gentile missions. New light is shed on Luke's literary techniques,
partly through a comparison with Plutarch.
2001 / 1-84227-035-4 / xviii + 386pp

Andrew D. Clarke
Secular and Christian Leadership in Corinth
A Socio-Historical and Exegetical Study of 1 Corinthians 1–6
This volume is an investigation into the leadership structures and dynamics of first-century Roman Corinth. These are compared with the practice of leadership in the Corinthian Christian community which are reflected in 1 Corinthians 1–6, and contrasted with Paul's own principles of Christian leadership.
2005 / 1-84227-229-2 / 200pp

Stephen Finamore
God, Order and Chaos
René Girard and the Apocalypse
Readers are often disturbed by the images of destruction in the book of Revelation and unsure why they are unleashed after the exaltation of Jesus. This book examines past approaches to these texts and uses René Girard's theories to revive some old ideas and propose some new ones.
2005 / 1-84227-197-0 / approx. 344pp

David G. Firth
Surrendering Retribution in the Psalms
Responses to Violence in the Individual Complaints
In *Surrendering Retribution in the Psalms*, David Firth examines the ways in which the book of Psalms inculcates a model response to violence through the repetition of standard patterns of prayer. Rather than seeking justification for retributive violence, Psalms encourages not only a surrender of the right of retribution to Yahweh, but also sets limits on the retribution that can be sought in imprecations. Arising initially from the author's experience in South Africa, the possibilities of this model to a particular context of violence is then briefly explored.
2005 / 1-84227-337-X / xviii + 154pp

Scott J. Hafemann
Suffering and Ministry in the Spirit
Paul's Defence of His Ministry in II Corinthians 2:14–3:3
Shedding new light on the way Paul defended his apostleship, the author offers a careful, detailed study of 2 Corinthians 2:14–3:3 linked with other key passages throughout 1 and 2 Corinthians. Demonstrating the unity and coherence of Paul's argument in this passage, the author shows that Paul's suffering served as the vehicle for revealing God's power and glory through the Spirit.
2000 / 0-85364-967-7 / xiv + 262pp

Scott J. Hafemann
Paul, Moses and the History of Israel
The Letter/Spirit Contrast and the Argument from Scripture in 2 Corinthians 3
An exegetical study of the call of Moses, the second giving of the Law (Exodus 32–34), the new covenant, and the prophetic understanding of the history of Israel in 2 Corinthians 3. Hafemann's work demonstrates Paul's contextual use of the Old Testament and the essential unity between the Law and the Gospel within the context of the distinctive ministries of Moses and Paul.
2005 / 1-84227-317-5 / xii + 498pp

Douglas S. McComiskey
Lukan Theology in the Light of the Gospel's Literary Structure
Luke's Gospel was purposefully written with theology embedded in its patterned literary structure. A critical analysis of this cyclical structure provides new windows into Luke's interpretation of the individual pericopes comprising the Gospel and illuminates several of his theological interests.
2004 / 1-84227-148-2 / xviii + 388pp

Stephen Motyer
Your Father the Devil?
A New Approach to John and 'The Jews'
Who are 'the Jews' in John's Gospel? Defending John against the charge of antisemitism, Motyer argues that, far from demonising the Jews, the Gospel seeks to present Jesus as 'Good News for Jews' in a late first century setting.
1997 / 0-85364-832-8 / xiv + 260pp

Esther Ng
Reconstructing Christian Origins?
The Feminist Theology of Elizabeth Schüssler Fiorenza: An Evaluation
In a detailed evaluation, the author challenges Elizabeth Schüssler Fiorenza's reconstruction of early Christian origins and her underlying presuppositions. The author also presents her own views on women's roles both then and now.
2002 / 1-84227-055-9 / xxiv + 468pp

Robin Parry
Old Testament Story and Christian Ethics
The Rape of Dinah as a Case Study

What is the role of story in ethics and, more particularly, what is the role of Old Testament story in Christian ethics? This book, drawing on the work of contemporary philosophers, argues that narrative is crucial in the ethical shaping of people and, drawing on the work of contemporary Old Testament scholars, that story plays a key role in Old Testament ethics. Parry then argues that when situated in canonical context Old Testament stories can be reappropriated by Christian readers in their own ethical formation. The shocking story of the rape of Dinah and the massacre of the Shechemites provides a fascinating case study for exploring the parameters within which Christian ethical appropriations of Old Testament stories can live.

2004 / 1-84227-210-1 / xx + 350pp

Ian Paul
Power to See the World Anew
The Value of Paul Ricoeur's Hermeneutic of Metaphor in Interpreting the Symbolism of Revelation 12 and 13

This book is a study of the hermeneutics of metaphor of Paul Ricoeur, one of the most important writers on hermeneutics and metaphor of the last century. It sets out the key points of his theory, important criticisms of his work, and how his approach, modified in the light of these criticisms, offers a methodological framework for reading apocalyptic texts.

2006 / 1-84227-056-7 / approx. 350pp

Robert L. Plummer
Paul's Understanding of the Church's Mission
Did the Apostle Paul Expect the Early Christian Communities to Evangelize?

This book engages in a careful study of Paul's letters to determine if the apostle expected the communities to which he wrote to engage in missionary activity. It helpfully summarizes the discussion on this debated issue, judiciously handling contested texts, and provides a way forward in addressing this critical question. While admitting that Paul rarely explicitly commands the communities he founded to evangelize, Plummer amasses significant incidental data to provide a convincing case that Paul did indeed expect his churches to engage in mission activity. Throughout the study, Plummer progressively builds a theological basis for the church's mission that is both distinctively Pauline and compelling.

2006 / 1-84227-333-7 / approx. 324pp

David Powys
'Hell': A Hard Look at a Hard Question
The Fate of the Unrighteous in New Testament Thought
This comprehensive treatment seeks to unlock the original meaning of terms and phrases long thought to support the traditional doctrine of hell. It concludes that there is an alternative—one which is more biblical, and which can positively revive the rationale for Christian mission.
1997 / 0-85364-831-X / xxii + 478pp

Sorin Sabou
Between Horror and Hope
Paul's Metaphorical Language of Death in Romans 6.1-11
This book argues that Paul's metaphorical language of death in Romans 6.1-11 conveys two aspects: horror and hope. The 'horror' aspect is conveyed by the 'crucifixion' language, and the 'hope' aspect by 'burial' language. The life of the Christian believer is understood, as relationship with sin is concerned ('death to sin'), between these two realities: horror and hope.
2005 / 1-84227-322-1 / approx. 224pp

Rosalind Selby
The Comical Doctrine
The Epistemology of New Testament Hermeneutics
This book argues that the gospel breaks through postmodernity's critique of truth and the referential possibilities of textuality with its gift of grace. With a rigorous, philosophical challenge to modernist and postmodernist assumptions, Selby offers an alternative epistemology to all who would still read with faith *and* with academic credibility.
2005 / 1-84227-212-8 / approx. 350pp

Kiwoong Son
Zion Symbolism in Hebrews
Hebrews 12.18-24 as a Hermeneutical Key to the Epistle
This book challenges the general tendency of understanding the Epistle to the Hebrews against a Hellenistic background and suggests that the Epistle should be understood in the light of the Jewish apocalyptic tradition. The author especially argues for the importance of the theological symbolism of Sinai and Zion (Heb. 12:18-24) as it provides the Epistle's theological background as well as the rhetorical basis of the superiority motif of Jesus throughout the Epistle.
2005 / 1-84227-368-X / approx. 280pp

Kevin Walton
Thou Traveller Unknown
The Presence and Absence of God in the Jacob Narrative
The author offers a fresh reading of the story of Jacob in the book of Genesis through the paradox of divine presence and absence. The work also seeks to make a contribution to Pentateuchal studies by bringing together a close reading of the final text with historical critical insights, doing justice to the text's historical depth, final form and canonical status.

2003 / 1-84227-059-1 / xvi + 238pp

George M. Wieland
The Significance of Salvation
A Study of Salvation Language in the Pastoral Epistles
The language and ideas of salvation pervade the three Pastoral Epistles. This study offers a close examination of their soteriological statements. In all three letters the idea of salvation is found to play a vital paraenetic role, but each also exhibits distinctive soteriological emphases. The results challenge common assumptions about the Pastoral Epistles as a corpus.

***2005** / 1-84227-257-8 / approx. 324pp*

Alistair Wilson
When Will These Things Happen?
A Study of Jesus as Judge in Matthew 21–25
This study seeks to allow Matthew's carefully constructed presentation of Jesus to be given full weight in the modern evaluation of Jesus' eschatology. Careful analysis of the text of Matthew 21–25 reveals Jesus to be standing firmly in the Jewish prophetic and wisdom traditions as he proclaims and enacts imminent judgement on the Jewish authorities then boldly claims the central role in the final and universal judgement.

2004 / 1-84227-146-6 / xxii + 272pp

Lindsay Wilson
Joseph Wise and Otherwise
The Intersection of Covenant and Wisdom in Genesis 37–50
This book offers a careful literary reading of Genesis 37–50 that argues that the Joseph story contains both strong covenant themes and many wisdom-like elements. The connections between the two helps to explore how covenant and wisdom might intersect in an integrated biblical theology.

2004 / 1-84227-140-7 / xvi + 340pp

Stephen I. Wright
The Voice of Jesus
Studies in the Interpretation of Six Gospel Parables
This literary study considers how the 'voice' of Jesus has been heard in different
periods of parable interpretation, and how the categories of figure and trope may
help us towards a sensitive reading of the parables today.
2000 / 0-85364-975-8 / xiv + 280pp

Paternoster
9 Holdom Avenue,
Bletchley,
Milton Keynes MK1 1QR,
United Kingdom
Web: www.authenticmedia.co.uk/paternoster

Paternoster Theological Monographs

(All titles uniform with this volume)
Dates in bold are of projected publication

Emil Bartos
Deification in Eastern Orthodox Theology
An Evaluation and Critique of the Theology of Dumitru Staniloae
Bartos studies a fundamental yet neglected aspect of Orthodox theology: deification. By examining the doctrines of anthropology, christology, soteriology and ecclesiology as they relate to deification, he provides an important contribution to contemporary dialogue between Eastern and Western theologians.

1999 / 0-85364-956-1 / xii + 370pp

Graham Buxton
The Trinity, Creation and Pastoral Ministry
Imaging the Perichoretic God
In this book the author proposes a three-way conversation between theology, science and pastoral ministry. His approach draws on a Trinitarian understanding of God as a relational being of love, whose life 'spills over' into all created reality, human and non-human. By locating human meaning and purpose within God's 'creation-community' this book offers the possibility of a transforming engagement between those in pastoral ministry and the scientific community.

2005 / 1-84227-369-8 / approx. 380 pp

Iain D. Campbell
Fixing the Indemnity
The Life and Work of George Adam Smith
When Old Testament scholar George Adam Smith (1856–1942) delivered the Lyman Beecher lectures at Yale University in 1899, he confidently declared that 'modern criticism has won its war against traditional theories. It only remains to fix the amount of the indemnity.' In this biography, Iain D. Campbell assesses Smith's critical approach to the Old Testament and evaluates its consequences, showing that Smith's life and work still raises questions about the relationship between biblical scholarship and evangelical faith.

2004 / 1-84227-228-4 / xx + 256pp

Tim Chester
Mission and the Coming of God
Eschatology, the Trinity and Mission in the Theology of Jürgen Moltmann
This book explores the theology and missiology of the influential contemporary theologian, Jürgen Moltmann. It highlights the important contribution Moltmann has made while offering a critique of his thought from an evangelical perspective. In so doing, it touches on pertinent issues for evangelical missiology. The conclusion takes Calvin as a starting point, proposing 'an eschatology of the cross' which offers a critique of the over-realised eschatologies in liberation theology and certain forms of evangelicalism.
2006 / 1-84227-320-5 / approx. 224pp

Sylvia Wilkey Collinson
Making Disciples
The Significance of Jesus' Educational Strategy for Today's Church
This study examines the biblical practice of discipling, formulates a definition, and makes comparisons with modern models of education. A recommendation is made for greater attention to its practice today.
2004 / 1-84227-116-4 / xiv + 278pp

Darrell Cosden
A Theology of Work
Work and the New Creation
Through dialogue with Moltmann, Pope John Paul II and others, this book develops a genitive 'theology of work', presenting a theological definition of work and a model for a theological ethics of work that shows work's nature, value and meaning now and eschatologically. Work is shown to be a transformative activity consisting of three dynamically inter-related dimensions: the instrumental, relational and ontological.
2005 / 1-84227-332-9 / xvi + 208pp

Stephen M. Dunning
The Crisis and the Quest
A Kierkegaardian Reading of Charles Williams
Employing Kierkegaardian categories and analysis, this study investigates both the central crisis in Charles Williams's authorship between hermetism and Christianity (Kierkegaard's Religions A and B), and the quest to resolve this crisis, a quest that ultimately presses the bounds of orthodoxy.
2000 / 0-85364-985-5 / xxiv + 254pp

Keith Ferdinando
The Triumph of Christ in African Perspective
A Study of Demonology and Redemption in the African Context
The book explores the implications of the gospel for traditional African fears of occult aggression. It analyses such traditional approaches to suffering and biblical responses to fears of demonic evil, concluding with an evaluation of African beliefs from the perspective of the gospel.
1999 / 0-85364-830-1 / xviii + 450pp

Andrew Goddard
Living the Word, Resisting the World
The Life and Thought of Jacques Ellul
This work offers a definitive study of both the life and thought of the French Reformed thinker Jacques Ellul (1912-1994). It will prove an indispensable resource for those interested in this influential theologian and sociologist and for Christian ethics and political thought generally.
2002 / 1-84227-053-2 / xxiv + 378pp

David Hilborn
The Words of our Lips
Language-Use in Free Church Worship
Studies of liturgical language have tended to focus on the written canons of Roman Catholic and Anglican communities. By contrast, David Hilborn analyses the more extemporary approach of English Nonconformity. Drawing on recent developments in linguistic pragmatics, he explores similarities and differences between 'fixed' and 'free' worship, and argues for the interdependence of each.
2006 / 0-85364-977-4 / approx. 350pp

Roger Hitching
The Church and Deaf People
A Study of Identity, Communication and Relationships with Special Reference to the Ecclesiology of Jürgen Moltmann
In *The Church and Deaf People* Roger Hitching sensitively examines the history and present experience of deaf people and finds similarities between aspects of sign language and Moltmann's theological method that 'open up' new ways of understanding theological concepts.
2003 / 1-84227-222-5 / xxii + 236pp

John G. Kelly
One God, One People
The Differentiated Unity of the People of God in the Theology of
Jürgen Moltmann
The author expounds and critiques Moltmann's doctrine of God and highlights the systematic connections between it and Moltmann's influential discussion of Israel. He then proposes a fresh approach to Jewish–Christian relations building on Moltmann's work using insights from Habermas and Rawls.
2005 / 0-85346-969-3 / approx. 350pp

Mark F.W. Lovatt
Confronting the Will-to-Power
A Reconsideration of the Theology of Reinhold Niebuhr
Confronting the Will-to-Power is an analysis of the theology of Reinhold Niebuhr, arguing that his work is an attempt to identify, and provide a practical theological answer to, the existence and nature of human evil.
2001 / 1-84227-054-0 / xviii + 216pp

Neil B. MacDonald
Karl Barth and the Strange New World within the Bible
Barth, Wittgenstein, and the Metadilemmas of the Enlightenment
Barth's discovery of the strange new world within the Bible is examined in the context of Kant, Hume, Overbeck, and, most importantly, Wittgenstein. MacDonald covers some fundamental issues in theology today: epistemology, the final form of the text and biblical truth-claims.
2000 / 0-85364-970-7 / xxvi + 374pp

Keith A. Mascord
Alvin Plantinga and Christian Apologetics
This book draws together the contributions of the philosopher Alvin Plantinga to the major contemporary challenges to Christian belief, highlighting in particular his ground-breaking work in epistemology and the problem of evil. Plantinga's theory that both theistic and Christian belief is warrantedly basic is explored and critiqued, and an assessment offered as to the significance of his work for apologetic theory and practice.
2005 / 1-84227-256-X / approx. 304pp

Gillian McCulloch
The Deconstruction of Dualism in Theology
With Reference to Ecofeminist Theology and New Age Spirituality
This book challenges eco-theological anti-dualism in Christian theology, arguing that dualism has a twofold function in Christian religious discourse. Firstly, it enables us to express the discontinuities and divisions that are part of the process of reality. Secondly, dualistic language allows us to express the mysteries of divine transcendence/immanence and the survival of the soul without collapsing into monism and materialism, both of which are problematic for Christian epistemology.
2002 / 1-84227-044-3 / xii + 282pp

Leslie McCurdy
Attributes and Atonement
The Holy Love of God in the Theology of P.T. Forsyth
Attributes and Atonement is an intriguing full-length study of P.T. Forsyth's doctrine of the cross as it relates particularly to God's holy love. It includes an unparalleled bibliography of both primary and secondary material relating to Forsyth.
1999 / 0-85364-833-6 / xiv + 328pp

Nozomu Miyahira
Towards a Theology of the Concord of God
A Japanese Perspective on the Trinity
This book introduces a new Japanese theology and a unique Trinitarian formula based on the Japanese intellectual climate: three betweennesses and one concord. It also presents a new interpretation of the Trinity, a co-subordinationism, which is in line with orthodox Trinitarianism; each single person of the Trinity is eternally and equally subordinate (or serviceable) to the other persons, so that they retain the mutual dynamic equality.
2000 / 0-85364-863-8 / xiv + 256pp

Eddy José Muskus
The Origins and Early Development of Liberation Theology in Latin America
With Particular Reference to Gustavo Gutiérrez
This work challenges the fundamental premise of Liberation Theology, 'opting for the poor', and its claim that Christ is found in them. It also argues that Liberation Theology emerged as a direct result of the failure of the Roman Catholic Church in Latin America.
2002 / 0-85364-974-X / xiv + 296pp

Jim Purves
The Triune God and the Charismatic Movement
A Critical Appraisal from a Scottish Perspective
All emotion and no theology? Or a fundamental challenge to reappraise and realign our trinitarian theology in the light of Christian experience? This study of charismatic renewal as it found expression within Scotland at the end of the twentieth century evaluates the use of Patristic, Reformed and contemporary models of the Trinity in explaining the workings of the Holy Spirit.
2004 / 1-84227-321-3 / xxiv + 246pp

Anna Robbins
Methods in the Madness
Diversity in Twentieth-Century Christian Social Ethics
The author compares the ethical methods of Walter Rauschenbusch, Reinhold Niebuhr and others. She argues that unless Christians are clear about the ways that theology and philosophy are expressed practically they may lose the ability to discuss social ethics across contexts, let alone reach effective agreements.
2004 / 1-84227-211-X / xx + 294pp

Ed Rybarczyk
Beyond Salvation
Eastern Orthodoxy and Classical Pentecostalism on Becoming Like Christ
At first glance eastern Orthodoxy and classical Pentecostalism seem quite distinct. This ground-breaking study shows they share much in common, especially as it concerns the experiential elements of following Christ. Both traditions assert that authentic Christianity transcends the wooden categories of modernism.
2004 / 1-84227-144-X / xii + 356pp

Signe Sandsmark
Is World View Neutral Education Possible and Desirable?
A Christian Response to Liberal Arguments
(Published jointly with The Stapleford Centre)
This book discusses reasons for belief in world view neutrality, and argues that 'neutral' education will have a hidden, but strong world view influence. It discusses the place for Christian education in the common school.
2000 / 0-85364-973-1 / xiv + 182pp

Hazel Sherman
Reading Zechariah
The Allegorical Tradition of Biblical Interpretation through the Commentary of
Didymus the Blind and Theodore of Mopsuestia
A close reading of the commentary on Zechariah by Didymus the Blind
alongside that of Theodore of Mopsuestia suggests that popular categorising of
Antiochene and Alexandrian biblical exegesis as 'historical' or 'allegorical' is
inadequate and misleading.
2005 / 1-84227-213-6 / approx. 280pp

Andrew Sloane
On Being a Christian in the Academy
Nicholas Wolterstorff and the Practice of Christian Scholarship
An exposition and critical appraisal of Nicholas Wolterstorff's epistemology in
the light of the philosophy of science, and an application of his thought to the
practice of Christian scholarship.
2003 / 1-84227-058-3 / xvi + 274pp

Damon W.K. So
Jesus' Revelation of His Father
A Narrative-Conceptual Study of the Trinity with Special Reference to
Karl Barth
This book explores the trinitarian dynamics in the context of Jesus' revelation of
his Father in his earthly ministry with references to key passages in Matthew's
Gospel. It develops from the exegeses of these passages a non-linear concept of
revelation which links Jesus' communion with his Father to his revelatory words
and actions through a nuanced understanding of the Holy Spirit, with references
to K. Barth, G.W.H. Lampe, J.D.G. Dunn and E. Irving.
2005 / 1-84227-323-X / approx. 380pp

Daniel Strange
The Possibility of Salvation Among the Unevangelised
An Analysis of Inclusivism in Recent Evangelical Theology
For evangelical theologians the 'fate of the unevangelised' impinges upon
fundamental tenets of evangelical identity. The position known as 'inclusivism',
defined by the belief that the unevangelised can be ontologically saved by Christ
whilst being epistemologically unaware of him, has been defended most
vigorously by the Canadian evangelical Clark H. Pinnock. Through a detailed
analysis and critique of Pinnock's work, this book examines a cluster of issues
surrounding the unevangelised and its implications for christology, soteriology
and the doctrine of revelation.
2002 / 1-84227-047-8 / xviii + 362pp

Scott Swain
God According to the Gospel
Biblical Narrative and the Identity of God in the Theology of Robert W. Jenson
Robert W. Jenson is one of the leading voices in contemporary Trinitarian theology. His boldest contribution in this area concerns his use of biblical narrative both to ground and explicate the Christian doctrine of God. *God According to the Gospel* critically examines Jenson's proposal and suggests an alternative way of reading the biblical portrayal of the triune God.
2006 / 1-84227-258-6 / approx. 180pp

Justyn Terry
The Justifying Judgement of God
A Reassessment of the Place of Judgement in the Saving Work of Christ
The argument of this book is that judgement, understood as the whole process of bringing justice, is the primary metaphor of atonement, with others, such as victory, redemption and sacrifice, subordinate to it. Judgement also provides the proper context for understanding penal substitution and the call to repentance, baptism, eucharist and holiness.
2005 / 1-84227-370-1 / approx. 274 pp

Graham Tomlin
The Power of the Cross
Theology and the Death of Christ in Paul, Luther and Pascal
This book explores the theology of the cross in St Paul, Luther and Pascal. It offers new perspectives on the theology of each, and some implications for the nature of power, apologetics, theology and church life in a postmodern context.
1999 / 0-85364-984-7 / xiv + 344pp

Adonis Vidu
Postliberal Theological Method
A Critical Study
The postliberal theology of Hans Frei, George Lindbeck, Ronald Thiemann, John Milbank and others is one of the more influential contemporary options. This book focuses on several aspects pertaining to its theological method, specifically its understanding of background, hermeneutics, epistemic justification, ontology, the nature of doctrine and, finally, Christological method.
2005 / 1-84227-395-7 / approx. 324pp

Graham J. Watts
Revelation and the Spirit
*A Comparative Study of the Relationship between the Doctrine of Revelation
and Pneumatology in the Theology of Eberhard Jüngel and of
Wolfhart Pannenberg*
The relationship between revelation and pneumatology is relatively unexplored.
This approach offers a fresh angle on two important twentieth century
theologians and raises pneumatological questions which are theologically crucial
and relevant to mission in a postmodern culture.
2005 / 1-84227-104-0 / xxii + 232pp

Nigel G. Wright
Disavowing Constantine
*Mission, Church and the Social Order in the Theologies of John Howard Yoder
and Jürgen Moltmann*
This book is a timely restatement of a radical theology of church and state in the
Anabaptist and Baptist tradition. Dr Wright constructs his argument in dialogue
and debate with Yoder and Moltmann, major contributors to a free church
perspective.
2000 / 0-85364-978-2 / xvi + 252pp

Paternoster:
thinking faith

Paternoster
9 Holdom Avenue,
Bletchley,
Milton Keynes MK1 1QR,
United Kingdom
Web: www.authenticmedia.co.uk/paternoster

www.ingramcontent.com/pod-product-compliance
Lightning Source LLC
Chambersburg PA
CBHW060332100426
42812CB00003B/961